ASHE Higher Education Report: Volume 34, Numbε
Kelly Ward, Lisa E. Wolf-Wendel, Series Editors

Faculty Careers and Work Lives:
A Professional Growth Perspective

KerryAnn O'Meara

Aimee LaPointe Terosky

Anna Neumann

Faculty Careers and Work Lives: A Professional Growth Perspective
KerryAnn O'Meara, Aimee LaPointe Terosky, and Anna Neumann
ASHE Higher Education Report: Volume 34, Number 3
Kelly Ward, Lisa E. Wolf-Wendel, Series Editors

ISSN 1551-6970   electronic ISSN 1554-6306   ISBN 978-0-4704-3971-5

The ASHE Higher Education Report is part of the Jossey-Bass Higher and Adult Education Series and is published six times a year by Wiley Subscription Services, Inc., A Wiley Company, at Jossey-Bass, 989 Market Street, San Francisco, California 94103-1741.

For subscription information, see the Back Issue/Subscription Order Form in the back of this volume.

CALL FOR PROPOSALS: Prospective authors are strongly encouraged to contact Kelly Ward (kaward@wsu.edu) or Lisa Wolf-Wendel (lwolf@ku.edu). See "About the ASHE Higher Education Report Series" in the back of this volume.

Visit the Jossey-Bass Web site at **www.josseybass.com.**

Printed in the United States of America on acid-free recycled paper.

The ASHE Higher Education Report is indexed in CIJE: Current Index to Journals in Education (ERIC), Current Abstracts (EBSCO), Education Index/Abstracts (H.W. Wilson), ERIC Database (Education Resources Information Center), Higher Education Abstracts (Claremont Graduate University), IBR & IBZ: International Bibliographies of Periodical Literature (K.G. Saur), and Resources in Education (ERIC).

Advisory Board

The ASHE Higher Education Report Series is sponsored by the Association for the Study of Higher Education (ASHE), which provides an editorial advisory board of ASHE members.

Contents

Executive Summary

This volume reviews and synthesizes recent research on faculty demographics, appointment types, work life, and reward systems, as well as prominent and/or promising theoretical perspectives for the study of faculty work, careers, and professional development. An overarching goal of the volume is to advance and challenge current dialogue on faculty careers by exploring the prevailing "narrative of constraint" that underlies much of the current research on higher education faculty. The authors define the major contribution of the "narrative of constraint" as highlighting barriers—to equity, quality, and productivity—in higher education, and thus as helping to eradicate those barriers, for example, by way of improved institutional policy and practice. For example, some researchers have pointed out multiple unseen constraints to work-family balance in academic women's careers; others have documented the extent and nature of racial discrimination in faculty work. In articulating such dynamics, researchers move higher education practice and policy forward with regard to equity, quality, and productivity.

Although the "narrative of constraint" has illuminated the myriad barriers that inhibit faculty careers, work, and work lives, the authors argue that it has—perhaps unintentionally—obscured what and how faculty grow and how they strive for their full potential in their intellectual and professional lives: for example, what faculty members seek, how they extend themselves through their pursuits, what they bring to their jobs and how that changes over time. Through their review of the extant literature on faculty careers, the authors found but few in-depth empirical considerations of faculty growth; nor was there much discussion of approaches for developing, sustaining, or deepening it in academic lives.

The authors define growth in four aspects: learning, agency, professional relationships, and commitments. They use these four aspects of faculty growth as conceptual "touchstones" as they review recent studies portraying massive change in the contemporary American faculty, for example, relative to demographics, appointments, work, and reward systems. The authors also use the four aspects as touchstones for consideration of theories for research on higher education faculty. The volume, then, considers how faculty identities, appointment structures, career paths and challenges, and reward systems can be reconsidered, and possibly revised, if connected to growth as a desirable career outcome. In the volume's view, growth offers some new directions for higher education academic policy, for campus communications with the public about the purposes of faculty work, and for future research. In brief, the volume positions "growth" as a counter narrative to the extant "narrative of constraint." It does not seek to displace research-based critiques of barriers that persist in the field, but rather, to engender a parallel view that strives, openly, for growth and learning among all faculty.

The counter-narrative of growth, presented in this volume, emphasizes the following themes:

- Learning is at the center of faculty work and their contributions.
- Faculty have and can develop a sense of agency to navigate barriers and put effort, will, intent, and talent into their work.
- Faculty learn, grow, and make contributions through professional relationships that are embedded in communities.
- Who a faculty member is—her history, identity, and experiences—will shape what and how she learns, the types and quality of contributions she makes to academe, and the ways in which she makes them.
- Faculty are professionals with capacities for deep commitment and vocation.

Given recent reviews and trend studies of faculty work (Gappa, Austin, and Trice, 2007; Schuster and Finkelstein, 2006), the synthesis herein offered does more than summarize these descriptively. It explores them, too, for implications for the faculty's growth—and in the hope that doing so will spur further consideration of growth as a worthwhile professional goal for all academics. The volume also focuses on a mounting realization in research, practice, and public communication: the idea that faculty growth has implications for the goals and effectiveness of higher education itself, institutionally and socially.

In sum, the core contribution of this volume is its synthesis of recent research on faculty work lives and careers in ways that suggest a new—or perhaps renewed—narrative. It considers how faculty can move beyond "managing" change brought on by external and/or institutional forces to how faculty can actively compose their own professional roles and work lives, and in ways that promote meaning, learning, and conscious commitment. The volume synthesizes recent research on trends in faculty work lives, and the theory relevant to them, to consider what the faculty do as they work, including how they may integrate multiple roles, fulfill multiple responsibilities, and at times, find satisfaction and joy in their efforts—even as they face challenges that, at times, feel unabated. Additionally, it presents several directions for future research on faculty work lives and careers, and how future research might contribute to transformation of the institutional structures, policies, and public discourses around faculty work.

This new narrative for faculty assumes that their primary work is to learn and grow, professionally and personally. It assumes that faculty face a set of constraints in approaching their work and learning, but that as they address them, they can hold on to drives for growth—in their teaching and mentoring; in their research or creative endeavor; in their institutional service and governance efforts; and in their community and broader public engagement. It is a fact of academic life that faculty work is judged by disciplinary norms, governance bodies, and the benefactors of research and scholarship—a fact gaining in momentum these days. The new narrative of faculty growth adds a voice to these "facts": that in all their work—research, teaching, service, community and public service—the faculty involve *themselves*: they themselves must "be there" and "be in it" to do their work. The volume offers a narrative of faculty assuming agency in the breadth of their work, in creating and maintaining professional relationships, and in pursuing their intellectual growth and career goals.

The volume closes with a wish that alongside the staunch "realism" of past research that has painted visions of barrier and constraint in higher education that the field begin to paint, as well, an alternative vision—an alternative narrative of research and practice: one that emphasizes growth, learning, and with an eye to the future, generativity.

Foreword

Every aspect of higher education is influenced by a talented and diverse faculty. Colleges and universities rely on their faculty to create a quality experience for students, to contribute to solving societal problems, and to develop new knowledge. Without the expertise and commitment of faculty, institutions of higher education would lack vitality. My research and that of many others have endeavored to contribute to greater understanding of faculty development, career advancement, diversity in the faculty ranks, and the meaningful combination of work and family. The intent of this research is to improve faculty work lives and the organizational environments where faculty work.

One aspect of research on faculty has always troubled me—the persistent negative perspective that exists about issues related to faculty work life. One does need to look far into research about faculty to find that as a group we are overworked and underpaid, criticized for being disinterested in students, and constantly under fire for the award of tenure. Yet my own experience and that of countless others substantiate that faculty work hard and are committed to every aspect of their job and the sense that the faculty career is "the last best job." The career is dynamic and everchanging, it provides the opportunity to pursue topics of societal and personal importance, it allows for creative expression, it provides the opportunity to work with students—the list goes on.

Why is it that research related to faculty work tends to paint a negative picture, yet the job itself tends to be satisfying, challenging, and rewarding? This question has many possible responses. One response lies in the difference between the work itself (which tends to be quite rewarding) and the environments where the work takes place (which can be frustrating). Another response lies in the view one adopts to look at the research related to faculty work life. KerryAnn O'Meara, Aimee LaPointe Terosky, and Anna Neumann in *Faculty Careers and Work Lives: A Professional Growth Perspective* build on this latter perspective by offering a holistic view of the faculty career. Their work provides a comprehensive overview of existing literature related to faculty and arrives at the conclusion that the dominant view of faculty work is defined by what they dub a "narrative of constraint." They recognize the importance of acknowledging the findings of existing research, but they also call for looking at the faculty career, adopting a generative view that looks at faculty work from the perspective of professional growth. Although it is important to acknowledge the narrative of constraint, it is also important to focus on the professional growth perspective of a career. The growth perspective has the potential to equip faculty members with the tools they need to navigate the nuances of the career. The growth perspective can also provide administrators and policymakers with the tools they need to maintain qualified and talented faculty and to provide workplaces that support a generative view of faculty work. Perhaps most significant, a growth perspective is important for graduate students and other prospective faculty members so they can see a holistic view of faculty work that can be marked by constraint at times but can also be an unprecedented opportunity for professional growth.

The monograph is sure to be of interest to faculty members, administrators, policymakers, and graduate students. The monograph is also sure to be of interest to those like myself who study the faculty career. This work provides a very thorough review of existing literature related to most every aspect of the faculty career. The juxtaposition of constraint and growth that grounds the monograph provides new and different ways to think about research related to faculty and the faculty career. In this way the monograph is not a generic review of the literature. Given the comprehensiveness of the review, synthesis, and analysis presented here, the monograph is very handy for faculty members, administrators who support them, and researchers who study them. The monograph has a useful place on the bookshelf of every faculty member, prospective faculty member, administrator, and faculty researcher.

Kelly Ward
Series Editor

Acknowledgments

The authors wish to thank two anonymous reviewers for their excellent suggestions, which improved both the content and organization of the monograph. Kelly Ward provided us editorial support and guidance as well as valuable feedback at multiple stages in this process, and we offer her our thanks. Sarah Norris carefully reviewed relevant literature, and Rebecca Thomas offered editing assistance; we thank them both.

We also benefited greatly from the wisdom of Cathy Trower, who reviewed the chapters on demographics and reward systems, and from Aaron Kuntz, who suggested some changes to the final chapter. Diane Dean served as a discussant on an AERA session based on this work, and we thank her for her helpful observations regarding language and discourse on faculty. Likewise, as we were putting the final monograph together, KerryAnn shared the narrative of constraint concept with her academic profession class at the University of Maryland; members of the class provided helpful advice on framing and language, along with helpful thoughts about the need to reconsider the extant narrative. We thank them for their contribution.

As always, we could not have undertaken this project without our partners and families, and to them we say, "Thank you, we did it!"

Published online in Wiley InterScience
(www.interscience.wiley.com) • DOI: 10.1002/aehe.3403

Setting the Stage

MUCH HAS BEEN SAID over the last two decades about American college and university faculty. For the 1990s in particular, a maelstrom of critique from trustees, legislators, the popular press, faculty unions, and policymakers addressed needs for "reform" in how faculty are recruited, socialized, and rewarded throughout their careers. What has followed has been much quieter, however. Efforts have been made to redefine scholarship in reward systems, to implement post-tenure review systems, and to make the system fairer for women and minority faculty. How faculty go about their work has changed fundamentally with increasing use of technology, and faculty have become more involved in what Boyer (1990), Rice (1996), and Shulman (2004) have called the scholarships of teaching and community engagement (see also Hutchings and Shulman, 1999). Additionally, the composition of the American faculty has begun to change as more women and faculty of color have joined the professoriate, though many still find glass ceilings hindering career advancement—at times ceilings that appear made of Plexiglas (Terosky, Phifer, and Neumann, 2008). Admittedly, American higher education leaders and policymakers have not done away with the tenure system; that said, dramatic increases in part-time and non-tenure-track appointments has rendered the tenure system as less relevant to increasing numbers of academics (Schuster and Finkelstein, 2006).

What is the history of the rhetoric, policy reform, and research on faculty over the last two decades, and what is missing in the dialogue? The purpose of this volume is to review and synthesize the literature on the American higher education faculty over the last fifteen to twenty years. As career-long students of higher education and the professoriate in particular, we have each studied the academic profession for many years, conducting hundreds of interviews with faculty in different types of institutions and in reference to all forms of professorial work: teaching, research, service, and blends of them. Our studies have taken us inside the classrooms of the most serious teachers, into their engagements with various communities, and into their learning, defined as "passionate discovery" or "creativity." All three of us have also investigated the balancing acts of the faculty work life—whether between work and family, institutional service and scholarship, or teaching and research. Systems and opportunities for reward, personal and professional, have also been a significant theme in our studies, whether viewed as a function of life and career, formal institutional evaluation (such as post-tenure review), or pursuits of teaching and service as personally meaningful career activities.

In addition to our own scholarship on the academic profession for this volume, we have reviewed more than one thousand books, articles, and chapters, a wide-ranging body of peer-reviewed research, and integrative scholarship on faculty written over the last fifteen to twenty years. Throughout the last two decades of public critique on faculty roles and rewards, and even in research and other scholarly writing on the faculty experience or on efforts to reform it, we see two things clearly: first, we see a clear narrative emerge, one that frames faculty as "just making it," "treading water," "dodging bullets," or barely "staying alive." Though this "narrative of constraint," as we call it, has helped us understand many important things about faculty work life, roles, reward systems, and careers, we see it as obscuring another far more important line of conversation: an image of faculty members growing, or as having potential to grow, regardless of career stage. This tendency toward growth is then the second thing we see and that our writing in this volume underscores. Our review leads us to propose that a missing piece in current research on faculty is an *explicit focus on faculty growth*. Although some work has touched on effective institutional strategies to facilitate structures for promoting faculty growth (see Gappa, Austin, and Trice, 2007), we believe that an explicit focus on faculty growth itself, through the lens of how and why faculty develop in their professional roles and lives, stands as a unique contribution to previous work.

Based on our concern regarding faculty growth, this monograph is organized as follows. The remainder of this chapter explains how we came to the conclusions we draw here—namely, that a strong narrative of constraint (including faculty responses to institutional and environmental constraint) has come to dominate scholarship on faculty and that though we view that narrative as important and "real," it misses the view from the other side of constraint: consideration of the faculty's professional growth even amid scarcity, turbulence, and ambiguity. To achieve this aim, we explore the history of public rhetoric on faculty, research on reform in faculty roles and rewards, and other major academic developments pertaining to faculty work and careers. We further define what we mean by a "narrative of constraint," offering specific examples, and we end the chapter with a rationale for why reviewing the literature with an eye toward faculty professional growth makes sense for the future of research and practice.

"A Framework for Faculty Growth" discusses an alternative narrative, one that centers on faculty professional growth. We define our working conception of "growth" and lay out its aspects. Each following chapter (on faculty demographics, appointment types, faculty work, and reward systems) begins with a short vignette centered on each chapter's key theme, presented through the experiences of a particular faculty member. These vignettes are informed by our review of the literature and by the hundreds of in-depth interviews that we have collectively conducted over the years. With the vignette as a starting point, each of these chapters then synthesizes the recent scholarship around its key theme. In the last third of each of these chapters, we "invite" the concept of faculty growth into the discussion. By "invite" we mean that we consider how recent trends and research findings relate to the concept of faculty growth, whether treated explicitly in the literature reviewed or implied and inferred. We also discuss what is missing in each of these major areas of study (who faculty are, what type of appointment they hold, the nature of their work, and rewards systems) that is relevant to faculty growth, asking questions and considering issues for future study.

Given the relative maturity of research on faculty compared with other areas of higher education study, we present and analyze, in "Perspectives Guiding Studies of Faculty," the key theoretical frameworks that higher education researchers have used over the years to study faculty. The chapter finds themes among the theories in use, presents their disciplinary origins, points out what each thematic cluster of theories reveals and obscures, and considers future research directions on faculty growth. The final chapter discusses the concept of metanarratives in recent research on faculty, ending with a discussion of various counternarratives that could guide future research and public discourse on faculty. Although much excellent work has been done on faculty from an international perspective (Altbach, 2003), we focus on American faculty for this monograph. From here on, when we say "faculty," we mean "American faculty."

We organized the volume in this manner for several reasons. First, given recent analytic reviews and trend studies of faculty work (Gappa, Austin, and Trice, 2007; Schuster and Finkelstein, 2006), we view our contribution not as "just one more synthetic review" but rather as a synthesis specifically focused on an emerging topic of interest: faculty growth. Thus we have sought to present and analyze past research in ways that bear specifically on faculty growth and to spark scholarly conversation about this topic. Second, we seek to focus the reader's attention on a rising challenge for research, practice, and public communication—the realization that faculty growth has implications for the goals and effectiveness of higher education. In focusing this synthesis of research, we build on the previous ASHE monograph by Austin and Gamson (1983), *Academic Workplace: New Demands, Heightened Tensions.* Here we hope to complement and extend the conversation they started on the intrinsic and extrinsic motivations of faculty and the challenges faculty face in the academic workplace, with consideration of how the way we study and write about faculty further influences their experiences and the types of faculty development we consider for them.

We have directed our synthesis specifically toward considerations of faculty growth because the concept of professionalism, as an aspect of the academic life, requires it (Colbeck, 2008; Sullivan, 2005). As professionals, faculty apply their developed knowledge, skills, and values to complex problems, challenges, and goals for the benefit of society. Professionals such as faculty have significant autonomy and privilege and are expected to commit themselves to the highest standards of excellence and ethical behavior in exchange for this autonomy. As Golde and Walker (2006) observe, faculty are entrusted to be "stewards" of their professions. A major part of this bargain is that faculty, as professionals, will continue throughout their careers to update their knowledge, skills, and ethical and practical competence in the service of their profession (Sullivan, 2005). As researchers, it is in our best interest to recognize and study the professional nature of the faculty's work—at the heart of which is deeply personal as well as professional learning, relationships, decisions, and commitments. By considering recent research on faculty in higher education this way, we hope to bring both the "personal" and the "professional" back into the conversation in ways that illuminate the highly contextual but highly important nature of the work that they do.

The remainder of this chapter provides a critical backdrop for the choices we have made in organizing this monograph. The next section explores the history of recent changes (and calls for change) in faculty roles and rewards, followed by a review of recent book-length works on faculty. The "narrative of constraint" that we see emerging from recent research and rhetoric is then outlined, followed by shorter discussions of the audience for the volume and its intended significance.

A Brief History of the "Attack on Tenure"

The late 1980s through the late 1990s was a period of great critique of the American professoriate. State legislators, trustees, and citizens pressured college campuses to provide greater accountability for student learning outcomes, faculty workload, and contributions to society. Research universities were critiqued for neglecting undergraduates in pursuit of esoteric research and for acting as ivory towers with little responsibility to apply knowledge to community problems (Checkoway, 1997; Rice, 1996). Charles Sykes (1988) wrote a scathing critique of faculty:

- They are overpaid, grotesquely under worked, and the architects of academia's vast empires of waste.
- They have abandoned their teaching responsibilities and their students. To the average undergraduate, the professoriate is unapproachable, uncommunicative, and unavailable.

- In pursuit of their own interests—research, academic politicking, cushier grants—they have left the nations' students in the care of an ill-trained, ill-paid, and bitter academic underclass.
- They have distorted university curriculums to accommodate their own narrow and selfish interests rather than the interests of their students. They have created a culture in which bad teaching goes unnoticed and unsanctioned and good teaching is penalized [p. 5].

In 1994, mandatory retirement ended, exacerbating a public concern that "deadwood" faculty would now be able to remain in faculty positions indefinitely. From the perspective of many trustees and administrators, tenure did no more than insulate professors from accountability for performance (Chait, 2002). Carlin (1999) observed in a now famous *Chronicle of Higher Education* article, "Basically, professors want to be accountable to no one" (p. A76). An article in *The Wall Street Journal* called college teachers the new leisure class (Maeroff, 1993), a *Washington Post* article considered the "greedy groans of academe," and many articles complained of faculty "double-dipping" by consulting for a majority of their time despite full-time appointments.

Chait (2002) observed that this critique of the tenure system and "over-indulged faculty" occurred at a time when many social groups were pressing for change. Following publication of *A Nation at Risk* in 1983, public schools and parent groups created charter schools to bypass teacher unions in the wake of widespread dissatisfaction with and distrust of public K–12 education.

In higher education, for-profit universities opened but without the protection of tenure offered to their faculties. Professional schools staffed by practitioners without tenure expanded in numbers, and women and faculty of color voiced concerns about racial and gender discrimination in the tenure system (Chait, 2002). Sullivan (2005) observes that such occurrences overlapped with growing distrust of other "professionals" in American society, including lawyers, physicians, and clergy. We might say that higher education's accountability movement, including critiques of the faculty, occurred amid a perfect storm of professional critique in American society.

A retrospective review of this period of public critique of higher education yields several observations. First, the critiques of the late 1980s and 1990s were rarely informed by data, collected and analyzed systematically, and trained on student outcomes. Legislators more often than not reacted to their constituents' stories of individual "deadwood" faculty rather than to longitudinal data on faculty workload, teaching outcomes, or other performance measures. In part, it happened because most campuses were not providing such data. But it may well have followed also on the public's distaste for academic culture: for that critique, the popular press needed no data. Internally, most campuses had not systematically collected data on the retention and promotion of women and faculty of color, and tenure processes were most often closed. Thus, the internal critique of tenure often was not backed up with concrete evidence.

Second, the critiques were rarely if ever analyzed relative to differences in discipline and institutional type. More often, images of tenured professors at research universities who were considered to "have it easy" by virtue of small teaching loads were presented as if they represented everyone, uncomplicated by course preparation or lab assignments, research experiences, or committee load. Although higher education research on faculty has done much over the last several decades to illuminate differences in the nature of work and careers by institutional type and discipline, somehow this research did not make it into the story.

Third, despite press oversight of higher education research, higher education researchers failed to counter public leaders' data-free and anecdotal claims with systematically collected and analyzed data on how faculty spend their time, how they construct their careers, and why. In response to the public critiques, college and university personnel did compile numerous institutional reports detailing instructional loads, grant activities, and research publications. Yet without a corresponding rationale—an authentic and compelling narrative—from faculty themselves as to how and why their work approaches do indeed support the missions of their institutions, these reports were meaningless. Without interpretation—without narrative contextualization—they meant very little. For example, given rising higher education costs, legislators needed to know why faculty research and publication ought to be preserved and why and how these activities enhanced the education of students. Without such explanation, reports on faculty research productivity were meaningless: research appears as an unnecessary luxury, conducted at taxpayers' expense. Without clear rationales as to the benefits of small learning environments for upper-level classes and for at-risk students, faculty might appear lazy or underworked, given small classes.

Interestingly, perhaps the strongest argument faculty could have made in defense of their own system of recruitment and tenure-track appointments would have been to compare and contrast their own teaching performance with that of persons in adjunct faculty appointments. In recent years, research has emerged showing that adjunct faculty are less likely to use active learning pedagogies (Umbach, 2007b) and that student retention in critical gatekeeper courses is higher when full-time tenure-track (as opposed to part-time) faculty teach the classes (Jaeger, Thornton, and Eagan, 2007). Given that teaching was most often at the center of public critique of the faculty, such response may well have provided useful information for the debate in process. It might possibly have explained some benefits of American higher education's historic tenure system.

Without data of this sort, however, the lax investigative reporting of the day took the deadwood faculty member with tenure and made him the poster boy for all other faculty, no matter the discipline, institutional type, career stage, or representation of the norm. One such example, illustrative of inter-actions between state systems and boards of regents at the time, occurred in Maryland. In 1991, the Maryland General Assembly began discussions of faculty productivity as a result of rising costs without perceived increases in course offerings or services (O'Meara, 1996). In 1992, the General Assembly's joint chairmen directed the Maryland Higher Education Commission to "discuss appropriate and realistic definitions and measures of faculty workload" and report back to the committee. After many submissions, including repeated responses to requests for additional information, the commission reviewed a report at its February 1994 meeting. During General Assembly hearings in 1994, however, legislators stated their dissatisfaction with the information provided in that report. What was the problem? Writers of the report had used the American Association of University Professors (AAUP) standards to account for maximum teaching load. Legislators withheld $21.5 million in fiscal year 1995 tuition revenues from the University of Maryland system,

Morgan State University, and St. Mary's College of Maryland until policies on faculty workload were developed for each campus (O'Meara, 1996). Though the university made a valiant and, on the face of it, an effective response (that is, the university system created a faculty workload policy that responded to legislators' concerns that research be balanced with teaching and service), this incident exemplifies institutional actors' struggle to clearly and meaningfully explain faculty work life to outsiders. Legislators were *not* interested in reports that used AAUP guidelines for comparison; those AAUP guidelines were not meaningful to them. They wanted to know exactly what University of Maryland faculty were doing during noninstructional hours and how their activities were serving their state. The original report, framed by the AAUP guidelines, in no way addressed the legislators' questions. Thus, regents seemed to be talking—or asking critical questions—in one language, while faculty and those leading them seemed to be speaking quite another, when in fact they were responding to lawmakers' questions.

The Response: Quieter Redefinition and Reorganization

As a result of and as part of this accountability movement, a new period of reform in faculty roles and rewards emerged. The American Association for Higher Education and Accreditation (AAHEA) created the Forum on Faculty Roles and Rewards to guide conversations about reform of the reward system inside the academy (Rice, 1996). Outside the academy, meanwhile, pressures from legislators resulted in myriad faculty workload reports and forced initiation of merit pay and other performance accountability measures, including post-tenure review.

A later chapter details the most significant alteration to the tenure system that occurred simultaneously with this movement—that is, the gradual replacement of retiring tenured faculty with part-time and full-time non-tenure-track faculty. Four other types of reforms that emerged during this time, however, have received significant attention in the literature and research: post-tenure review, modifications toward greater equity for balance of work and family, new attention to teaching and community engagement as forms of learning and scholarship, and redefining scholarship in reward systems.

One early reform spurred by the accountability movement was post-tenure review—periodic evaluation of tenured faculty (Licata, 1999). The AAUP denounced post-tenure review in 1983 as a threat to academic freedom and tenure and in 1995 further argued that it "dampens creativity and collegial relationships and threatens academic freedom" (American Association of University Professors, 1999). Yet in 1998 as the AAUP realized that post-tenure review was spreading despite its concerns, the organization established "minimum standards" for good practice. By 1996, 61 percent of 680 institutions belonging to the Association of American Universities had instituted one form or another of post-tenure review, and by 1999, 37 state systems had engaged in some level of post-tenure review or discussion (Licata, 1999). Almost a decade after the 1999 count by Licata, most state systems and a majority of private institutions have some system of post-tenure review in place. A current topic of research is the degree to which these post-tenure processes were merely a management fad that were "virtually adopted" or were institutionalized toward some real change (Birnbaum, 2000).

Another set of tenure reforms aims to fix the equity problems of tenure processes, particularly for women who have children while on the tenure track. The Sloan Foundation, the National Science Foundation, AAHEA or the former American Association for Higher Education, and several large research universities have been very active in suggesting and enacting reforms to "stop the clock" for individuals involved in family care and to make tenure systems overall more family friendly for both female and male academics. Expanded childcare centers, part-time options, and subsidy programs for child care have been put in place. National studies of equity among female and male professors, particularly in some of the most prestigious institutions such as Berkeley, the Massachusetts Institute of Technology, Harvard, and Yale and carried in both *The Chronicle of Higher Education* and *The New York Times,* catalyzed much of the current efforts at reform of academe for women. Covered later in this volume are the specific barriers women on and off the tenure track face in balancing work and family, including discussion of where reforms seem to have been successful and where they are lacking.

Perhaps among the most important reforms were efforts to redefine scholarship and introduce the idea of multiple forms of scholarship. Following on the heels of Sykes's indictments (1988), The Carnegie Foundation for the Advancement of Teaching, Gene Rice, Ernest Boyer, and Lee Shulman in particular tried to reframe the national conversation about faculty and what they do in higher education. Ernest Boyer, then president of The Carnegie Foundation for the Advancement of Teaching, made famous a framework for redefining scholarship developed by Gene Rice while a scholar in residence at the foundation. The now famous 1990 Carnegie Report, *Scholarship Reconsidered,* argued that institutions should return to their roots and reward faculty involvement in the scholarships of discovery *and* of teaching, integration, and application of knowledge (subsequently reframed as engagement). This report also argued that faculty reward systems should stress the forms of scholarship most closely aligned with institutional mission (for example, baccalaureate institutions stress teaching scholarship). Boyer (1990) asserted that if reward systems were formally changed to encourage discovery *and* teaching, integration, and application of knowledge, faculty and administrators would accept and appreciate these multiple forms of scholarship more readily and faculty rewards and institutional mission would be more aligned. The framework was intended primarily to reframe the national conversation about faculty work and to start an internal conversation about faculty work and priorities.

Scholarship Reconsidered became the best selling special report ever issued by The Carnegie Foundation (Glassick, Huber, and Maeroff, 1997). It was followed by a report by Glassick, Huber, and Maeroff (1997) filling in the details of what these forms of scholarship might entail and how they might be assessed. Hundreds of campuses nationwide and abroad have changed their promotion and tenure language and put other structures in place to encourage and reward multiple forms of scholarship since 1990 (Braxton, Luckey, and Helland, 2006; Diamond, 1999; Glassick, Huber, and Maeroff, 1997; O'Meara, 2002b; O'Meara and Rice, 2005; Rice and Sorcinelli, 2002). While what has become known as the "Boyer framework" is not without its critics, no reasonable person would argue that the report has not shaped how administrators and faculty developers talk about faculty roles and rewards.

An important question can be raised as to how much of the movement to redefine scholarship has influenced the daily work of individual faculty that is the crux of the problem—at least in the eyes of state legislators and other resource providers. We view the work of Shulman (2004), Huber (2002, 2004), and Hutchings (Hutchings and Shulman, 1999)—especially their efforts to conceptualize and advocate for a scholarship of teaching—as making the greatest claim to real change in the faculty's local work practices. Many examples are available, including Barr and Tagg's pivotal discussion (1995) of moving from a teaching to a learning paradigm and the increased use of Angelo and Cross's classroom assessment techniques (1993). Moreover, the work of Bass (2005) and others in advocating for how technology can make learning visible and the work of Shulman, Huber, and Hutchings in making "teaching community property" (Hutchings and Shulman, 1999) suggests that they have all infiltrated national associations, training for teaching assistants, and workshops for department chairs and become part of the vocabulary of teaching. Similar efforts have been made nationally to engage faculty with their surrounding communities (the scholarship of application or engagement). The sheer numbers of faculty reporting themselves as involved in service learning over the last twenty years suggest that some important shifts have occurred in how faculty think about their teaching and research in relation to their communities (Hollander and Hartley, 2000; Ward, 2003).

Returning to the topic of teaching, however, we think it is important to observe that the work of Lee Shulman and The Carnegie Foundation for the Advancement of Teaching has been primarily a movement about teacher learning and growth "in the trenches" where it really happens and less about policy, reward systems, or definitional orientation, which we see as the emphasis of Boyer and Rice in their fashioning of the four forms of scholarship. Shulman and colleagues have focused primarily on practice and on getting inside faculty mind-sets in everyday academic practice. As such they have attended to teacher-learner interactions, syllabus construction, developmentally oriented peer classroom visits, and development of teaching portfolios of teachers' reflections on their own growth and learning. By focusing on everyday practice, or on what Schön (1983) refers to as the "swamp" of daily professional practice, Shulman and others were shaping faculty work where real change and growth is most likely to happen: in classrooms with students and in interactions with colleagues about what goes on in classrooms.

Both sets of contributions—those by Boyer and Rice on the one hand and those by Shulman, Hutchings, and Huber on the other—are important, but we may find evidence of their import and impact in different places. Evidence of change in the reward system will be present more in policy, symbols of what we value, promotion and tenure decisions, and institutional rhetoric. Evidence of change relative to teachers' growth, including growth toward improved teaching practice, will be present in teachers' classroom-based work with their students.

Major Recent Research on Faculty

As the topic of higher education faculty roles and rewards underwent national scrutiny, higher education researchers investigated many different facets of faculty work. Some of these research projects openly fueled reform movements (Chait, 2002), while others, perhaps equally important, seemed to fly under the radar. We summarize here several major book-length works on faculty over the last twenty years, and we will refer to this summary in arguing for what we see as missing from the conversation about faculty careers, roles, work and rewards, and suggestions for future research. In light of the preceding discussion on growing public scrutiny of higher education, we observe with interest that although the research on faculty has tended to portray faculty careers as overloaded, underpaid, and undervalued, public (nonacademic) critics have presented the faculty (at least doctoral or research-oriented faculty) as underworked, overpaid, and not accountable.

In the 1980s, Finkelstein's *The American Academic Profession* (1984) comprehensively assessed faculty members' work activities, including their preferences in teaching and research, while Bowen and Schuster's *American Professors: A National Resource Imperiled* (1986) described the activities and characteristics of academics. As mentioned, Boyer tried to reframe the conversation about faculty in his 1990 Carnegie Report, *Scholarship Reconsidered,* while Fairweather (1996), in *Faculty Work and Public Trust: Restoring the Value of Teaching and Public Service in American Academic Life,* showed why it was so important by outlining the preeminence of research in academic reward systems. Likewise, Licata and Morreale (2002) considered the impact of post-tenure review on faculty and institutions, Braskamp and Ory (1994) considered how to assess faculty work and performance, and Diamond (1999) and McMillan and Berberet (2002) discussed how to align faculty rewards with institutional mission. Chait (2002) and colleagues considered how tenure faired in the firestorms of controversy. At the same time, Braxton, Luckey, and Helland (2006) and O'Meara and Rice (2005) and colleagues considered the impact of efforts to reform reward systems to acknowledge broader definitions of scholarship.

Several major lines of inquiry explored specific career stages, issues, or sectors of academic life. For example, Wulff, Austin, Nyquist, and Sprague (2004) and Weidman, Twale, and Stein (2001) explored pathways to the professoriate, Sorcinelli and Austin (1992) and Tierney and Bensimon (1996) explored early career socialization in academe, and Bland and Bergquist (1997) explored senior faculty experiences. Altbach (2003) has helped us more than anyone else in understanding how the current status of the American professoriate compares with the status of colleagues around the world in *Decline of the Guru: The Academic Profession in Developing and Middle Income Countries.*

Toward the end of the 1990s, Finkelstein, Seal, and Schuster's *The New Academic Generation* (1998) explored trends among new cohorts of faculty, revealing the increasing trend of non-tenure-track appointments. This growing sector of the faculty had been documented previously by Gappa and Leslie (1993) in *The Invisible Faculty* and more recently by Baldwin and Chronister (2001) in *Teaching Without Tenure: Policies and Practices for a New Era.* Meanwhile, breakthroughs were made in our understanding of the experiences of women faculty and faculty of color by Glazer-Raymo (1999) in *Shattering the Myths: Women in Academe,* Turner and Myers (1999) in *Faculty of Color in Academe: Bittersweet Success,* Aguirre (2000) on women and minority faculty, and Cooper and Stevens (2002) in *Tenure in the Sacred Grove: Issues and Strategies for Women and Minority Faculty.* We also learned about gay, lesbian, and bisexual faculty experiences through research by McNaron (1997), Tierney (1997), and Talburt (2000).

The issue of faculty and teaching was taken up by Braxton and Bayer (1999) in *Faculty Misconduct in Collegiate Teaching* and Chism (2007), while Breneman and Youn (1988) explored faculty experiences in academic labor markets. The intersection of faculty and academic capitalism, entrepreneurial activity, faculty unions, and restructuring of academic labor has likewise been taken up by Geiger (2004), Slaughter and Leslie (1997), Slaughter and Rhoades (2004), and Rhoades (1998).

As we began the research for this volume, two new works emerged that deserve special recognition for their comprehensive treatment of the current state of faculty and future directions: Schuster and Finkelstein's *The American Faculty: The Restructuring of Academic Work and Careers* (2006) and Gappa, Austin, and Trice's *Rethinking Faculty Work: Higher Education's Strategic Imperative* (2007). Developed from national faculty survey data (such as the National Study of Postsecondary Faculty [NSOPF] and information from the Higher Education Research Institute [HERI] and the National Center for Education Statistics [NCES]), *The American Faculty* (Schuster and Finkelstein, 2006) presents trends in faculty appointments, demographics, work, and careers. Although this volume contributes much to the body of work, two stand out: a compendium of faculty survey results ranging generally from 1969 to 1997 that notes major changes over time and an in-depth analysis of how external forces such as globalization, entrepreneurialism, and consumerism influence the professoriate. Using national databases on faculty (NSOPF, HERI, NCES) and focus groups, Gappa, Austin, and Trice (2007) noted trends and factors shaping faculty workplaces and identified five essential elements of academic work: equity, academic freedom and autonomy, flexibility, professional growth, and collegiality. Like *The American Faculty, Rethinking Faculty Work* contributes much to current knowledge, though three stand out: an analysis of how trends in faculty workplaces and careers compare with those in other organizations and professions, implications for institutions transforming into more diverse workplaces, and recommendations for how higher education institutions might change so as to support the five essential elements of faculty work.

The Narrative of Constraint in Faculty Work

Over the last two decades of public critique of faculty roles and rewards and in research on faculty experiences and academic reform, we see a consistent narrative emerge. Though we discuss the concept of *narrative* further in the last chapter, including its significance in this book, we offer here a user-friendly definition: *narrative* refers to a commonly told story, in this case one used to explain faculty careers, work, and roles (Birnbaum, 2000; Postman, 1995).

We identify the faculty's commonly told story as a *narrative of constraint*. The *Merriam-Webster Dictionary* defines constraint as "the state of being checked, restricted or compelled to avoid or perform some action" (www. merriam-webster.com/dictionary/constraint). Interestingly, *Merriam-Webster* goes on to use as an example "the constraint and monotony of a monastic life" and includes references also to constraints in military life—both typically masculine images. Constraint is further defined in *Merriam-Webster* as "repression of one's feelings, behavior, or actions." Synonyms of constraint are restraint, restriction, constriction, limit, check, and control. We choose the concept of constraint to reflect a common faculty story line that, we think, assumes a limiting view of the faculty career while obscuring, no doubt unintentionally, other possible stories about accomplishment of goals, actions, and professional growth.

What is the content of the narrative of constraint? Our analysis suggests the following elements:

Graduate students face many barriers to entering academe as professors, not the least of which is their own assessment that pursuit of an academic career may not be worth the sacrifice.

Faculty face many constraints in their careers, some growing out of personal identity relative to gender, race, or ethnicity and others growing out of affiliation with underresourced campuses or institutions striving for prestige.

An overloaded plate and lack of ability to manage it pervades academic life.

Faculty are subject to unfair tenure systems, work expectations, mission creep, managerial reform, chilly climates, and a lack of support and mentoring.

These constraints and poor working environments impact faculty satisfaction, stress, turnover, and productivity.

Although some faculty reach beyond their own socialization to take teaching seriously, engage with communities, and carry out interdisciplinary work, these actions are more exceptions than norms, as most faculty are simply "treading water," given increasing pressures from technology, changing student demographics, entrepreneurism, and economic retrenchment.

As they face these constraints, faculty are most often pictured as alone—lone rangers in often isolated departments or programs.

Moreover, many of the books mentioned in the previous section (for example, Altbach, 2003; Gappa and Leslie, 1993; Bowen and Schuster, 1986) consistently repeat the words *decline, imperiled,* and *invisible.* Alongside such assessments of the current condition of the academic profession are words that consistently describe challenge such as *barrier, prevent,* and *survival* (see, for example, Armenti, 2004a; Heilman, 2001; Schrier, 1997) and the action verbs *restructuring, rethinking, reframing,* and *reconsidering* (see Boyer, 1990; Gappa, Austin, and Trice, 2007; O'Meara, 2004b; Rhoades, 1998). The literature has emphasized reforming the structures that support faculty work, amid change that threatens basic values and benefits of the faculty career.

It is important to acknowledge that despite our critique, the narrative of constraint and the research that supports it have served us well in many ways. An explicit emphasis on how faculty "survive" institutions of higher education that provide continuing roadblocks to their success and satisfaction has been helpful in understanding how to reform higher education working conditions, especially in ways that make workplaces equitable. For example, unless we understand the nature of constraints to work and family balance, fair assessment of scholarship, and career advancement for women and faculty of color, we will not be able to remove them. This focus, however, has perhaps unintentionally obscured what and how faculty grow, striving for their full potential in their intellectual and professional lives. Rare if present at all in our assessment of recent research on faculty was any in-depth empirical consideration of faculty growth and how it might be developed, sustained, or deepened in academic lives.

What does the narrative of constraint offer, and what does it keep us from seeing and thinking about? Exhibit 1 highlights aspects of the faculty career that this narrative reveals and others that it obscures.

EXHIBIT 1

What the Narrative of Constraint Emphasizes and Obscures

By revealing and emphasizing. . .	We simultaneously obscure. . .
Constraints on faculty work—what is holding faculty back, limiting their potential, careers, and work	Catalysts for faculty work, the nature of commitments and talents that fuel potential, careers, and work
The talent left behind and the work not done	The talent that is there and the accomplishments of work done today
Faculty as lone rangers, limited by isolation	Faculty in webs of professionals with whom they work and learn
Faculty as victims of chilly climates, lack of mentoring and support, reward systems that deemphasize teaching and community engagement or are overtly political	Faculty who find agency to craft work lives that make distinct contributions to higher education and are personally meaningful
Faculty productivity as measured by teaching and advising loads, number of publications, awards, and grant dollars	Faculty learning as measured by concrete changes in understanding that positively influence and improve faculty work
Faculty satisfaction as measured by turnover and whether faculty would choose the career again	Faculty growth as measured by whether faculty are seeking and finding opportunities for learning and growth
Faculty development as something we do to faculty to get them to behave in certain ways	Faculty growth as having the potential to be self-directed, to unfold and deepen throughout the academic life, building on individual goals and talents
Treading water and just making it as faculty	Becoming and growing as faculty

We identify several reasons that the narrative of constraint may dominate higher education research and practice. First, higher education researchers have tended to study faculty in research universities and to represent faculty experiences in those environments as representative of faculty work life and experiences everywhere. Given that research universities often are competitive and individualistic and present special challenges for women and faculty of color in career advancement, pay, and work climate, it makes sense that constraint would be a dominant theme. Second, in some ways, the narrative of constraint may be a response to the public perception of faculty as overindulged, underworked, and living a life of relative privilege and ease. In fact, research has shown the long hours, barriers, and complexity of faculty work life that refute this perception. It is noteworthy that faculty who engage in research have a stake in refuting this perception. Third, the narrative of constraint is in many ways "a good news story." Ask any *Chronicle of Higher Education* reporter which story will get attention: a faculty member who does not get tenure as a result of departmental politics or a faculty member involved in a local outreach project? The negative case typically wins the spotlight. Critique, conflict, even ineffectiveness attract commentators and scholars alike. We need to move this narrative of constraint, in its many versions, into a new phase—a new phase that aims to acknowledge what is wrong with the structure of academic careers while simultaneously recognizing what is right. In this way, we strive to point out what can be torn down but also offer building blocks to reconstruct the faculty's academic home.

Faculty Growth

We propose this challenge for scholars who study faculty, academic leaders, faculty development specialists, and the faculty themselves: *identify ways to foster, in faculty members, the desire and will to craft themselves as teachers, researchers, and partners in service and community engagement who have actively chosen—and continue actively to choose—the academic career as a way to lead their lives.* We associate such desire and such will with a perspective on the faculty's development that we refer to as "faculty members' professional growth." The next chapter outlines a conceptual framework for studying professional growth. It highlights four aspects of faculty professional growth, which we use in subsequent chapters to frame discussion of faculty demographics, appointments, work, and reward systems. In the last two chapters, we consider what a focus on professional growth might mean for the theoretical frameworks and perspectives that researchers have used in recent years to study faculty. We consider also those perspectives and theories that might contribute to the new narrative—of growth—that is the focus of this book.

Significance

There is a long history of research on the academic workplace. The signs of interest in research on faculty continue today, with new journals emerging on faculty (for example, *Journal of the Professoriate*) and high numbers of research proposals featuring faculty topics submitted to organizations such as the Association for the Study of Higher Education (ASHE) or to Division J (Postsecondary Education) of the American Educational Research Association (AERA). This volume provides a distinct contribution in its synthesis of recent research on faculty in at least four major areas of study while also considering disciplinary perspectives for the study of faculty. By focusing our attention on what these findings and strategies might mean for the understudied area of faculty growth, we intend to contribute to a new narrative about what it means to be a faculty member in higher education.

And there has never been a better time for reframing the narrative on faculty toward improved understandings of faculty growth. Higher education is about to hire a significant number of people to replace retiring professors (Austin, 2002a; Gappa, Austin, and Trice, 2007; Schuster and Finkelstein, 2006). Research shows that the development of professional identity is significantly shaped through processes of socialization in graduate school and in early career (Sweitzer, 2008; Weidman, Twale, and Stein, 2001). Currently, many graduate students hear and read about a half-empty view of faculty work that as we see it is highly individualistic, competitive, and faltering in meaning and balance. Yet graduate students have said in multiple studies over the past ten years that what they want from the academy are careers that enable them to find meaning, balance, and flexibility in their personal and professional lives (Austin, 2002b; Rice, Sorcinelli, and Austin, 2000). They want a work environment where they can pursue their scholarly passions and find personal and professional meaning. Implicit in what future faculty say they want from their careers is the opportunity for significant personal growth. Is such growth possible?

We believe that it is. Faculty can and are in fact carving out strategies to make meaningful contributions to diverse higher education goals. Such faculty are putting students first (Braskamp, Trautvetter, and Ward, 2006), making long-term commitments to community engagement (O'Meara, 2008), taking teaching seriously (Terosky, 2005), and making their scholarly learning—their learning of meaningful subject matter (Neumann, in press)—top priorities. Each year, national surveys ask faculty whether they would become faculty if they were to do it all over again, and repeatedly more than four-fifths say "yes!" This story—this narrative—about faculty members' pursuing and in many cases achieving their higher education goals (even saying they would do it all over again) needs to be in the headlines, much as is other news about problems, barriers, challenges, and constraints. But we also need to study the narrative and ways of enacting it—including how faculty learn to craft it. We need to study it and then communicate it to individuals entering and building faculty careers.

This is not to say the story of faculty careers needs to ignore persistent problems. Rather, a new narrative needs to be one of constant vigilance about workplaces and how they can become better homes for everyone involved, which means, in part, questioning "what we define and accept as normal" (Bracken, Allen, and Dean, 2006, p. 7) in faculty work life so that alternative visions of academic careers and contributions can be accommodated. Sensitivity to how certain academic values associated with higher education—such as individualism and competitiveness (Creamer, 1998)—both negatively and positively influence our academic cultures is likewise important.

In sum, the core contribution of this volume is its synthesis of recent research on faculty work lives and careers in ways that suggest a new narrative. The book explores how faculty can move beyond "managing" changes brought on by external and institutional forces to composing new professional roles and work lives where they can find meaning, continue to learn, and make commitments to rigorous and meaningful research, teaching, and engagement. We synthesize recent research on trends in faculty work lives and the theory relevant to them to offer possible new views of what faculty do as they work and how they integrate multiple roles, fulfill multiple responsibilities and, occasionally at least, find satisfaction and joy in their work. Additionally, we synthesize research to understand where the research agenda on faculty work lives and careers needs to go next and what the research suggests for transformation in institutional structures and policies and policy narratives governing faculty work.

Audience for This Volume

We write this volume with three audiences in mind: those who study faculty careers, current and prospective faculty, and those who sustain faculty careers by way of policy, professional development, reward systems, and advocacy. Those who sustain faculty careers include faculty developers, senior faculty (mentors), provosts, deans, department chairs, and other faculty and institutional leaders dealing with academic matters. Likewise, students in higher education graduate programs looking for summaries of recent research on major areas of faculty study may find them in this volume. Finally, we hope to influence the ways in which major studies of faculty work in professional associations and think tanks frame narratives around faculty, careers, and work.

Conclusion

Higher education in the end is a very human endeavor (Neumann, in press), touching people's lives—those of students but also those who work at its "core," the faculty. It is, at its best, as Bowen (1977) observed, "about change in people." As such, we need to better understand the professional growth of individuals charged with fulfilling this potential. This volume synthesizes the current state of research on faculty appointments, demographics, work, and reward systems and how both trends and research in these areas might influence key aspects of faculty growth over a life span.

Social science researchers have been criticized for dwelling on dysfunction at the expense of working toward more positive aspects of organizational and individual action (Seligman and Csikszentmihalyi, 2000). If we too "dwell," we do so in light of the research questions, frameworks, and directions that promise to shed light on faculty growth.

A Framework for Faculty Growth

THIS CHAPTER PRESENTS THE LENS WE USED to focus our literature review on the concept of faculty growth. Changes to the "academic core" of higher education are challenging to invoke (Birnbaum, 1992), and leaders may well look to their faculty development specialists to help them institute academic change: for example, helping faculty adjust their teaching in light of new demands and helping them respond to heightened performance expectations. We suggest, however, that something quite other than "institutional response" must happen under the rubric of faculty development: faculty development specialists must do something other—something more—than address administrative imperatives. We foresee future faculty development specialists, academic leaders, and the faculty themselves as struggling to address the challenge of fostering, in faculty members, the desire and will to craft themselves as teachers, researchers, and agents of thoughtful change with others in service and community engagement and thereby becoming practicing scholars and scholarly practitioners who have actively chosen—and continue actively to choose—the academic career as a way to lead their lives. We associate such will, and such desire, with a perspective on the faculty's development, which we refer to as "faculty members' professional growth."

This chapter presents a conceptual framework that defines this concept and lays out its content. The framework is intentionally interdisciplinary, drawing on research on human development and sociology and drawing from a range of cross-disciplinary studies of individual and organizational learning, faculty career stage, human cognition and learning, and agency. Our assumption in this presentation is that faculty growth, as a concept warranting attention, has

---

been underemphasized in most prior representations of the faculty. We do not pretend to develop a definitive, empirically tested model applicable to all career stages, types of institutions, and disciplines and fields. Rather, we present this framework to propel the national narrative on college and university faculty toward explicit consideration of faculty growth and to suggest directions for future research on this topic.

Defining Faculty Professional Growth

We define faculty members' professional growth as *change that occurs in a person through the course of her or his academic career or personal life and that allows her or him to bring new and diverse knowledge, skills, values, and professional orientations to her or his work.* Though useful as a starting point, this definition forces three questions: (1) How does change, in the form of growth, occur—by what means, and in what contexts? (2) How is such change manifest? (3) What is it about the person specifically that changes? Our efforts to address these questions are informed, in part, by Magnusson's integrative theory of development (1995), which posits that an individual functions and develops as a total integrated system. Growth in this view involves a process of "continuous reciprocal interaction among psychological, biological, and environmental factors" (pp. 25–29)—that is, between a person and his or her environment (pp. 25–29). To expand beyond immediate growth environments, we relied also on Bronfenbrenner's representations of human development (1979) as rooted in an ecology of nested environments, each of which may itself change.

We choose to frame faculty professional growth in terms of a broad range of disciplinary adult development and adult learning theory as well as theory on human development and life span (Erikson, 1993), because they allow consideration of the individual and social contexts of faculty careers and work.

In defining something, it is often helpful to think through the thing being defined in relation to what it is not. Researchers have used the term "vital" to describe faculty who are productive scholars, active university citizens, or engaged teachers (Baldwin, 1979, Baldwin, 1990; Boice, 1992, 1993). Likewise, the terms "stuck" (Kanter, 1977) and "stagnant" (Baldwin, 1990) have been used to describe what Dweck (2006) has more recently referred to as a "fixed mind-set" wherein a person cannot imagine new possibilities for him- or herself in learning new skills, knowledge sets, or orientations. Additionally, we recognize that faculty development, as itself a field of professional practice, has used the word "development" to describe some of what we term "growth."

These theories and related terms are relevant to our concept of faculty growth and provide a foundation for our definition of it. Our definition is distinct, however, in that we position "faculty growth" in professors' "professional lives." In doing so, we portray faculty growth as (1) ongoing and in a constant state of becoming as opposed to being fixed, (2) a process that is facilitated by external environments but that also must be viewed in terms of what individuals themselves want and need as developing persons, and (3) set in a specific sociocultural and personal context relative to faculty members' identities, roles, and work. This third feature of faculty growth takes into account Huston, Norman, and Ambrose's observation (2007) that specific attributes of individual institutions will affect faculty in specific ways. While we assume, as Magnusson (1995) does, that faculty growth involves interaction between a person and her or his multiple environments, we focus more specifically on the interaction between a person and her or his professional work as itself an "environment."

Having said so, we do find existing theories on faculty development, vitality, and generativity useful in identifying professors and instructors who exhibit professional growth in different contexts. Faculty growth is deceptively complex, however, in that many faculty do grow out of "stuckness" in the long run; moreover, "stuckness" may in fact be a feature of a growing career (Dweck, 2006). The next section further explores the concept of faculty growth by outlining four of its aspects as represented (though usually indirectly) in the writings about higher education.

Aspects of Faculty Members' Professional Growth

Drawing on educational, philosophical, sociological, organizational, and psychological reviews of human and professional development, we explore faculty members' professional development through four aspects:

- Learning (ability to engage, personally and professionally);
- Agency (ability to assume);

- Professional relationships (ability to create, nurture, and sustain);
- Commitments (ability to act on and form).

These aspects are not mutually exclusive, nor is this list exhaustive. Distinct aspects interact and no doubt influence one another. Our review of the literature suggests that faculty growth, framed through these aspects, has not been previously studied, though its existence has in some cases been assumed. Each of the four aspects might be considered active expressions of growth in faculty careers. In the following sections, we define each of these four aspects of faculty professional growth.

Learning

We build on the assumption that learning is at the center of faculty work and that all faculty are expected to be "master learners" (Neumann, in press). We assume also that faculty members *can* learn and develop throughout their careers, though varying in what, how, and why they learn. Faculty carry out their learning in their many different work roles (teaching, research, internal service, and outreach), in different ways with different groups (students, colleagues, the public), and in different organizational contexts (institutional or appointment type). Given that faculty need to learn to do their work (Neumann, in press), it is critical to look at how the changing conditions of professorial careers shape faculty members' capacities for and engagement in learning.

Our definition of learning is informed by theories of human development and sociocultural theory. We build on the research of Neumann (2005), who previously defined learning: "Learning, as changed cognition, involves the personal and shared construction of knowledge; it involves coming to know something familiar in different ways, or to know something altogether new, from within one's self and often with others" (p. 65). From a sociocultural perspective, we emphasize a vision of learning whereby "individuals are active participants in social environments that have accepted meanings and values that are not only learned but affect learning and what is learned" (Creamer and Lattuca, 2005, p. 4). Thus, individuals learn in situated environments such as through interactions with colleagues (Creamer and Lattuca, 2005). Faculty learn in disciplines, departments, and programs; through research, teaching, and engagement in partnerships; and alongside colleagues. Even the scholar who learns alone may do so in interaction with other scholars' prior work. Thus, learning is a collective experience (Neumann, in press). It is at one and the same time "highly personal because it involves unique experiences of mind" and "highly interactive in that it draws on and produces cognitive connection among individuals who come to know related things" (Neumann, 2005, p. 65). Learning involves making and remaking specific knowledge. Understanding learning requires understanding *what* is being learned (Neumann, in press).

Given the different natures of their appointments and disciplines, faculty have different opportunities to learn in their work—for example, supervising research projects, using technology in new ways to strengthen teaching, or engaging in conversation with colleagues. The experiences and identities (such as different genders, races, and ethnicity) they bring to their work may pull them toward some forms of learning more than others. For example, research on post-tenure women faculty has shown that many "pulls" exist away from "scholarly learning," defined as meaningful subject-matter learning (Neumann, in press), including interpersonal, organizational, and social forces, some of which are specific to gender (Terosky, Phifer, and Neumann, 2008). After receiving tenure, for example, women may feel a pull toward increased administrative leadership or institutional service, a pull toward research management that excludes scholarly learning, or a pull toward involvement in institutional efforts to make workplaces more equitable and fair for all who work there (Terosky, Phifer, and Neumann, 2008).

Likewise, the changing nature of the work that faculty are asked to do influences opportunities for learning. Many faculty are caught off guard by the newest changes in academe such as requirements related to use of technology, pressures to become entrepreneurial, or requirements to connect their work with teacher education and K–16 programs. All these new demands can detract from faculty learning at any career point, or they could greatly enhance learning, depending on whether faculty have the skills, strategies, mind-set, and capacity to respond to challenges and opportunities in generative ways (Dweck, 2006; Erikson, 1993). As such, learning is a core aspect of faculty professional growth. Given that higher education is centered on learning,

learning should be considered at the center of how faculty grow throughout their careers.

Agency

We build on the work of sociologists who state "in exerting agency, individuals garner power, will, and desire to create work contexts conducive to their thought over time" (Elder, 1997, pp. 964–965). In this sociological tradition, we define agency as "the human capacity . . . to act intentionally, planfully and reflexively and in a temporal or a biographical mode" (Marshall, 2000, p. 11). In higher education research, agency speaks to a feature of the faculty *person* in the faculty role as she or he strives to construct the contexts of her or his own learning and development in professional and intellectual ways (Neumann, in press; Neumann, Terosky, and Schell, 2006). We wish to highlight three aspects of this concept that we find particularly rich for further support of faculty through research and practice.

First, we distinguish *agency* as complementary to but different from the related concepts of *academic freedom* and *autonomy*, which are rooted in professional and political views of higher education. Faculty need their institutions to guarantee autonomy ("the right to decide how to do one's work within one's particular assignment") as well as academic freedom ("freedom in the classroom to discuss their subjects, freedom to conduct research and publish its results, and freedom to speak and write as citizens") (Gappa, Austin, and Trice, 2007, pp. 226–227). As indicated earlier, however, agency exceeds both autonomy and academic freedom: It originates from within the faculty member herself or himself and is nurtured in a professional community that provides resources to develop and sustain it. Whereas *academic freedom* speaks to professional rights and responsibilities in the professional collective, *agency* applies to the lives of persons more broadly, higher educators among them. For example, Baez's work (2000) on critical agency among faculty of color adds identity to the mix by illustrating that rather than race-related service always being a burden, it can be an agency-enhancing opportunity to make meaningful contributions that faculty find personally satisfying. As such, agency is often intimately connected to who we are as well as what we are doing.

Second, like our earlier definition of learning, agency bears a close relationship to social context. Faculty members' abilities to activate agency may relate to the resources available for their so doing (Marshall, 2000). Agency is entwined with social structure, as acting freely takes place in structures that present various opportunities and constraints (Elder, 1994). Social stratification, for example, may influence individuals' access to context-embedded resources and privileges (Elder, 1994; Neumann, Terosky, and Schell, 2006). For example, appointment type and job security may change faculty access to important work resources or feelings of agency in gaining access.

Third, faculty sense of agency is influenced by the flow of time. Marshall's definition of agency above notes a temporal element. Likewise, Emirbayer and Mische (1998) theorize agency as "the temporally constructed engagement by actors of different structural environments—the temporal-relationship contexts of action—which, through the interplay of habit, imagination, and judgment, both [reproduce and transform] those structures in interactive response to the problems posed by changing historical situations" (p. 970). As such, faculty agency is influenced by past, current, and future projection assessments of social structure and one's place in it. Mason and Goulden (2002) have found women seem to be more likely to take advantage of parental leave policies if they have achieved certain career milestones such as prestigious fellowships, grants, or publication. It may be that these career conditions enhance a sense of agency around parental leave decisions.

Whether it be to balance work and family issues, to do the research one thinks is important but not valued in a department, or to gain needed teaching resources while in a non-tenure-track appointment, faculty agency seems critical in navigating workplaces and composing meaningful careers. It is also embedded in the concept of the professional, who must have the confidence and agency to assert herself to powerful organizations around her when she believes them to be wrong—whether an HMO, a public defender's office, a religious body, or a university dean (Sullivan, 2005). As such, agency needs to be a central focus for studies of faculty.

Professional Relationships

By *relationships* we mean interactions that provide personal and professional support; that stimulate, facilitate, and shape learning; and that strengthen faculty capacity to bring the best of their talents to their work roles.

Research indicates that faculty members' capacity to form relationships with students and colleagues figures heavily in their job satisfaction and motivation (Austin and Gamson, 1983; Blackburn and Lawrence, 1995; Hagedorn, 2000; Rosser, 2004). For example, Ropers-Huilman (2000) found that faculty women may reap deep satisfaction from teaching and learning relationships with their students. Other researchers have shown that relationships with colleagues may influence faculty satisfaction (Astin and Davis, 1993; Dickens and Sagaria, 1997; Hagedorn, 2000). The higher education literature portrays colleague connections as supporting scholarship (Creamer and Lattuca, 2005; Dickens and Sagaria, 1997) and as providing access to mentors and allies (Tierney and Bensimon, 1996). As Argyris (1964) noted, professional relationships may offer, too, a sense of "confirmation" by way of heightened self-esteem that enhances motivation.

Neumann's study of the learning of forty recently tenured university professors (2006) explicitly brings out the theme of professional relationships among faculty that she terms "colleagueship." For example, in an analysis of emotion in university professors' research, Neumann indicates that "passionate thought" may arise in "the person-with-person relationships of scholars' lives, which, as in all people's lives, are central to development" (p. 405). Several scholars participating in this study described moments of passionate thought as occurring amid classroom conversations or in subject-anchored conversations among colleagues. A conclusion of this study is that a significant part of creative work, captured by Neumann as "flow" and "passion," is the product of one or more persons' learning a particular subject and having a conversation that illuminates, that transforms, that creates. The interaction, whether through teaching or research, is one of learning together (p. 413). In this view, professional relationships are sites of professors' scholarly learning and thus their intellectual growth. Emerging research on mentoring relationships, colleagueship, and intellectual community provides a strong foundation for better understanding how professional relationships exist at the center—as opposed to periphery—of the faculty's learning and thereby their growth.

Commitments

Commitments are long-term, conscious, personal, and professional investments that scholars make in certain people, programs, places, and social concerns through concrete activity that furthers the goals of higher education. Drawing on the work of developmental psychologists and sociologists, we define commitment in terms of conscious choice, active nature, and content.

Conscious Choice. In describing the intellectual and ethical development of college students, Perry (1968) defined commitment as "affirmation of personal values or choice . . . a conscious act or realization of identity and responsibility" (p. 135). Perry used this term to describe integrative, affirmative investments, as opposed to unquestioned or unexamined beliefs. A professor who scans his or her field and sees the need for and decides to create a new interdisciplinary center for environmental policy, then develops it over time has made such a conscious commitment.

Active Nature. Conscious choice yields more than emotion. It requires time and energy as well as clear action. Perry (1968) observes, "Commitment refers to an act, or ongoing activity relating a person as agent and chooser to aspects of his life in which he invests his energies, his care and his identity" (p. 135). Perry refers to commitments as "ongoing creative activities" that require "the courage of responsibility" (p. 135). A faculty member who works diligently week after week with at-risk students in private English tutorials because he or she wants the students to succeed has made a commitment to retention and persistence of at-risk students that is enacted through each tutorial session.

Content. As with learning, we are interested in commitment concretely rather than abstractly—in *what* one commits to, the content and focus of commitment. Scholars have conceptualized commitment as conscious personal dedication to *particular* people, groups, or social concerns. In a study of scholars' work in the field of agriculture, Peters, Jordan, Adamek, and Alter (2005) identified and explored individuals' commitments to specific farm communities, agricultural processes, and ways of growing and selling organic foods. Similarly, in an examination of what it means for research-active university professors to "take teaching seriously," Terosky (2005) found that exemplary faculty consistently devote attention and reflective energy to their teaching, an act that we cast further as commitment to teaching. As these examples suggest, we consider faculty commitments in reference to the furthering of key higher education processes: teaching, research, community engagement, and shared governance and institutional effort.

Two additional features of commitment merit attention: its inherent reciprocity and its bearing on professionalism. As Daloz, Keen, Keen, and Parks (1996) indicate, people sustain commitment, but commitment in its turn sustains the people who commit. Our approach to commitment considers what those people both give and derive through commitment. And with regard to professionalism, Sullivan (2005) noted that capacity and responsibility for commitment to public purposes mark the "professional" of contemporary times. Integrity is in Sullivan's view a part of commitment. The "outline of integrity in professional life," he says, depends on individual commitments embedded in "communities of professional purpose" (p. 290). Long-term personal and professional commitments seem to us an important though too rarely used lens to consider the daily work and long-term growth of faculty.

Summary

We view the four aspects of our conceptual framework for faculty growth, though presented separately, as potentially synergistic and self-reinforcing. For example, we view a faculty member's learning (one aspect) as substantively related to the sense of agency (another aspect) that brings it into being: A person who learns in personally meaningful ways typically has a hand in making that learning happen. Further, such learning and the related agency occur and are reinforced in the social context of relationships between students and colleagues and other partners inside and outside academe (a third aspect), some portion of whom may be linked through commitment to common learning or work goals (a fourth aspect). Opportunities for learning, a sense of agency to plan for and seize such opportunities, professional relationships, and a sense of community or connection, anchored in commitment, all shape the degree to which faculty make contributions to students, colleagues, institutions, and society.

We challenge readers to consider implications of change and challenge in faculty demographics, appointments, work, and reward systems, with an eye toward what these findings mean for professional growth, an area we revisit at the end of each remaining chapter of the volume.

New Architects and Composers of Faculty Work

"Shall I leave the door open or closed?" Sharon's doctoral student says as she prepares to leave her office. "Half-open sounds good," Sharon says as she turns back to her half-written manuscript. She works on it for about twenty minutes and then checks her e-mail.

She received an e-mail from the associate dean, letting her know she had the highest teaching evaluations of any faculty member in her college that past semester. She takes great pride in this e-mail and decides to print it out and save it for her contract renewal next year. She also reads an e-mail noting an important new conference in her research field but observes it is being held around her son's birthday: Could she make it home in time to throw his party? A few hours later at home, after putting the children to bed, making lunches, and doing laundry, she returns to her manuscript. After turning out the light that night, she wonders about how many of her "daily happenings" influence what she researches and what she has to say.

WHAT WE HEAR FROM SHARON—the emphasis on teaching, her non-tenure-track status, how she works at balancing work and family in day-to-day decisions, and her reflection on how identity and experience may intertwine with scholarship—are all themes in recent research on faculty demographics. This chapter discusses current demographic data and projected trends about faculty gender, race or ethnicity, and age. Then it considers how these patterns influence the socialization of faculty, their campus work experiences, and the contributions they make to higher education. Toward this end, we rely on Schuster and Finkelstein's book *The American Faculty* (2006), which analyzes annual faculty survey data between 1969 and 2001; the National Education Advocate's *Special Issue* (2007); the annual Survey of Earned Doctorates (Association of American Colleges and Universities, 2005), which was sponsored by six federal agencies and released in 2006 (summary report at www.aacu.org/ocww/volume 35); recent data provided by the NCES, in particular the *National Study of Postsecondary Faculty;* and faculty survey data from the UCLA Higher Education Research Institute.

Though we address age and generational differences broadly, we emphasize especially the experiences of women and minority faculty. This emphasis reflects the slant of recent research discourses in the field and allows us to consider how gender, race, and ethnicity may interact with faculty growth. We build on a smaller body of research on age and generational differences to also suggest new research on intersections with faculty growth.

Contextualizing Demographic Changes in the Professoriate

It is important to contextualize faculty demographic shifts in relation to other key shifts: increases in the faculty, changes in where faculty work, and increasing diversity in society overall. According to Schuster and Finkelstein (2006), "In 1969 the full-time professoriate was predominantly male (83 percent) and overwhelmingly white (96 percent), in all perhaps 80 percent white males. But the white male domination has steadily eroded to 64 percent male and 85 percent white or, in all, not much more than one-half, about 54 percent white males" (p. 71). This shift has occurred as the number of faculty has clearly increased (for example, NCES data show 474,000 faculty in 1970 [369,000 of them full time], compared with 1.11 million in 2001) (p. 40). The rise in the number of women faculty occurred through a time when the percentage of women working full time in U.S. society and in the number of baby boomers retiring increased overall.

Although higher education faculty overall is less dominated by white men than three decades earlier, *we have more faculty overall* than before and more faculty working in two- and four-year public institutions. For example, in 1969, 48.3 percent of all full-time American professors were employed by research and doctoral universities, which slipped to 42.2 percent in 1998. Whereas in 1969, two-year colleges were home to one in eight of all full-time faculty, they were home to one in five by 1998 (Schuster and Finkelstein, 2006, p. 43). As such, although we recognize that more women and faculty of color have moved into higher education, they are perhaps more likely than generations before them to move into institutions that do not emphasize research. Likewise, the diversity of the faculty by race and ethnicity is *not* keeping up with the increasing diversity of society. Currently, 28 percent of U.S. undergraduates are students of color (Umbach, 2006), and experts predict that whites will make up less than half of the population of the United States by the middle of the twenty-first century (Cole and Barber, 2003; Umbach, 2006). Based on these demographic trends, the number of faculty of color do not and will not represent the composition of the American population. For example, African American, Hispanic, and American Indian faculty numbers in 2005–2006 were well below parity with the 2025 population projections, while Asians have surpassed parity (NEA Higher Education Advocate, 2007, p. 14). Given projected increases in the number of Hispanic undergraduates, a serious gap will occur in the number of Hispanic students and Hispanic faculty, thereby resulting in fewer Hispanic students seeing members of their own racial or ethnic class in professorial positions.

As a sign of promise, in 2004, 20 percent of doctorates awarded to U.S. citizens were earned by racial or ethnic minorities (Addams, 2008) which is the largest percentage to date. Although this data point indicates progress, scholars who study the recruitment of minority scholars have observed that "the predominant barrier is racial and ethnic bias resulting in unwelcoming and unsupportive work environments for faculty of color" (Turner and Meyers, 1999, p. 3). Additionally, the majority of African American Ph.D.'s are granted in fields like education and the social sciences, not science, technology, engineering, and mathematics (STEM) (Hoffer and others, 2005), which tend to have greater prestige and salaries, especially in research universities.

Moreover, we have to contextualize demographic shifts by considering that both Generation X and Generation Y faculty are replacing baby boomer faculty and that they want different things from their workplaces than previous generations did (Cook, 2008). Although definitions vary somewhat, Generation X is generally considered to include people born from 1965 to 1982, Generation Y from 1980 to 1994 (en.wikipedia.org/wiki/Generation_X, Y). Culture clashes are inevitable as these newcomers make their way into structures that have existed for decades and critique and try to change them—both on the tenure track and beyond (Cook, 2008). A ripe area for future research but difficult to tease out are the intersections among gender, race or ethnicity, and generation (age). With demographic shifts contextualized, the next section provides more specific facts broken down by gender, race or ethnicity, and age.

New Authors and Composers of Faculty Work

There is little doubt that there are new groups of faculty entering academic careers. However, the challenges they face can be very different. Also, faculty that enter previously homogenous and older academic environments who are women, younger in age, *and* faculty of color face special challenges negotiating their work with colleague and student response to these identities. While a full discussion of faculty negotiating multiple identities is beyond the scope of this chapter, we recognize its importance to future research.

Gender

The headline news on diversification of the professoriate is that over the years significant numbers of women have been appointed to faculty positions and more will be appointed in the future. Nationally, women make up 43 percent of the faculty (West and Curtis, 2006), yet progress to this point has been decades in the making. Schuster and Finkelstein (2006) found that between 1969 and 1998, the proportion of women among full-time faculty doubled from approximately one in six (17.3 percent) in 1969 to more than one in three in 1998. By 1998, 44.2 percent of faculty in the first seven years of their academic careers were women (p. 51). The *NEA Advocate Online* (2007) likewise confirms the slow steady trend of an increasing number of women joining faculty ranks in recent decades. In the last sixteen years, the number of full-time women faculty at public institutions has increased 74 percent, and the number of full-time women at private institutions has increased 54 percent. As such, women represent "nearly all of the increase in the teaching faculty over the past [sixteen] years" (p. 14).

The increase in women faculty varies greatly by institutional type, discipline, and rank, however (Perna, 2001b, 2005). Women are disproportionately represented in two-year colleges (for example, 53.6 percent in the new entry cohort in 1998) compared with research universities (40 percent in the new entry cohort in 1998) (Schuster and Finkelstein, 2006, p. 51). Although women comprise more than half the faculty at community colleges, they come in at below half in all other sectors of higher education, with the greatest disparity between males and females in doctoral universities (NEA Higher Education Advocate, 2007, p. 14). With regard to rank, scholars have noted that women have historically faced challenges in entering academe and moving up from lower ranks (assistant or associate) to higher ranks (full or senior) (Glazer-Raymo, 1999; Harding, 1991; Neumann and Peterson, 1997; Perna, 2001b, 2005; Rossiter, 1982; Terosky, Phifer, and Neumann, 2008).

Likewise, the feminization of the professoriate varies considerably by discipline. Whereas women accounted for 67 percent of appointments in education and the health sciences in the new entrant cohort in 1998, women account for only 12 percent of new entrants in engineering (Schuster and Finkelstein, 2006, p. 53). These patterns reappear in pipeline studies. Whereas in 2005 more than 50 percent of the doctorates earned in the social sciences, humanities, and education were earned by women, only 26 percent of physical science doctorates and 20 percent of engineering doctorates were awarded to women (Association of American Colleges and Universities, 2005). Men are overrepresented in STEM fields, whereas women are concentrated in social work, elementary education, and nursing (Umbach, 2006; West and Curtis, 2006).

In summary, we know that there has been and will continue to be a significant increase in women faculty. To date, however, women's appointments are not concentrated in the ranks (tenure track and full professor), in the types of institutions (research universities), and in the disciplines (STEM fields) where the greatest power and prestige reside (Perna, 2001b, 2005; Umbach, 2006; West and Curtis, 2006). Though many scholars have noted the barriers and limits that women aspiring to professional careers face (see, for example,

Glazer-Raymo, 2008), some have noted too that academic careers are not structured to mesh with the roles of wife and mother (Astin, 1997; Morrison, Rudd, Nerad, and Picciano, 2007) or family caretaker more generally. Some writers have taken the culprit to be institutional reward systems that devalue traditional academic "women's work" such as service, teaching, and advising (Clark and Corcoran, 1986; Park, 1996).

Race and Ethnicity

Academe has seen some progress relative to desires to increase ethnic and racial diversity among the faculty, but such change has been slow and uneven (Turner and Myers, 1999). The percentage of nonwhite faculty nearly quadrupled between 1969 and 1998 (Schuster and Finkelstein, 2006). In 1969, "fewer than one in twenty-six full-time faculty (3.8 percent) were members of racial or ethnic minorities. By 1998 that proportion had grown to about one seventh (14.5 percent) overall" (Schuster and Finkelstein, 2006, p. 53). However, by 1998, 19.8 percent of the new entrant cohort of faculty were minority (p. 54). Asian and Asian Americans show the greatest increase in proportion of full-time faculty members (1.3 percent in 1969 to 5.5 percent in 1998). Other groups show increases as well, albeit at a slower pace: African American faculty increased from 2.2 percent in 1969 to 5 percent in 1998, and Hispanic faculty increased from 1 percent in 1984 to 3.4 percent in 1998 (Schuster and Finkelstein, 2006, pp. 53–54). Umbach (2006) observed that 9 percent of all college faculty in 1983 were of color. In 2003, the estimate was 14 percent, similar to Schuster and Finkelstein's total (2006). Researchers and commentators agree that a 5 percent increase over twenty years is not much to be proud of, especially when compared with progress relative to gender. Rather, these numbers represent "too little diversity, for too long" (Trower and Chait, 2002).

Improvements in the racial and ethnic diversity of faculty have also been uneven across discipline, type of institution, and appointment type. Among the faculty in the new entrant cohort at universities, minorities accounted for 32.6 percent in the humanities, 19.4 percent in the social sciences, 13.7 percent in the fine arts, 14.4 percent in the health sciences, and 33.3 percent in engineering (Schuster and Finkelstein, 2006, p. 55). Asian faculty numbers have grown largely in engineering and natural sciences; African American faculty in education, social sciences, and fine arts; and Hispanic faculty in the humanities (Schuster and Finkelstein, 2006, pp. 55–56). As such, the growth in numbers of faculty of color in colleges and universities has been slow and uneven, and it has not kept pace with the diversity of the student body across higher education.

Age and Career Stage

Demographics are also changing in relationship to faculty age. The professoriate is growing considerably older as faculty hired in the 1960s during expansion in higher education near traditional retirement age. In 1969, 22.5 percent of faculty were fifty years or older, compared with 51.7 percent in 1998. In 1969, 33.1 percent of the faculty were thirty-five years of age or younger, compared with 8 percent in 1998 (Schuster and Finkelstein, 2006, p. 58). The NSOPF:99 report on full-time faculty found that 29 percent of the faculty left their 1997–1998 academic year positions because of retirement, while the NSOPF:04 report found this same statistic had increased to 36 percent (Conley, 2006).

The graying of the professoriate has occurred across all types of institutions, but it is most noticeable at two-year colleges (12.2 percent of the faculty) and four-year public comprehensive institutions (18 percent of the faculty) (Schuster and Finkelstein, 2006, p. 58). This age shift has been explained as resulting from increases in postdoctoral fellowships in the life sciences and related fields, the uncapping of the mandatory retirement age, and the creation of retirement incentive programs (Schuster and Finkelstein, 2006). Regardless, the new entry cohort of faculty is large, and their values, work habits, and preferences will no doubt have a pervasive influence on academic work in the years to come (Finkelstein, Seal, and Schuster, 1998). In addition to the work of Schuster and Finkelstein (2006), Austin (2002a, 2002b) and Cathy Trower and Anne Gallagher (described in an article by Cook, 2008) have studied who these new faculty are, what they want, and how they differ from previous generations.

We note also the relative absence of discussion of the experiences of gay, lesbian, and transgender faculty members. With the exception of a handful of writings (Bensimon, 1992; McNaron, 1997; Tierney, 1997), we know relatively little about this portion of the faculty population, though clearly in future years, the conditions of their work and their experiences on the job will require researchers' attention as the American public takes up the issues of the legalization of gay marriage, creation of equal work benefits, and so on.

How Difference Matters

This section reviews research on how demographics, especially race or ethnicity and gender, interact with graduate socialization and career experiences, work commitments and contributions, and work stress and satisfactions.

Graduate Student Socialization and Career Experiences

Before discussing how gender, race or ethnicity, age, and career stage shape one's preparation for the professoriate, we first review theories of socialization. Weidman, Twale, and Stein (2001) reviewed literature on graduate student socialization and found that graduate school serves as a key place for future faculty to acquire the knowledge and skills needed for their roles as scholars. Austin and McDaniels (2006) further point out that the knowledge, skills, and professional networks that students acquire in graduate school shape their capacities as early career faculty to contribute to their disciplines and to "hit the ground running" (Whitt, 1991) in teaching, mentoring, institutional service, and outreach. By building on models of preparation of lawyers, doctors, engineers, nurses, and clergy, Golde (2008) elaborates on this view by observing that doctoral students engage in at least three apprenticeships to acquire the requisite knowledge, skills, and professional orientation: an intellectual apprenticeship of knowledge in a field, a skills apprenticeship of skills learned in practice, and a values apprenticeship in which identity is learned through observation, reflection, and experience. Austin (2002a, 2002b) discusses needs and approaches to preparing future faculty for current and forthcoming changes in the technologies of academic work, racial and ethnic diversity, accountability, and new forms of scholarship.

As is true for the faculty generally, novice scholars (notably graduate students) who are women or people of color report distinctive, in fact challenging, socialization experiences (Aguirre, 2000; Helmke, Kurtz-Costes, and Ülkü-Steiner, 2006; Rayle and others, 2006; Tierney and Bensimon, 1996). Common challenges include addressing barriers to the establishment of mentoring relationships, enduring a "chilly climate," and struggling for access to professional and research opportunities to learn grant writing or writing for research publications. Some writers (Helmke, Kurtz-Costes, and Ülkü-Steiner, 2006; Rayle and others, 2006) have begun to uncover the experiences of female students in graduate school and found that they experience difficulty in locating female advisors in senior positions who are willing to advise and are not already at capacity with advisees, view themselves as disadvantaged and marginalized compared with male students (who develop relationships with male faculty more readily), and feel stressed in efforts to balance their work and personal lives. Others have similarly found that female graduate students often benefit from strong mentor relationships and supports provided by horizontal relationships—though in an academic culture marked by vertical and hierarchical relationships (Rayle and others, 2006). Such findings suggest the need to guard again the potentially negative consequences of having too few women mentors and role models in departments that aspire to gender diversity. Much like women graduate students, minority doctoral students suffer from inadequate mentoring but also from social isolation and from persistent needs to "work against the grain" of academic cultures that often devalue scholarship on race and ethnicity (Aguirre, 2000). Graduate students who are aspiring academics experience such barriers in a larger context of generational difference. Researchers have consistently shown that current graduate students lack the knowledge, skills, and professional orientation needed to meet current challenges they will face in the professoriate and that the majority—whether white or students of color, male or female—struggle with finding mentors to help them balance life and work, develop research agendas and acquire funding, and engage in new forms of scholarship (Austin, 2002a, 2002b).

Like graduate school socialization, the transition to early career is wrought with similar challenges for faculty of color and women. As women and minority faculty enter early careers, they often encounter distinct challenges in establishing themselves as teachers, scholars, and colleagues. In particular, faculty of color on predominantly white campuses typically experience poor mentoring, disproportionate advising and service loads, an isolating work environment, and lack of scholarly recognition when their research focuses explicitly on matters related to ethnic minority populations (Antonio, 2002; de la Luz

Reyes and Halcon, 1991; Turner and Myers, 1999). An environment that is isolating and that devalues research on minority groups is unlikely to facilitate these scholars' intellectual learning. It has been pointed out that women and people of color in professorial positions suffer from diverse forms of "cumulative disadvantage" (Clark and Corcoran, 1986): with low access to growth-oriented resources at one point stretching out into the future.

Commitments and Contributions

Helen Astin (1997), professor emeritus at UCLA and author of *Race and Ethnicity in the American professoriate,* has observed, "It is disheartening that higher education has not done a better job in recruiting and sustaining a more diverse group of people for its faculty ranks, especially when faculty of color have shown greater commitment to what the public says it wants from its colleges: more attention to undergraduate education and greater service to the community" (www.gseis.ucla.edu/heri/race_pr.95.html). With Astin, we believe that current higher education discourses largely overlook the extent to which gender and race or ethnicity may shape the content and meaning of faculty work and scholarship. This section reviews writings that suggest the extent to which gender, race, and ethnicity can intertwine with faculty work: teaching, research, shared governance, and community engagement.

Several studies of faculty work suggest that the emphasis and the nature of commitments fueling the work of minority and women faculty may differ from those of their white male counterparts (Aguirre, 2000; Antonio, 2002; Baez, 2000; Rosser, 2004; Umbach, 2006). Drawing on the HERI 1995 faculty survey of 21,467 full-time undergraduate teaching faculty from 313 four-year institutions, Antonio (2002) found faculty of color to be one third more likely than other faculty to advise student groups involved in community service and to pledge to provide services to the community, and more likely to value the affective, moral, and civic development of students (p. 594). Significantly, Antonio found that faculty of color were 75 percent more likely than white faculty to pursue an academic position in hopes of effecting change in society through their position. Although Antonio (2002) found faculty of color having lower publication rates (journal articles and books) compared with white faculty, he observed that faculty of color hold higher levels of commitment to research in terms of its personal importance to them, time per week devoted to it, and effect on the decision to pursue a faculty career. In brief, Antonio notes that many faculty of color view their scholarship and teaching as enactment of their commitment to social change.

Continuing this line of inquiry, Umbach (2006) explored the extent to which faculty of color engage students in ways that are significantly different from their white colleagues; in doing so he considered also whether and how structural factors such as diversity influence the degree to which faculty of color engage students in and out of the classroom. Umbach (2006) analyzed self-report survey responses from a sample of 13,499 full- and part-time faculty at 134 colleges and universities in spring 2003. Approximately 8 percent of the faculty who responded were faculty of color. As with Antonio's study, Umbach found significant differences between the white faculty and the faculty of color with regard to teaching activities:

1. African American and Native American faculty reported more frequently interacting with students.
2. Faculty of color from all racial groups reported employing active and collaborative learning techniques with greater frequency than white faculty.
3. With the exception of Native American faculty, faculty of color were more likely than white faculty to report emphasizing higher-order cognitive experiences for their students.
4. Except for Asian Pacific Americans, faculty of color more frequently reported engaging students in activities related to diversity than white faculty, even when controlling for institutional type, rank, years teaching, and discipline.

Umbach's research (2006) is further complemented by Schuster and Finkelstein's analysis of thirty years of faculty survey data and subsequent observation (2006) that minority faculty diverge by about 5 percent from majority faculty in attending to students' development of moral values (p. 136).

With regard to gender, Umbach (2006) found that women faculty differed from their male counterparts with regard to teaching. Women faculty more frequently reported interacting with students, employing student-centered active and collaborative learning techniques, engaging students in higher-order cognitive activities, and using diversity in their classes more than male faculty. Umbach's findings are consistent with the results of previous research suggesting that women report behaviors that suggest they are more highly committed than men to teaching and advising (Fairweather, 1996; Finkelstein, Seal, and Schuster, 1998; Harlow, 2003; Park, 1996); this line of research shows women reporting more time spent preparing for courses and advising students and using more techniques that elicit active learning than do men. In addition, Schuster and Finkelstein (2006) show that women are more likely to endorse broad liberal arts education and diversity goals for undergraduate education and to emphasize career preparation (p. 136).

Rosser (2005b) used 1993 and 1999 NSOPF data to assess whether and how women and minority faculty members' workload responsibilities have changed over time. One key finding is that the only group of faculty that "consistently contributed their time to teaching activities over time and in both subsets are ethnic minorities . . . supporting previous research [that] suggests that ethnic minority faculty members continue to conduct their teaching activities differently than their colleagues" (p. 27). Likewise, women ethnic minority faculty members tended to be less productive in research but continued to teach more courses and provide more student contact hours than their white colleagues (p. 28). Rosser (2005b) acknowledged that focusing on teaching and student contact poses challenges for these faculty members in pursuit of tenure and promotion in doctoral-granting institutions. The work activities that faculty of color and women value often go unrewarded in higher education. Higher education scholars note that the scholarship of faculty of color and women is often not viewed as "legitimate" knowledge, thereby locking faculty out of the "room of academic knowledge construction" (Terosky, Phifer, and Neumann, 2008). Moreover, the activities described above (Antonio, 2002; Rosser, 2005b; Umbach, 2006) such as teaching and social change work can "pull away from scholarly learning" (Terosky, Phifer, and Neumann, 2008), which is detrimental to the efforts of faculty to pursue their scholarly interests as well as promotion and tenure. This configuration of work—deemphasizing research, scholarly interests, and efforts to gain tenure and promotion—for faculty of color contributes also to the paucity of diverse voices heard in disciplinary scholarship.

With regard to career stage demographics, recent research shows few major differences between new faculty and senior faculty in terms of work commitments, with the exception that new faculty emphasize research productivity to a greater extent. Using NSOPF:93 data, Finkelstein, Seal, and Schuster (1998) contrasted characteristics of new entrants (defined as full time with up to seven years of faculty experience) with those of senior faculty (defined as full time with seven or more years of experience). The authors found that new entrants had more diverse educational and work backgrounds than their senior colleagues. New faculty were also, as previously noted, more demographically diverse than their senior counterparts. Finkelstein, Seal, and Schuster (1998) found no significant differences in instructional methods used or in other major aspects of work such as time engaged in teaching. They concluded that although the new entry cohort is less satisfied with job security (as more are entering non-tenure-track positions), "the two cohorts differ more in who they are than what they do" (p. 102).

Workload Stress and Satisfaction

Women and faculty of color tend to be less satisfied with different aspects of their careers than their white male counterparts. A study of new scholars in Harvard's Graduate School of Education, conducted under the auspices of the Collaborative on Academic Careers in Higher Education, found that of twenty-eight measures of workplace satisfaction, junior faculty women were significantly less satisfied than men on nineteen measures; in no area were males significantly less satisfied than females (Trower and Bleak, 2004a). The Harvard study also found that women faculty were significantly less satisfied than men in terms of commitment of the department chair and senior faculty to their success; the interest senior faculty take in their professional development; opportunities to collaborate with senior faculty; professional interactions with senior colleagues; quality of mentoring from senior faculty; how well they fit in their department and pressure to conform to departmental colleagues' political views, personal behavior, and attire; expectations for how to spend their time; expectations for research output and external funding; time and resources available for research; clarity, transparency, and fairness of tenure decisions; professional assistance for writing proposals; and salary level (Trower and Bleak, 2004a).

In addition to these areas of dissatisfaction, scholars note that women faculty face significant obstacles to balancing academic careers and family responsibilities (Colbeck and Drago, 2005; Mason and Goulden, 2002; Ward and Wolf-Wendel, 2007). Wolfinger, Mason, and Goulden (2006) and Erskine and Spalter-Roth (2005) found that women faculty report having fewer children than they had originally planned as a result of career constraints. Moreover, satisfaction and the ability to balance work and family differ greatly by institutional type. Ward and Wolf-Wendel (2007) interviewed women faculty working at different types of institutions (comprehensive research, regional comprehensive research, liberal arts, and community college). Women faculty at comprehensive striving research institutions expressed great discontent over balancing the mixed messages they received about priorities for tenure (research demands versus teaching versus engagement) and their family lives. Women at regional comprehensive universities (that were not striving) described having more balanced lives with teaching and service (as opposed to research and pursuit of grants) as focal points of their work. Women with young children at liberal arts colleges found the academic "mothering" aspects of their jobs "draining" and felt as though the family-oriented campus mission of the liberal arts campus complicated their own family lives. Finally, women with young children at community colleges expressed their overall contentment with life, both with regard to the balance between work and family and feelings of work and family success. Interestingly, women faculty at community colleges felt camaraderie and empathy with their students, as many of their students were also struggling to balance work and family issues (Ward and Wolf-Wendel, 2007).

Patterns of work and career satisfaction and dissatisfaction evident among women are replicated in data provided by faculty of color. Trower and Bleak (2004b) found that faculty of color were significantly less satisfied than white faculty with clarity of expectations for tenure and types of evidence required for tenure decisions; confidence that tenure decisions were based on performance rather than politics, relationships, or demographics; pressure to conform to departmental colleagues' political views; and influence they felt they had on their research focus. A stream of research over the last two decades on the experiences of faculty of color has shown similar findings to those provided by

Trower and Bleak (2004b): Current faculty of color are generally less satisfied with multiple aspects of their institutional reward systems, department climates, and workloads (Aguirre, 2000; de la Luz Reyes and Halcon, 1991; Johnsrud and Rosser, 2002; Johnsrud and Sadao, 1998; Lackritz, 2004; Rosser, 2004; Turner, 2002, 2003).

Shifting to generational issues, three studies of aspiring or junior faculty have noted differences emerging between what these newcomers want and what they feel they are getting in faculty careers. Rice, Sorcinelli, and Austin (2000) conducted focus groups with aspiring and early career faculty and found these faculty yearning for community and balance of work and life that they were not finding. Moreover, Austin's research (2002a, 2002b) with graduate students preparing to be future faculty confirms these earlier findings. Cathy Trower and Anne Gallagher surveyed pretenure faculty at nearly eighty institutions about their satisfaction and concerns (Cook, 2008). These authors observed specific differences between Generation X (currently in place) and Generation Y (emerging) faculty and their predecessors in what they are looking for from an academic career. For example, Trower and Gallagher (Cook, 2008) observe that when most traditionalists and even baby boomers began their positions, many had stay-at-home wives and were willing to work long hours. Traditionalists and even many baby boomers prefer a traditional top-down organizational structure, dislike changing jobs, and are motivated by jobs well done, money, titles, and promotion. Generation X faculty, on the other hand, prefer (but are not finding) flatter organizational structures (Cook, 2008). They are more often motivated by self-fulfillment and want flexibility in work to balance it with family or fun. Trower and Gallagher (Cook, 2008) found a balance between work and family to be a major goal, but leveling the playing field for men and women, making higher education more transparent, and finding greater collegiality and community were also important. As mentioned, teasing out which of these preferences and experiences are based on generational differences and which are based on other identity characteristics is ripe for further exploration.

Issues of age and life stage and shifts in historical time and how these two factors intertwine are very rare in the study of higher education. One recent study, by sociologist Joseph Hermanowicz (1998), is a strong exception to this rule. Hermanowicz conducted a study of physicists divided across three degree-award historical periods (time) and working at multiple institutions differentiated by culture and mission (space). His simultaneous cross-age (anchored in year of Ph.D. award) and cross-institutional comparisons yield unprecedented views into the shaping and curbing of professional ambition in the contexts of time (lifetime, historical time) and space (type of institutional culture). Though Hermanowicz's ten-year follow-up of the physicists (2009) was in process at the time of our own volume's publication, it is clear that his baseline study invited longitudinal analysis of the sort that higher education scholars will pursue in future years. We raise this point as a way of noting that time (career stage and historical period in interaction) is an issue that will require significant attention in future years, especially as considerations of change in the academic life become salient, and that site-comparative and longitudinal (long-term) studies of faculty careers will in the long run help to address the complex questions that single point-in-time studies now raise. It is not enough to look just at differences, now in the present, of the experiences of faculty of diverse backgrounds, for all we can do is *guess* at what their future will be. Ultimately, we need to track what *does* happen to them over time—in terms of work and growth—and why. Doing so will require the conduct of tightly designed cross-institutional (multisite), longitudinal studies that rely on diverse forms of data.

Summary and Implications

In sum, the number of women in the American higher education faculty has significantly increased over the last two decades—both in gross numbers and in the proportional space they occupy in the profession. Women still occupy minority status in the faculty, however: overrepresented in less prestigious institutions, disciplines, and lower academic ranks and underrepresented on more elite campuses, selected disciplines (some of the sciences and engineering), and, importantly, at senior career ranks where faculty can exert both intellectual and professional leadership. The number and percentage of minorities entering the faculty has improved modestly, but progress has been slow, varying by discipline and institutional type, and has not kept pace with the more rapidly growing diversity of the postsecondary student body and U.S. society. Additionally, the academic profession is growing considerably older, and retirements are on the rise.

A summary of major findings suggests that in comparison with their male counterparts, women faculty are more likely to:

- Experience difficulty in identifying mentors to guide them in their careers and to provide models for the balancing of work and family lives (this pattern is especially pronounced in graduate school);
- Employ student-centered pedagogies;
- Spend significant time preparing for teaching and advising and embrace liberal arts goals;
- Face pulls away from scholarly learning toward "academic mothering" roles or toward righting gender inequity in their institutions;
- Not enter the tenure track, leave institutions prior to receiving tenure, or take longer to achieve tenure or promotion for family related reasons (varying of course by discipline and institutional type);
- Experience discrimination and feel the consequences in their careers of needs to provide family care despite advances in parental and family leave policy;
- Perceive discrimination, experience social isolation, feel less satisfied with their positions, and feel more pressure to conform to normative political views, personal behavior, and attire.

A summary of major findings suggests that in comparison with their white counterparts, faculty of color are more likely to:

- Experience difficulty in establishing mentoring relationships in graduate school and finding support for their scholarly interests;
- Experience poor mentoring, social isolation, and lack of scholarly recognition for research (notably studies focusing on ethnic and minority populations);
- Leave institutions before receiving tenure;

- Articulate and enact commitments to the holistic development of students and to out-of-class experiences, goals for social change, community engagement, and the scholarship of application;
- Use student-centered pedagogies such as collaborative learning and diversity-related classroom activities;
- Be dissatisfied with their institution's tenure process (its fairness, sense of their own prospects of achieving tenure) and feel less control over their research trajectory. (It must be noted, however, that recent studies show that when career stage and institutional type are controlled, fewer differences emerge between faculty of color and white faculty [Trower and Bleak, 2004b].)

A summary of major findings suggests that compared with their full-time senior counterparts, full-time junior faculty are more likely to:

- Be diverse in their educational backgrounds and work histories;
- Be oriented toward research;
- Enter the professoriate in non-tenure-track appointments;
- Employ student-centered approaches to teaching;
- Search for professional community and feel less satisfied with job security;
- As Generation X or Generation Y faculty, seek balance between work and family, more flat organizational structures, and job flexibility.

Relative disadvantage—and concerns about its cumulative effects (Clark and Corcoran, 1986; Park, 1996)—are common themes in research on the academic careers of women and faculty of color. Various studies cited in this chapter draw attention to the challenges that women and faculty of color face. They range from the so-called "leaky pipeline" into graduate school and lack of mentoring opportunities in graduate school and early career to the glass ceilings that halt individuals' advancement in rank and accession toward intellectual and professional leadership (Glazer-Raymo, 1999; Terosky, Phifer, and Neumann, 2008). A variety of theories have been employed to help us understand these differences. For example, Valian's work (2000) on cultural schemas and Kanter's work (1977) on tokenism provide platforms for understanding stereotyping and bias against faculty by race or gender in the workplace, whereas human capital theory has helped us to understand how individual faculty experiences, skills, and knowledge sets in interaction with the academic market explain differences among men and women in academe (Perna, 2001b; West and Curtis, 2006). Likewise, feminist policy analyses and related discourse analyses have shown how women and faculty of color might be unintentionally positioned as weak or victims in advocating for reform by their own advocates (Allan, 2003; Bensimon and Marshall, 1997).

Beyond the constraint of inequality, however, what does the demographic research suggest for faculty growth as we define it in this monograph? The constraints facing women and faculty of color result in several challenges to their growth, in particular, the challenge of contributing to the knowledge construction or, for that matter, the research agendas of their academic disciplines and subjects (see Terosky, Phifer, and Neumann, 2008; Neumann, in press). Even after receiving tenure, being excluded from many of the invisible colleges, "intellectual parlors," and significant disciplinary networks have left women and faculty of color bereft of critical learning opportunities. In brief, overt and subtle racism, sexism, and tokenism have created environments for faculty that limit faculty learning and growth (Glazer-Raymo, 1999; Glazer-Raymo, 2008).

Yet a gap remains in exploring the more positive experiences of women and faculty of color, particularly with regard to scholarly learning experiences and distinct commitments and contributions to higher education (Fairweather, 1996; Finkelstein, Seal, and Schuster, 1998; Harlow, 2003; Park, 1996; Umbach, 2006). Given that a majority of the evidence on this topic derives from survey-based self-reported data, it must be noted that observational, interview-based, and artifact-based studies documenting distinct contributions would complement these findings. Moreover, recent research is beginning to examine faculty demographics beyond the mere numbers of the male versus female or white versus faculty of color dichotomy; some scholars have begun to probe beyond the numbers, signifying merely "presence" (or bluntly, "head count"), to assess what occurs when women and faculty of color are kept from reaching senior levels and when they are pulled away from construction of academic knowledge (Glazer-Raymo, 2008; Neumann, 1999a; Neumann and Peterson, 1997; Terosky, Phifer, and Neumann, 2008; Turner and Myers, 1999). Continued study in this area will benefit higher education.

From the standpoint of research, we need to locate and highlight ways in which women and faculty of color push past the overt racism and subtle discrimination that is found in teaching evaluations, committee assignments, and assumptions about the kinds of scholarship that count more than others. Likewise, researchers need to uncover how women faculty may resist normative practices that impede a balance between work and family and how junior faculty and non-tenure-track faculty may advocate for the types of professional development and other resources and opportunities that they truly need as growing professionals. Understanding how some faculty, especially those currently in the minority, successfully advocate for their own growth among their colleagues and how they garner support for important but unfamiliar causes in "chilly climates" is an important next-generation issue for faculty research. Baez (2000) and Kuntz (2005) provide examples of such work in studies of faculty of color working with students of color and of faculty activists in the social sciences.

We also know from previous research that professional relationships support both the faculty's learning and the faculty's sense of agency. Future research needs to build on the extant literature on faculty learning communities, communication networks, and invisible colleges to understand how and why they might enhance or detract from faculty learning and agency, especially among groups that have traditionally been excluded from the "sacred grove" of power in departments, institutions, and disciplines. How do or how might alliance building, boundary spanning, and forming social identity groups influence faculty growth? How do they encourage faculty to resist accommodation to norms that do not fit their identities, interests, and commitments? What aspects of agency can be learned, and can faculty be socialized to adopt them, for example, through peer networks?

From a cultural standpoint, it will also be very interesting to understand how Generation X and Generation Y faculty are navigating structures that do not fit their needs and accommodating, remaking, or resisting them. Trower and Gallagher's research (Cook, 2008) cited earlier has begun this line of inquiry, and no doubt more will come.

From the standpoint of practice, this chapter speaks to various steps that colleges and universities could take to better recruit, retain, and support women, faculty of color, and junior Generation X and Generation Y faculty. As departments attempt to strengthen the pipeline to facilitate the passage into higher education of increasing numbers of minority and women scholars and as campuses attempt to gear the faculty workplace toward equity (in effect, warming up the chilly climate for women and faculty of color), it will be critical for them to consider how to make their cultures more than fair. Rather, campuses that will be successful in recruiting faculty of color, women, and junior faculty will consider what it is about the profession that attracts them and what it is they most want to learn—and then find ways to support their growth in that area. To do so means much more than professional development accounts with conference funds. Rather, it means listening to and creating scaffolding around the professional dreams of these faculty members. In other words, the goal for women, faculty of color, and junior faculty overall at a university that "gets it" will not be trying merely to "survive" the tenure track: These universities will be places where faculty of color, women, and junior faculty overall feel themselves being challenged intellectually and are conscious of what they are learning and contributing.

As noted earlier in this chapter, women and faculty of color make distinct contributions to higher education, often despite inhospitable work environments. A number of scholars have studied ways to transform recruitment processes and create support networks for faculty of color to retain faculty through tenure decisions and beyond (Turner and Myers, 1999) and to transform academic cultures to make them more hospitable academic homes for faculty and students of color (Aguirre, 2000; Antonio, 2002; Astin, 1997; Cole and Barber, 2003; Trower and Chait, 2002; Turner and Myers, 1999; Turner, 2003). This research suggests that the worst problems identified for women and faculty of color need to be addressed through leadership, culture change, and investments in professional development rather than huge endowments of funding. For example, women faculty and faculty of color report social isolation and a lack of professional networking, for which numerous models of peer mentoring could be employed. Many women faculty, even those who are tenured, feel inadequately empowered to set their own work priorities, balance work and family, and make room for scholarship. Again, we need to examine how department chairs, peer and senior mentoring, policy changes, and preparation while in graduate school—rather than just doling out dollars for unspecified support—can address these issues. Though not unimportant, the granting of funds without more active, directed institutional support may have less impact on the faculty's growth than its strategized investment.

Indeed, demographics do influence faculty work experiences, just as demographics influence students' learning experiences. This chapter suggests that demographic statistics provide just one part of the picture of the current (and projected) state of the professoriate; the other part of the picture involves a deep analysis of what these demographic statistics tell us about the experiences of faculty as well as what they fail to address. The next chapter looks at another area of the academic career—type of appointment—and employs a similar analysis of statistical information, coupled with an exploration of the experiences of faculty (and students).

Faculty Appointments

1958: "I'll be home in time for dinner. I just have to show my one graduate student, Mike, how to use the lab's new microscope at 4 P.M.," Tom Smith explained to his wife on the telephone. As he hung up, Tom's department secretary brought him his mail. Tom noticed that he had received a letter from his dean describing what he would need to prepare and otherwise do in support of his senior colleagues' deliberations of the possibility of his own promotion to full professor. He could hardly believe that his lifelong dream of becoming a full professor at State University was in reach. After obtaining his Ph.D. in biology in 1948, Tom was immediately hired by State University, then tenured six years later in 1954. Tom plans to remain at State University until he retires. As he reviewed the promotion guidelines, Tom felt himself growing in confidence about his chances of being promoted to full professor. After all, he did just publish two articles this past year in a well-respected journal with his research group of five graduate students. His undergraduate teaching evaluations were high. Further, he had just accepted an invitation to become the chair of the biology department's curriculum committee, a highly respected faculty leadership position. As he continued to reflect on how satisfied he is with his work, he realized he had better get some of his course grading finished so that he can head home right after his 4 o'clock meeting. His wife had been home all day with their two children, and she might want him to read their bedtime stories to them.

2004: "Oh, shoot, did I leave the handout for my class at home?" Norma Anthony, a part-time non-tenure-track adjunct professor at State University (four-year institution) and Town College (two-year community college), said absentmindedly to herself. Because her Town College classes are new to her schedule, she finds it difficult to stay organized with her hectic commuting schedule. Because she commutes between two institutions and because she does not have an office at either one, Norma keeps all of her teaching files in the trunk of her car or in her home office and meets with her students in the schools' cafeterias or coffee shops. Although she is getting used to this structure, there are times, like today, when she forgets something at one of her locations. As she raced home to get her handout, Norma wondered whether and when she might obtain a full-time position at either institution. It does not seem likely because she has been hoping for a full-time position since she obtained her Ph.D. in sociology in 2000. Although she loves the flexibility of her part-time work, which includes two evening courses at Town College and two day courses at State University, she worries about job security because her contract has to be renewed each year at both institutions. As Norma rushes into her house, she takes a moment to watch her husband play with their toddler in the backyard. She is thankful that her husband has summers off from his high school guidance counselor position; it is one time of the year that she does not have to worry about juggling her daughter's day care, relatives, and her husband's schedule. Sprinting to her car, Norma's husband yells out a reminder that she needs to find child care on Wednesday when, she had told him, she would attend the Town College faculty meeting; he has a meeting at the same time at his school. Norma had already spent an hour trying to find someone to watch her daughter on Wednesday, and with no luck, she decided to skip her Town College faculty meeting, because after all, as an adjunct, she was not required to attend. As she pulled out of her driveway, Norma wondered whether her husband would mind if she went to the coffee shop for a few hours on Saturday to work on her research. It has been more than three months since she has had time to get back to her research, but she knows that her husband could probably use some time away from family duties as well. He has a fair amount of professional work preparation to attend to as well. "Oh, well, I'll think about that later," she said to herself as she pulled onto the highway leading her to State University.

AS THESE TWO VIGNETTES SHOW, the traditional (full-time tenure-track) academic career as we once knew it—as in the case of Tom Smith—is being augmented (and possibly replaced) by another type of appointment, as represented by Norma Anthony. The contrast is obviously extreme here: not all 1958 faculty lives were as simple as Tom's, and not all 2004 faculty lives were as frantic as Norma's. Yet higher education statistics indicate that nontraditional—temporary, non-tenure-track, part-time— appointments are rising dramatically. Recently, scholars have examined the rise of nontraditional appointments, and they have explored too how being employed as a "contingent faculty member" may shape a new faculty work life (Baldwin and Chronister, 2001; Gappa, Austin, and Trice, 2007), requiring new images of research and teaching productivity (Benjamin, 2002; Bland and others, 2006; Jaeger, Thornton, and Eagan, 2007; Umbach, 2007b) and new conceptions of faculty satisfaction (Gappa, 2000; Gappa and Leslie, 1993).

This chapter defines nontraditional appointments, examines their recent proliferation, and discusses their content, including their perceived performance. It then discusses implications of nontraditional appointments for overall faculty growth.

Defining Nontraditional Faculty Appointments

Faculty appointments are changing. Gappa, Austin, and Trice (2007) describe this change by referring to the work of Handy (1994), who discusses the reconfiguration of work on a global level. Handy (1994) observes how workers in the current global economy can be divided into three groups: professionals (who form the core of an organization), freelance professionals (who are hired project by project), and part-time or full-time non-tenure-track workers (who are hired on an hourly basis). Gappa, Austin, and Trice (2007) suggest that a similar movement is reshaping faculty appointments. The professional core consists of full-time tenure-track professors who engage in teaching, research, and service; freelance professionals are faculty with renewable contracts who specialize in teaching or research; and part-time or full-time non-tenure-track workers are faculty who are hired temporarily to teach specific courses.

What kinds of academic-professional positions make up the core of the part-time or full-time non-tenure-track faculty? Gappa and Leslie (1993) present the following four contingent faculty categories: (1) the *professional/ specialist/expert,* who is employed in his or her disciplinary field but is also interested in teaching at a college or university; (2) the *career ender,* who is retired or planning to retire from his or her primary employment; (3) the *freelancer,* who holds multiple positions at higher education institutions; and (4) the *aspiring academic,* who hopes to obtain full-time tenure-track work. These categories take into account the intent of the individual in their appointment, something not often done in discussing such appointments from an organizational perspective. Beyond these categories, institutions and writers often refer to such faculty as part-time faculty, adjunct faculty, non-tenure-track faculty, term faculty, contract faculty, freelance faculty, and part-time or full-time non-tenure-track faculty. For simplicity and consistency, we use the terms part-time and full-time non-tenure-track faculty in these appointments (Gappa, 2000; Schuster and Finkelstein, 2006). The next two sections examine these two types of appointments in more detail.

Part-Time Faculty Appointments

Part-time faculty are usually hired to teach a specific course or courses. Their work consists of designing and preparing for the course(s), teaching them, and interacting with students on course-related matters (through office hours and e-mail, for example). The faculty member is usually paid per credit hour of the course taught and is not responsible for other duties traditionally associated with the professorial ranks such as participating in faculty governance or service, conducting research, or advising students. Although teaching-intensive positions dominate part-time work, faculty are occasionally hired to perform administrative or research-related duties part time.

Higher education institutions increasingly hire part-time faculty to perform the duties previously mentioned. Data show that the proportion of faculty employed in part-time positions nearly doubled over a thirty-year span between 1970 (22 percent) and 1999 (43 percent) (Conley and Leslie, 2002). Moreover, between 1969 and 2001, the number of part-time faculty increased by 376 percent—five times faster than the increase in the number of full-time faculty (Schuster and Finkelstein, 2006). Almost all part-time faculty positions (95 percent) are non-tenure-track (Gappa, 2000), and rarely does a part-time position turn into a full-time position (Schuster and Finkelstein, 2006).

Although all types of institutions of higher education rely increasingly on part-time faculty, variation by institutional type and discipline is apparent. Public and private comprehensive, private liberal arts, and public two-year institutions report relying on greater numbers of part-time faculty than do public and private research and doctoral institutions (Antony and Valadez, 2002). Recent reports indicate that 21 percent of faculty at public research institutions hold part-time appointments, versus 65 percent at two-year institutions (National Center for Education Statistics, 2001). The lower number of part-time faculty at research and doctoral institutions may be explained by the increased use of graduate students to cover a certain number of teaching positions (Gappa, 2000). Graduate students are not considered part-time faculty in these or most counts, despite their roles as teaching assistants. With regard to discipline, part-timers make up more than 49 percent of the faculty in several disciplines or fields: law, fine arts, English and literature, computer science, and mathematics. In engineering, education, business, health sciences, humanities, and natural and social sciences, part-timers are also highly represented. The smallest numbers of part-time faculty are in the fields of agriculture, home economics, economics, political science, and biological and physical sciences (Gappa, 2000).

The people who fill part-time positions have several distinguishing characteristics. First, part-time faculty typically hold multiple jobs. Seventy-seven percent hold other part-time jobs in addition to their part-time faculty appointment; 64 percent hold a full-time job in addition to their part-time faculty appointment (Gappa, 2000). Approximately one fifth (16 percent) of part-timers are "aspiring academics" (Gappa and Leslie, 1993), hoping one day to obtain a traditional faculty appointment. Second, part-time faculty appointments are largely filled by women. As of 1998, 48 percent of all part-time faculty were female, while only 36 percent of all full-time faculty were women (Conley and Leslie, 2002). Despite women's increasing success in obtaining doctorates, they continue to be overrepresented in part-time faculty positions (Conley and Leslie, 2002; Gappa, 2000; Laursen and others, 2007; Perna, 2005).

Full-Time Non-Tenure-Track Faculty Appointments

Full-time non-tenure-track faculty are typically hired for teaching, research, or administration-intensive positions on a full-time basis without the option of tenure. Of the three, most full-time non-tenure-track faculty (83 percent) are hired solely to teach (NEA Higher Education Advocate, 2007). Full-time non-tenure-track faculty members often do not (yet sometimes do) perform the full range of traditional academic duties (that is, teaching, research, *and* service) associated with traditional tenure-track faculty positions.

Non-tenure-track faculty appointments are on the rise, a noted trend by scholars such as Schuster and Finkelstein (2006) and Gappa (2000). Based on analysis of data from 1993, 1995, and 1997 national faculty surveys (HERI and NSOPF), the majority of new faculty appointments were non-tenure-track (Finkelstein and Schuster, 2001). By 1998, full-time non-tenure-track faculty accounted for 28.1 percent of all full-time faculty and 16 percent of all faculty (Conley and Leslie, 2002). In community colleges, 35 percent of all full-time positions were off the tenure track (Conley and Leslie, 2002).

Reports indicate too that the hiring of full-time non-tenure-track faculty varies by institutional type and discipline. Based on 1993 NSOPF data, full-time non-tenure-track faculty were employed in the following concentrations in diverse types of institutions: research universities (39.5 percent), doctorate-granting institutions (18.5 percent), comprehensive institutions (16.9 percent), community colleges (12.3 percent), and private liberal arts colleges (7.8 percent). Relative to discipline, the health sciences employed the largest proportion of full-time non-tenure-track faculty (28 percent), followed by the natural sciences (15.7 percent) and the humanities (12.5 percent).

When compared with tenure-track faculty, full-time non-tenure-track faculty (in particular, those in teaching-intensive appointments) were half as likely to hold a doctorate degree (31.2 percent versus 61.4 percent), almost twice as likely to be under age 45 (57.8 versus 32.3 percent), and more than twice as likely to be at the earliest stage of the academic career (52.2 percent new entrants versus 22.9 percent at other stages) (Schuster and Finkelstein, 2006). If the faculty member is hired into a teaching-intensive appointment, he or she is less likely to publish or be involved in funded research when compared with their tenure-track counterparts (Schuster and Finkelstein, 2006). When comparing genders, women are twice as likely as men to hold full-time non-tenure-track teaching appointments, especially in the liberal arts such as English and modern languages (Schuster and Finkelstein, 2006).

Examining the Rise in Contingent Appointments

As higher education scholars have noted, part-time or full-time non-tenure-track faculty appointments are on the rise. Why? Writings on this topic present several responses.

First, part-time or full-time non-tenure-track faculty appointments represent immediate (though perhaps short-term) financial advantages (cost savings) for institutions, as part-time and full-time non-tenure-track faculty compensation is low when compared with full-time faculty compensation (Bland and others, 2006; Finkelstein and Schuster, 2001; Gappa, 2000; Schuster and Finkelstein, 2006). Part-time faculty compensation is approximately one quarter that of full-time faculty pay (Jacoby, 2006). Curtis (2005) conducted another study based on 2003–2004 and 2004–2005 NSOPF compensation data, finding that part-time faculty were compensated less per class hour than full-time faculty and that part-time non-tenure-track professors were paid 64 percent less than tenured professors. Similar to part-time faculty, full-time non-tenure-track faculty are paid less than tenure-track faculty (Gappa, 2000; Harper, Baldwin, Gansneder, and Chronister, 2001). A study by Curtis (2005) also found that full-time non-tenure-track professors were paid 26 percent less than tenured professors. Besides savings in compensation, part-time or full-time non-tenure-track faculty, especially part-time faculty, are usually hired without benefits, which is the greatest point of job dissatisfaction among part-time or full-time non-tenure-track faculty (Gappa, 2000).

Second, because part-time or full-time non-tenure-track faculty usually are appointed on renewable contracts (as opposed to having the assurance of continued employment that comes with tenure), these faculty appointments guarantee colleges and universities a fair amount of flexibility, allowing them to change course (in curriculum or financing, for example) relatively quickly in response to emergent environmental opportunities or constraints. Such flexibility represents a clear policy advantage in times of fluctuating state and federal funding (Gappa, 2000). This appointment strategy would allow a department to fill a staffing gap that otherwise would not warrant appointment of a full-time faculty member, for example, because of the rigidity of the department's tenure profile or emergent budgetary constraints (Antony and Valadez, 2002).

Third, part-time or full-time non-tenure-track faculty can focus in on one area of a career—presumably their strength—rather than attempting to cover the full spectrum of faculty responsibility, that is, teaching, research, and administrative goals (Bland and others, 2006). The traditional three-part career model (teaching, research, service or outreach), though valuable in previously unarticulated ways (Neumann, in press), is complex and takes time and support for faculty to learn, and it requires a financial investment that institutions may at times choose to forgo (though doing so requires a judiciousness that has not been well articulated to date). Part-time or full-time non-tenure-track faculty also may add significant practical experience and expertise to selected courses (Bland and others, 2006; Gappa, 2000), for example in applied areas like business and education.

Last, as we noted in "Setting the Stage," the public has voiced its discontent with higher education, especially with the lack of accountability on the part of faculty. As a result, neither the public in general nor its leaders (including state legislators) nor institutions' trustees have come to the rescue of traditional modes of doing business in higher education. Few public leaders cry out openly in favor of the unchecked, lifetime tenured position. Few public leaders have tried to stem the forward creep of appointment change among higher education faculties—perhaps as the result of a growing belief that faculty in non-tenure-track positions may be more easily held accountable to institutional and societal goals than can faculty in tenured positions (O'Meara, Kaufman, and Kuntz, 2003).

Analyzing Performance

As we explained earlier, proponents of moves to use contingent faculty for cost savings cite enhanced financial well-being, responsiveness, and efficiency as the upside of their preferred strategy. Critics of these moves counter, however, that their costs—to productivity, teaching performance, and job satisfaction—are still largely unknown and likely outweigh benefits (Bland and others, 2006; Jaeger, Thornton, and Eagan, 2007; Umbach, 2007b).

This section reviews three criticisms of the increased use of part-time and full-time non-tenure-track faculty appointments. First, however, we observe that the larger campus in which faculty appointments reside must be looked at in any assessment of change in faculty appointment structure. In other words, change in appointment structure must be assessed in context. Consider, for example, that a newly appointed part-time faculty member will have a very different experience in an institution where 70 percent of the faculty are already part time (and have been for many years) than she will in an institution where 70 percent are full-time tenure-track appointments (and have been historically). Overall increases in contingent faculty must be viewed against a threshold that differentiates a faculty member's experience—namely, how the institution knows itself and treats faculty in appointments differing from an "ideal." Likewise, some institutions do not subscribe to the tenure system. At these institutions, multiyear contracts replace traditional tenure. Institutions without a tenure system are likely to treat contingent appointments quite differently from institutions whose tenure system is alive and well. Finally, many professional fields have historically depended on adjunct faculty, especially in graduate programs requiring expertise in clinical practice such as medical and allied health fields, business, and education to some extent. Increasing part-time temporary faculty in these settings is likely to have a very different effect than increasing such appointments in an institution that has historically relied on tenure-track faculty to teach core sophomore English literature courses.

Research Productivity

A key consideration for institutions with research missions in considering increases in contingent faculty is what happens to the research productivity of the faculty when appointment structures change so as to bring in more part-time or full-time non-tenure-track faculty. Several studies have shown that research productivity is hindered for contingent faculty; these faculty publish less than tenure-track faculty (Bland and others, 2006; Finkelstein and Schuster, 2001; Schuster and Finkelstein, 2006). Further, because part-time faculty have limited time on campuses, they are less likely to be involved in formal or informal conversations about their scholarly interests. As such, they may add minimally to the development of a local research culture.

Teaching and Advising

Research on the implications of part-time or full-time non-tenure-track appointments for student learning is largely negative (Benjamin, 2002; Bland, 2004; Umbach, 2007b). The prevailing view is that the full-time tenure-track professors who teach, research, and perform service for an institution serve students better. Why? Researchers note several reasons.

First, because part-time faculty teach mostly first-year courses (Harper, Baldwin, Gansneder, and Chronister, 2001), it is conceivable that in an institution with a prominent contingent-faculty workforce many first-year foundational courses are taught by individuals with lower-level (not terminal) degrees. Part-time or full-time non-tenure-track faculty, and especially part-time faculty, are more than half as likely to hold doctorates as full-time tenure track faculty (Jacoby, 2006). Some researchers argue, however, that part-timers are professionally qualified for the teaching positions they fill: 11 percent of part-time faculty hold a professional degree, and 52 percent hold one or more master's degrees (Gappa, 2000).

Second, part-time faculty spend less time out of class interacting with students than do full-time faculty (Finkelstein and Schuster, 2001; Umbach, 2007b). Drawing on 2003–2004 self-report data from Indiana University's Faculty Survey on Student Engagement ($n = 20,319$), Umbach (2007b) notes that part-time faculty interact less with students than do full-time faculty (in fact, two-thirds less). In a study using 1992 and 1993 NSOPF data, Antony and Valadez (2002) found that full-time faculty reported greater satisfaction with student interactions than did their part-time colleagues. Why do part-time faculty interact less with students than tenure-track faculty do? Part-time faculty members' compensation is typically per class hour, resulting in fewer hours that they physically spend on campus. Moreover, many part-time faculty members piece together a full-time position by teaching several classes at several institutions, resulting in little time for out-of-class and informal interactions with students. Third, institutions usually provide fewer professional development opportunities for temporary faculty; physical resources such as office space, computer equipment, and supplies often are lacking for part-time faculty (Gappa, 2000; Jacoby, 2006).

Further, concerns have been raised about the teaching practices of non-tenure-track faculty. Often these faculty have lower office-hour loads, use technology less, make more use of traditional examination techniques, maintain lower writing expectations, and grade significantly higher than do tenure-track professors (Benjamin, 2002; Jacoby, 2006). The contrast is most stark between part-time and full-time contingent faculty. Drawing on 2003–2004 data from Indiana University's Faculty Survey on Student Engagement, Umbach (2007b) reports that part-time faculty employ fewer collaborative learning tools and challenge students less than do full-time faculty. Jacoby (2006) contends that part-time faculty use less time-intensive instructional practices because they are rarely compensated for class preparation. As previously mentioned, the part-time appointment system is not designed to foster informal and high-quality interactions between these faculty and students, thereby hindering the development of a campus learning environment that explicitly includes them. All these activities conflict with what is known about effective practices for students' success.

Fourth, researchers contend that increases in part-time faculty negatively affect student persistence (Benjamin, 2002; Harrington and Schibik, 2001; Jacoby 2006; Jaeger, Thornton, and Eagan, 2007), thereby heightening the possibility of student attrition. Harrington and Schibik (2001) indicate that freshmen who took larger numbers of courses taught by part-time faculty at a large university were less likely to persist toward the degree of their choice than did freshmen who took classes from full-time faculty. The study calculated that for each 10 percent increase in part-time faculty at four-year institutions, graduation rates decreased by 2.65 percent. Relatedly, Burgess and Samuels (1999) found that students enrolled in sequentially ordered courses whereby earlier courses were taught by part-time faculty performed worse in the later classes than did their peers who took the early courses with tenure-track faculty. This finding is consistent with Jaeger, Thornton, and Eagan's finding (2007) that full-time and tenure-track faculty are more likely than part-time faculty to be associated with high retention in gatekeeper courses.

Thus a significant policy issue arises: In which institutions are any of the teaching-learning-related downsides of the changes in appointment structure most visible? Research by Benjamin (2002) indicates that the greatest effect on student learning of a policy of increasing contingent hires is felt typically at community colleges—primarily because of the large numbers of part-time or full-time non-tenure-track faculty employed at these institutions. Drawing on a broad range of national government-sponsored studies, Benjamin (2002) found strong negative correlations between the percentage of part-time faculty at community colleges and student graduation rates. Benjamin's explanations for this negative correlation include lax hiring and personnel policies around part-time or full-time non-tenure-track faculty and among contingent faculty, less availability for students, lower academic expectations, less use of technology, and use of pedagogy that is not consistent with other core courses at the community college level. However, it must be acknowledged that community colleges serve some of the most at-risk students in terms of retention regardless of instructor. As such, comparisons of appointment type are most relevant within institutional types where students are more similar.

Job Satisfaction

On the other hand, some research on faculty satisfaction concludes that part-time or full-time non-tenure-track faculty find their work more satisfying than tenure-track faculty (Bland, Center, and Finstad, 2000). A study conducted at the University of Minnesota Medical School in 2000 found that although tenure-track faculty published more articles and worked more hours, non-tenure-track faculty reported greater levels of satisfaction with their work (Bland, Center, and Finstad, 2000). Though this finding bears close consideration, it must be recalled that it was conducted in a medical school; medical campuses have historically used nontenured appointments for clinical positions, and thus they are likely to be better institutionalized than they are in other parts of the university or in other types of institutions. Yet looking across different types of institutions of higher education, Gappa (2000) notes that teaching-intensive part-time or full-time non-tenure-track faculty describe their positions as satisfying; her report suggests that these faculty are intrinsically drawn to teaching and are able to focus purely on that work. Similarly, Antony and Valadez (2002) found that the part-time faculty they studied were content in their positions because they had the opportunity to do what they most enjoy—teaching.

Recent research suggests that one of the key reasons for higher levels of satisfaction for part-time or full-time non-tenure-track faculty is workload. Workload relates to the actual activities one completes as part of a job. Whereas tenure-track faculty have claimed ambiguity in institutional priorities for their workload and an overloaded plate, it seems to be less true for part-time and non-tenure-track faculty. Clearly the landscape of satisfaction varies greatly by situation (the part-time-aspiring-to-be-full-time faculty member versus the full-time non-tenure-track faculty member at an institution without tenure versus the nontenured faculty member at an institution with tenure). Despite being less satisfied with their second-class citizenship and their minimal levels of student interaction, some part-time faculty are more satisfied with their workload and personal control over their professional time (Antony and Valadez, 2002; Schuster and Finkelstein, 2006). Part-time faculty might choose this path over the tenure-track path because of lower levels of stress and increased possibility of balance in one's work life afforded by jobs that allow faculty to focus on particular responsibilities (Antony and Valadez, 2002). Full-time non-tenure-track faculty at non-tenure-bearing institutions may be more content in some ways than tenure-track faculty at other institutions that do grant tenure, as issues of power and prestige may be minimized in the former, at least with regard to the messages that tenured status carries. Further, some non-tenure-track faculty may be uninterested in tenure-track positions because they prefer a different lifestyle, because they know they can obtain employment in nonacademic fields that are more lucrative than are academic jobs, or because they are senior faculty who view themselves as nearing the end of their careers (Gappa, 1996, 2000).

Despite these prominent leanings toward satisfaction, some research does indicate some faculty members' dissatisfaction with their part-time or full-time non-tenure-track appointments, particularly around issues of job security and worker's rights. In one study, 45 percent of part-timers expressed dissatisfaction with their job security (Gappa, 2000). Because part-time or full-time non-tenure-track appointments require only minimal commitment from the institution, turnover is high. Finkelstein and Schuster (2001) note that only a quarter of all part-time faculty appointments extend beyond two terms. A lack of job security may put part-time or full-time non-tenure-track faculty in a vulnerable situation with regard to navigating institutional politics, advocating for resources, and maintaining rigorous classroom standards. Although no definitive stream of research proves a correlation, some evidence also suggests part-time faculty give higher grades as a reaction to negative student evaluations and job security (Greenwald and Gilmore, 1997; McArthur, 1999).

Part-time or full-time non-tenure-track faculty also voice frustrations about their capacities to develop campus-based relationships and to make meaningful commitments to the institution. Many part-time faculty note feelings of second-class citizenship or marginalization. According to Gappa (2000), part-timers may become frustrated because they do not feel integrated into campus life. In the part-time or full-time non-tenure-track faculty system, especially part-time faculty are paid by task (class-contact hours or research projects, for example), and usually they are not paid to be involved in other workings of the institution such as academic planning, curriculum committees, or governance. Some part-time or full-time non-tenure-track faculty are prohibited outright from membership on governance committees. Kezar, Lester, and Anderson (2006) observe that there is "no tradition or systematic policy for including contingent faculty in governance" (p. 122). Yet Gappa and Leslie (1993) and Baldwin and Chronister (2001) have found interest among part-time or full-time non-tenure-track faculty in being involved in institutional governance.

The argument cuts both ways. From the standpoint of the contingent faculty, increased campus involvement beyond specific tasks assigned (like teaching) might prompt stronger commitment by these faculty to the campus and its work, though this supposition needs to be tested, given assertions that a fair amount of institutional governance is likely to be more symbolic than instrumental (Birnbaum, 1988). Alternatively, from the standpoint of an institution and the core faculty, it must be acknowledged that decisions to involve short-term faculty in long-term institutional matters in which the permanent faculty core is deeply invested must be treated judiciously, given likely differences among group members in their career agendas. This topic is for future institutional leaders to take up.

Summary and Implications

Part-time and full-time non-tenure-track appointments are on the rise.

Part-time or full-time non-tenure-track appointments are renewable appointments in which a faculty member is hired to perform specific professorial duties (such as teaching, research, or administration), with teaching the most common.

Women are significantly more likely than men to hold part-time and full-time non-tenure-track faculty positions.

Two-year institutions hire the largest number of part-time faculty; research universities hire the largest number of full-time non-tenure-track faculty.

Professional fields, English, and literature hire the largest number of part-time faculty; the health and natural sciences and the humanities hire the largest number of full-time non-tenure-track faculty.

Institutions of higher education hire part-time and full-time non-tenure-track faculty to save costs, promote logistical flexibility, and boost accountability practices.

Research productivity differs for part-time and full-time non-tenure-track faculty versus tenure track faculty; full-time non-tenure-track faculty have been found in several studies to publish less than tenure-track faculty.

In terms of teaching, part-time faculty have been found to interact less with students out of class, use technology less, use traditional examination techniques more and active-learning techniques less, and maintain lower expectations for writing than tenure-track professors.

When questioned about their work, part-time and full-time non-tenure-track faculty express high levels of job satisfaction, primarily because of the lessened workload and stress of balancing conflicting roles.

Whether part time or full time, however, non-tenure-track faculty voice concerns about the instability of their positions, their status as second-class citizens, and the challenge of building collegial relationships at their institutions.

As we considered the implications of the trend toward part-time and non-tenure-track appointments and recent research on them for faculty growth, a recurrent theme was the reservoir of *resources* from which part-time or full-time non-tenure-track faculty can draw to continue to learn and grow professionally. In making this statement, we employ a broad definition of the word *resources* to include physical resources (office or laboratory space), intellectual resources (opportunities to learn in scholarly ways), professional development resources (instructional technology workshops, teaching center consultations), interpersonal resources (opportunities for professional relationships, a voice in and contributions to governance), financial resources (compensation, benefits), and general resources (time). Although such resources—or the lack of them—are of paramount concern for all faculty members, they are likely to matter a great deal to contingent faculty, given their needs frequently to establish their legitimacy, status, and base of operations in institutions.

What are the implications of this discussion of availability (and unavailability) of resources for the work of part-time or full-time non-tenure-track faculty? We construe the connection between resources and faculty relative to a hierarchy of needs. As previously presented, many resources typically afforded to individuals in traditional faculty appointments are inaccessible to part-time or full-time non-tenure-track faculty. For example, part-time faculty's compensation is typically directly tied to class hours (financial resources), thereby resulting in their spending fewer hours on campus and thus accessing fewer campus-sponsored opportunities for professional development. Moreover, physical resources such as office space, computer equipment, and supplies are often lacking for part-time (and at times full-time) non-tenure-track faculty (Gappa, 2000; Jacoby, 2006). One can assume that if a part-time or full-time non-tenure-track faculty member is struggling to meet lower-level needs such as finding a space to meet with students, worrying about basic job security, or attempting to figure out the course management system without proper training, then the faculty member might not have the time to foster higher-level work such as advancing his or her scholarly learning through reading or research or redesigning a course to better fit a new group of students. The resources available to many part-time appointments do not support effectiveness in teaching, much less research. Many full-time non-tenure-track faculty do not have access to research support. The cumulative cost of basic resource availability and concomitantly lost productivity on the output side of academic organization versus the benefits of part-time or full-time non-tenure-track appointments ("auxiliary inputs to the system") is not well known. Large-scale comparisons of costs and benefits have not been carried out to date.

The absence of basic resources creates a continuous cycle of renewable contracts. Because most part-time or full-time non-tenure-track faculty are not paid to conduct research—thereby an absent resource—they have to further their scholarly learning through research on their own time and own dollar, like Norma in our introductory vignette. This situation not only makes it difficult to carve out time for scholarly research but also keeps part-time or full-time non-tenure-track faculty in a cycle of renewable appointments if they cannot meet tenure-track research expectations in ways that will help them land tenure-track jobs. Further, because part-time faculty spend limited time on campuses, they are less likely to be involved in formal or informal conversations about their scholarly interests.

Another relevant theme is the idea of power or agency in shaping career priorities and commitments. Part-time and full-time non-tenure-track appointments can create caste-like systems in institutions of higher education, with the full-time tenure-track positions representing the top class and the part-time positions the lowest. This caste-like system is likely to reinforce past patterns of discrimination as women and faculty of color may become overrepresented in lower-ranking appointments. Faculty unions have historically played a critical role in advocating for faculty across appointment types. New faculty unions have formed for part-time and non-tenure-track faculty. The role of unions in supporting the professional growth, learning, and agency of part-time and non-tenure-track faculty is largely unsung and ready for further research.

Moreover, future research should extend understanding of the resources that some individuals in non-tenure-track appointments may bring to their jobs and hence their institutions. For example, faculty with strong jobs and connections outside an institution may bring power and influence to their positions that allow them to push for institutional change, as they may have other options for employment and identification. In such cases, institutional leaders and colleagues need to think through the desirability (or nondesirability) of such change for the collective faculty and organization—both at the point of hire and once such faculty come on board. Likewise, some contingent faculty members may bring with them sets of rich connections to other organizations and social activities, positioning some of them as ideal boundary spanners (Milem, Sherlin, and Irwin, 2001). Contingent faculty often are hired because they have knowledge and skills that help enrich the curriculum in ways that current faculty cannot.

In brief, appointment type brings with it a diverse array of resources and opportunities—for learning, development of professional relationships, and abilities to realize personal commitments. Though appearing initially as a bureaucratic shell, appointment type provides a scaffolding of power and opportunities for access to professional endeavor that must be recognized. And as this chapter shows, different faculty appointment types imply both differential access and differential power—for the faculty's professional endeavors and professional learning—on many levels. Future research would do well to consider how persons in a diversity of academic appointments may enact a viable agency for scholarly learning and for professional growth that will be of benefit to their students, colleagues, fields, institutions, communities, and, not least, themselves.

Having considered who the faculty are and what types of appointments they hold as a backdrop, we now turn to the nature of faculty work.

Faculty Work

"Just tell me about a typical day or week in the life of Professor Samson," asked the doctoral student who was interviewing Judy, a recently tenured associate professor of education at a small liberal arts college. Inside her head, Judy laughs at the student's question because it seems like there is no typical day in her life. "OK, let's give this a shot," Judy says to herself. "Well, I guess it's easiest to start with my teaching schedule, since I think that is the only thing that remains consistent around here. I typically teach three undergraduate courses a day, with Friday being discussion sessions rather than lecture sessions. I try to hold my classes in the late morning or early afternoon so that I can spend my mornings preparing for class, responding to e-mails from students, or grading papers. After my courses are over, I usually have to attend a meeting or two in the afternoon. Right now I am on a grant committee that is trying to get money from a private foundation for a service-learning project in which education majors at our college would tutor local children at an after-school program. It seems like this committee is taking up all my free time right now. I mean I am even dreaming about the grant at night. I actually hate working on grant committees because you are not guaranteed a return on all that work. We might not get the grant, and then I feel like all of that time is wasted. But my dean asked me to do it, and it is a great idea. I would just prefer doing something else. Anyway, after my meetings, I try to do something that resembles a personal life such as meet a friend for dinner, see a

movie, or work out. Then I try to put in two to three hours of work late at night. I try to use that time to read the latest education journals or rewrite an article of mine that I am trying to publish. I made the mistake early in my career of getting heavily published and now my department seems to expect me to keep publishing at these levels but without the time or support to do it. I feel completely strapped for time now, but that doesn't seem to matter to the college that is trying to improve its national rankings—and we all know how to improve your rankings . . . increase faculty publication rates. I usually collapse into bed around midnight and then start it all over again the next day. Of course, this 'typical' day or week is usually messed up by some type of drama in the department, or a slew of urgent e-mails, or a deadline for a student's or colleague's recommendation letter, or any other uncontrollable factor in my life!" As the student takes copious notes, Judy wonders if she just scared off an aspiring academic.

A S JUDY SAMSON'S VIGNETTE ILLUSTRATES, the faculty career is one filled with diverse activities. And Judy's career—that of a recently tenured associate professor in education at a liberal arts school—is just one example of what a faculty day might look like. The tone of the vignette, somewhat frenetic, also aptly describes what has been revealed in recent research on faculty work (see, for example, Gappa, Austin, and Trice, 2007; Menges and Austin, 2001; Neumann and Terosky, 2007; Neumann, Terosky, and Schell, 2006; O'Meara, Kaufman, and Kuntz, 2003; Schuster and Finkelstein, 2006; Terosky, 2005). The next section draws on the extant literature to review the nature of faculty work and how it is changing. Following this literature review, we consider these findings through the lens of faculty growth.

Faculty Work Uncovered

What is faculty work today? Most commentators on higher education use the triumvirate of teaching, research, and service to describe what it is that faculty do—explaining that it will differ greatly by discipline and institutional type.

This scheme of teaching, research, and service as framing the content of faculty work serves as scaffolding for considerations of what counts in terms of faculty productivity. Policy analysts and many educational researchers also use it to trace trends in faculty work. Although they are familiar to higher education audiences, we briefly define these faculty work activities.

Teaching is often considered the clearest faculty work activity, because in the most basic administrative terms, it can be viewed through the lens of needed staffing of for-credit courses. Teaching as commonly represented in the higher education discourse involves designing a course, preparing lessons, remaining current in a discipline's literature, grading students' work, meeting with students outside class, and exchanging e-mail with students about course content. We present this definition in the most basic of "work" terms, setting aside for now knowledge-anchored views prominent in the scholarship of teaching (Shulman, 2004; for a review, see Terosky, 2005).

Research is less clear, because research productivity and success are defined differently by institutional type and academic discipline or field. With regard to institutional type, the research role of a professor at a research university might include generating new knowledge through empirical studies and publishing findings in top-tier peer-reviewed journals, while the research role of a professor at a liberal arts college (or a college whose primary mission is not research) might include updating a course to reflect the most current knowledge and preparing articles for local news outlets. In regard to academic discipline or field, the research role of a professor in the natural sciences might involve running a lab of undergraduate or graduate students and publishing findings in a professional journal, while the research role of a professor in an applied profession might involve clinical work and writing practical articles for a trade journal (Schuster and Finkelstein, 2006). What counts as research varies from site to site. As in the case of teaching, we present research here as a work form, though recognizing that it may include as well notions of "scholarly learning" (Neumann, in press) that expand its scope.

Service, the third career activity, is the least understood of the three. Service, inconsistently defined in higher education research, varies by institutional type, academic discipline or field, and career stage (Fear and Sandmann, 1995; Lynton, 1995; Lynton and Elman, 1987; Neumann and Terosky, 2007;

O'Meara, 2002a; Ward, 2003). For the purposes of this monograph, we divide service into several categories, including institutional service, disciplinary service, community service, and scholarly service. We define "institutional service" as contributions to the operation of the employing college or university, "disciplinary service" as contributions to professional associations and the discipline or field in general. External to the higher education institution, we distinguish between scholarly service, which draws on a professor's area of expertise and nonscholarly or community service, which does not draw on a professor's area of expertise (Neumann and Terosky, 2007, p. 283; Bowen and Schuster, 1986; Centra, 1979; Checkoway, 1997; Fear and Sandmann, 1995; Glassick, Huber, and Maeroff, 1997; McCallum, 1994; O'Meara and Jaeger, 2007; Taylor, 1997; Ward, 2003). External service has most recently been discussed under the rubric of community engagement, which includes service learning and participatory action research. Like the prior two activities, service has the potential to embed professors' scholarly learning (Neumann, in press).

Beyond the three-part framework of faculty work, faculty perform a myriad of activities that either do not fit neatly into the three categories or are unnoticed or unrewarded. The American Association of University Professors created a working list of these activities, which include three categories of faculty work (student-centered work, disciplinary- or professional-centered work, and community-centered work), much of which is largely unrecognized. Although the level and type of work vary by institutional type, the AAUP created a sampling of faculty work activities, which included among others such diverse activities as:

- Counseling students about personal problems, learning difficulties, or life choices;
- Writing letters of recommendation to help students enter graduate programs or secure jobs or internships;
- Participating in a departmental self-study;
- Applying for a grant for the department or helping to raise money for the university;
- Answering phone calls from citizens and offering professional expertise;

- Serving on the boards of local, state, or national groups
(see http://www.aaup.org/AAUP/issues/facwork/facultydolist.htm for the full list).

A key point from this list is that although we may have a common under-standing of many aspects of teaching, research, and service, *much* of what faculty do daily in the name of maintaining the infrastructure and mission of a campus involves activities that extend beyond such categorization or recognition.

Emerging Trends in Faculty Work

A literature review of research studies on faculty work reveals several emerging trends: redefining scholarship and new involvements in teaching and community engagement as forms of scholarship, integrating responsibilities, rising workload, interdisciplinary work, and increasing role specialization.

Redefining the meaning of scholarship and identifying those types of scholarship that count in the realm of faculty work are part of a prominent national movement. As described earlier, the redefining scholarship movement has resulted in faculty's thinking about and engaging in teaching as a form of scholarship, integrating knowledge for lay audiences, and pursuing community engagement in scholarly ways (O'Meara and Rice, 2005). As such, practitioners and researchers have explored the nature of teaching and community engagement as new forms of scholarship, studied why faculty are motivated to engage in such forms of scholarship, and promoted institutional recognition for these types of scholarship (Huber, 2002, 2004; O'Meara, 2008; Terosky, 2005; Ward, 2003).

Another trend is the increase in studies focused on faculty's integrating the various roles and responsibilities facing them as academics. Rather than compartmentalizing research, teaching, and service into isolated "silos," researchers have noted ways in which roles are integrated (Bloomgarden and O'Meara, 2007; Colbeck, 1998, 2002a). Likewise, studies have examined how faculty integrate work and family roles (Colbeck and Drago, 2005). Scholars argue that workload studies viewing faculty work as compartmentalized provide skewed results. For example, Colbeck (1998) notes that faculty workload studies do not allow reporting of work that fulfills more than one purpose, thereby skewing the estimations of time allocated. In two workload studies at single institutions, faculty were permitted to estimate time spent on activities that contributed to more than one work category. The studies found that faculty accomplished multiple goals for as much as 45 percent of their working hours (Colbeck, 1998).

Similar to role integration, interdisciplinarity is another trend in both faculty work and studies of faculty work (Lattuca, 2001; Trower, 2008). Research has found Generation X and Y faculty as well as aspiring faculty interested in and pursuing interdisciplinary research. They often struggle with some of the structural and cultural issues that go with it, however. For example, many scholars doing interdisciplinary work are in joint appointments, thus living in two "academic homes" whose members may not see eye to eye on their priorities. This situation can make the pursuit of tenure a challenge (Trower, 2008). A steep learning curve is involved in becoming fluent in the languages, norms, and perspectives of more than one discipline simultaneously, and faculty often need to learn new ways of thinking about problems, develop boundary scanning skills, and learn to work collaboratively in ways other faculty do not (Lattuca, 2001).

A fourth trend relates to rising workloads. In 1984, faculty reported working forty hours per week; by 1998, faculty reported working 48.6 hours per week, which amounts to a 21.5 percent increase (Schuster and Finkelstein, 2006). The number of faculty working fifty hours per week, a group that Schuster and Finkelstein (2006) refer to as "driven" or "committed," doubled between 1972 and 1998 to the point of accounting for nearly two fifths of the faculty body (p. 81). And one in four faculty members work more than fifty-five hours per week (Schuster and Finkelstein, 2006). This increase in work hours per week has occurred in all types of institutions, but research universities have faced the most dramatic increases because of increased pressure to publish and to improve instructional practices. Studies have examined how pursuit of institutional prestige, entrepreneurism, and other forces are pushing faculty to publish and to work increasing numbers of hours (Creamer, 1998; O'Meara, 2007a). These statistics stand in stark contrast to some of the more critical commentaries of faculty work, for instance, accusations that faculty maintain minimal workloads and contribute inadequately to student learning.

Fifth, researchers note that the role of the professor is narrowing as the number of community college and part-time non-tenure-track faculty increases. In contrast to what Rice (1996) refers to as the "whole scholar" or what Colbeck (2008) refers to as the "integrated scholar"—wherein faculty are engaged in multiple forms of scholarship and faculty work—it is growing increasingly more common for faculty to engage in just one role: that of a teacher, a researcher, *or* an administrator. The point has been made that faculty focused on teaching can enhance their teaching through research on student learning and pedagogy. Regardless of the type of research, researchers have long tried to demonstrate the tangible benefits to teachers who are also scholars. The implications of an increase in faculty positions without an explicit role for scholarship have been noted and requires careful exploration in the future (Bland and others, 2006; Gappa, 2000; Schuster and Finkelstein, 2006). Clearly an opportunity exists for faculty who emphasize teaching to focus their discovery on student learning and pedagogy through the scholarship of teaching (Huber, 2004)—but only if that time is considered part of their role and they are rewarded.

Each of these themes and lines of inquiry into faculty work has several things in common. First, none of these work phenomena appeared out of nowhere; they grew out of a larger professional, organizational, and social world that is itself changing. Second, each of these evolving shifts in faculty work calls on faculty to develop new knowledge and skills—both in preparation for the professoriate and through mid- and advanced career. The next section discusses some of the major social and political contexts that have no doubt shaped these trends. The last section points out the types of new academic skills, knowledge, and orientations we believe this work calls for.

Measures of Accountability

Over the past decade, institutions of higher education have faced pressure to do more and to do it more efficiently. A loud cry has been raised for higher education to become more accountable and more effective than it has been in the past, especially in terms of undergraduate instruction (Schuster and Finkelstein, 2006; U.S. Department of Education, 2006). Such calls have strong implications for the future of faculty work. During a time of reduced public trust in higher education, both the faculty and their work have come under increased public scrutiny (Honan and Teferra, 2001). Distrust comes through in negative media portrayals of the professoriate (see Sykes, 1988) as well as in state systems' increased efforts to regulate faculty work (Colbeck, 2002b; Gappa, Austin, and Trice, 2007). One example of unprecedented government efforts to regulate faculty work is Ohio's legislative mandate requiring a 10 percent increase in time spent on teaching by all faculty at four-year public institutions (Colbeck, 2002b). Gappa, Austin, and Trice (2005) note that universities are demanding increased efficiency and original research from faculty as financial constraints and state oversight increase.

What are the implications for faculty work in light of rising accountability movements such as that in Ohio? Scholars argue that faculty are becoming more and more like "managed professionals," a term borrowed from Rhoades (1998). In other words, both increasing calls for accountability and governmental efforts to regulate faculty work challenge the autonomy and self-governance that once characterized the faculty career. Faculty are finding themselves in a new context of public distrust of their work and of public (lay) intrusion into it.

Out of the accountability movement, as discussed in the first chapter, came reforms such as post-tenure review, detailed annual reporting procedures, new accreditation movements, and strategic planning exercises. This new layer of institutional activity has become yet another source of faculty work, but rarely is this new work acknowledged in institutional reward systems.

Rise in Fiscal Challenges, Competition, and Entrepreneurism

As higher education faces reduced financial support from government sources and as it faces rising costs in the form of operating costs, technology costs, compensation benefits, and student services, among others, it is assuming a distinct competitive and entrepreneurial feel (Gappa, Austin, and Trice, 2007; Slaughter and Rhoades, 2004). The entrepreneurial spirit is especially palpable at research universities but also at institutions that are striving to emulate research universities or improve their national rankings (O'Meara, 2007a; Slaughter and Rhoades, 2004).

The competitive and entrepreneurial milieu of contemporary American campuses has implications for faculty work. Professors are being asked to publish more and to obtain more grant money and other forms of revenue. Academic departments are being asked to initiate revenue-producing programs (Gappa, Austin, and Trice, 2007) and decide which courses to offer based on revenue, which undermines the faculty's authority over curricular decision making (Slaughter, 1997). For instance, the new technology available for producing courses, especially online, blurs the lines of faculty ownership of a course and its content (Gappa, Austin, and Trice, 2007).

Research on entrepreneurism and academic capitalism has begun to provide pictures of both the benefits that can be provided to graduate education and faculty research from partnerships with industry (Mendoza, 2007) and ways in which these forces can harm academic freedom and faculty autonomy in matters of knowledge production. Some studies have found that professional relationships developed with industry can actually provide faculty a source of power on their own campuses, especially when the partnerships bring in significant funding. Other studies have outlined ways in which faculty have been strongly guided to study topics that benefit industry (Slaughter and Rhoades, 2004). In the future, we need still more studies that help us understand how faculty (especially junior, women, and faculty of color) navigate the waters of entrepreneurism when their research may be at odds with or just not related to industry or government priorities. We also need further study of what faculty learn from entrepreneurial partnerships and how such learning shapes their teaching and research on campuses.

Changes in Students

The number of students enrolled in higher and postsecondary education has been increasing by approximately 50 percent over the past twenty-five years, and it is expected to increase another 15 percent from 2003 (Austin, 2002a; Gappa, Austin, and Trice, 2007). Beyond the growing enrollments, students are increasingly more diverse with regard to age, gender, race, nationality, ethnicity, and educational expectations (Gappa, Austin, and Trice, 2007). A major trend is the rise in nontraditional students, with current data indicating that students twenty-five years and older account for approximately 40 percent of the undergraduate population (Gappa, Austin, and Trice, 2007). Nontraditional students have differing expectations for their higher education experiences, including expectations of convenient class times and locations, lower costs for courses and services, and specific curricula that directly connect course material to professional practice. In addition to diversifying student ages, recent statistics note that ethnic and racial minority enrollments have increased from 16 percent to 25 percent since 1980 (Gappa, Austin, and Trice, 2007).

Like the rise in accountability and competitiveness, a diversifying student population also has implications for faculty work. Faculty members need to learn how to work with a multicultural and multigenerational group of students. Gappa, Austin, and Trice (2005) argue that a continually diversifying student population has dramatically affected faculty, which does not have the institutional support they need to respond to these changes. This contextual factor will shape the way higher education and faculty do their work, ranging from increased awareness of diversity issues, to family-friendly class meeting times, to calls for developmental education for struggling students, to new forms of instruction that meet the interests and needs of a student population that is increasingly diverse in age, gender, race, and preferred modes of instruction.

As we look at the diversification of higher education and the continuing shift toward expanding access, we need to better understand the ways in which faculty can assist students in engaging inside and outside the classroom. Portraits of individual faculty who have made commitments to student retention and who have found distinct ways to support minority students and first-generation students are as important as national surveys that consider the characteristics of faculty who report such commitments.

Technology

Another factor affecting faculty work is the rise in technology and its use in instruction and day-to-day operations. Faculty are being called on to integrate technology into their teaching and work lives (Groves and Zemel, 2000; Okojie and Olinzock, 2006; Schuster and Finkelstein, 2006). New technologies have been created to assist the learning experience—for example, through online discussions, course management systems, out-of-class student-faculty communication, online courses, multimedia presentations, and so forth. Besides teaching and student communication, technology is also touted as a means of fostering collaboration among colleagues. For example, Ma and Runyon (2004) suggest that faculty maintain their own Web sites (grouped by department or discipline) where they can post their syllabi, class notes, and related course materials. Web sites could also house a community area to post group work, suggestions for other faculty, and so forth.

These new technologies require faculty to reconsider the way they go about working and their teaching especially. Technology does open up possibilities for better communication (including outside the classroom) between professors and students. But increased communication also poses a challenge as faculty face a growing expectation that they be available to students all day, every day. This change in faculty-student interaction poses a challenge to faculty time management. Moreover, the "Net" generation of students (students who grew up with technology and the Internet) learns in ways that are often dramatically different from their professors. The need for faculty to learn and adapt to the new way of doing business can contribute to information and cognitive overload for faculty, a condition that may freeze action, change, and learning. Birnbaum's references (1988, 1992) to administrators who at times purposefully "overload a system" with new information while pursuing more substantive policies elsewhere that will have real impact on faculty work are relevant here. For example, faculty may have their attention cued to new requirements to have all syllabi on a Blackboard system by the following semester, when in fact the student evaluation system is being put online and changed in ways that faculty fail to attend to. Such changes on campus, on top of the ever-expanding amount of research online to keep up with, are often too much. It is important that as more aspects of faculty work are put online or enhanced through technology, critical questions must be asked about how change will affect the daily work of faculty—in positive *and* negative ways.

As with any major change in the conduct of one's work, faculty also need professional development opportunities to learn how to make good use of technology to enhance student learning, fostering collegial interactions, and simplify the administrative work associated with faculty careers.

Researchers have also begun to look at faculty experiences and satisfaction with online courses and programs of study. Given the increase in online programs, especially at community colleges and doctoral colleges that primarily use adjuncts for such programs, it behooves higher education practitioners and researchers to better understand how to support faculty in updating their skills and knowledge and working with administrators on their campuses to ask for needed resources. It is important to understand how academic programs can facilitate relationships among online faculty in hopes of fostering faculty learning. The long-term implications of online programs that face a "revolving door" of faculty (mainly adjunct faculty) because of turnover must be studied for the sake of program development and student learning.

Each of these forces and trends will continue to influence faculty satisfaction, a topic that has been a target of research over the past two decades.

Faculty Satisfaction

Faculty satisfaction has been studied in great detail (see Hagedorn, 2000; Rosser, 2004, 2005a; Schuster and Finkelstein, 2006). Although the NSOPF:04 shows high degrees of overall job satisfaction for faculty (87.5 percent), regardless of appointment, career stage, institution, gender, or ethnic background (Gappa, Austin, and Trice, 2007), data analyses indicate a significant decline in job satisfaction over the past generation. In 1969 and 1975 surveys, half the faculty defined themselves as "very satisfied"; by 1998 approximately one third of the faculty defined themselves as "very satisfied." Moreover, the amount of faculty who reported being dissatisfied doubled from 7.2 percent in 1975 to 15.3 percent in 1998 (Schuster and Finkelstein, 2006). This trend in decreasing satisfaction holds in all institutional types, although community college faculty report higher levels of satisfaction (51.1 percent of tenured community college faculty report they are "very satisfied"). Another survey of tenure-track faculty at six research universities found that 25 percent were dissatisfied or very dissatisfied with their work or workplace (Trower and Bleak, 2004a, 2004b).

Compared with other professional fields, higher education enjoys an overall high level of faculty satisfaction (Gappa, Austin, and Trice, 2007). Scholars have explored areas of faculty dissatisfaction—including rising workloads, rising publication expectations to achieve tenure and promotion, reduced capabilities to balance personal and professional lives, and declining collegial interactions—in hopes of bringing awareness and action to these areas of discontent (Hagedorn, 2000).

One of the main sources of dissatisfaction for faculty is rising workloads, or trying to keep up with the overflowing plate of faculty work. Fiscal constraints and the rise in part-time faculty appointments have left fewer permanent full-time faculty to do the work. Rice (2006) also suggests that the array of late-twentieth-century postsecondary education reforms that were often added onto the faculty plate, often without clear guidelines or sufficient support, contribute to the feel of overload. Rice, Sorcinelli, and Austin (2000) found that professors participating in their study viewed their careers as hectic and relentless.

Another area of dissatisfaction is rising expectations for tenure and promotion (Gappa, Austin, and Trice, 2007; Rice, 2006; Schuster and Finkelstein, 2006). This phenomenon, often referred to as "publish or perish," is linked to some institutions' desire to improve their rankings and prestige, which is linked further to research productivity. Lindholm, Szelenyi, Hurtado, and Korn (2005) found that 44 percent of faculty listed tenure and promotion review as a key area of stress.

The rising workload and increasing expectations about tenure and promotion connect to another key area of faculty dissatisfaction—the inability to balance one's personal and professional lives (Gappa, Austin, and Trice, 2007; Hagedorn, 2000). As the workload and competition increase, faculty find that their career tasks are continuously growing and that they must be meshed with the responsibilities of one's home, family, or personal responsibilities (all of which may increase at various times of life). Lindholm, Szelenyi, Hurtado, and Korn's study (2005) found that 73.5 percent of faculty reported managing household responsibilities and 73.8 percent the lack of personal time as major areas of stress in relation to their work. Although issues of balancing work and personal life affect both men and women, women on and off the tenure track are particularly dissatisfied with regard to this issue, as they find it difficult to bear and raise children because of the lack of flexibility in their careers or the fear of impeding tenure (Armenti, 2004b; Gappa, Austin, and Trice, 2007; Glazer-Raymo, 1999, 2008; Mason and Goulden, 2002; Ropers-Huilman, 2000; Ward and Wolf-Wendel, 2003). Sixty-one percent of assistant professors in a study by Finkel and Olswang (1996) state that having children is an impediment to obtaining tenure.

Another area of faculty dissatisfaction that may disproportionately affect women is a shrinking collegial atmosphere in colleges and universities. The rising workload and the transient nature of contingent appointments are antithetical to collegial interaction. Despite research that points consistently to the benefits of collegial interactions for faculty satisfaction (Hagedorn, 1996; Kadar, 2005; Riger, Stokes, Raja, and Sullivan, 1997; Ropers-Huilman, 2000), the current environment is moving away from this ideal (see Neumann, in press; Neumann, Terosky, and Schell, 2006). This shift away from a collegial environment may be especially detrimental to women because of the value women place on connecting with others (Astin and Davis, 1993; Ropers-Huilman, 2000) and because of the importance of mentoring for the career success of women (Tierney and Bensimon, 1996).

The decline in faculty satisfaction with their work raises concerns about higher education's ability to recruit and retain future and current faculty, especially faculty from diverse backgrounds. Lindholm, Szelenyi, Hurtado, and Korn (2005) found that 31 percent of faculty are considering work outside the academy and that women, with or without children, and people of color are disproportionately choosing nonacademic careers (Wolfinger, Mason, and Goulden, 2004). Bieber and Worley (2006) noted that graduate students often find their idealized notion of the academic career conflicting with the realities of the profession, thereby leading to the possibility of graduate students' being less likely to pursue an academic career. In fact, Wimsatt and Trice (2006) found that 62 percent of faculty in a national survey believe that graduate students are less likely to pursue an academic research career than they were in the past. The same concerns apply to new faculty. Rice, Sorcinelli, and Austin (2000) found that the stress of finding enough time to do their work leads aspiring and new faculty to question whether a faculty career is viable.

As faculty members question whether an academic career is a good idea for them, given the changing roles and expectations of that career, higher education leaders worry about losing good people who are already in professorial positions. One third of faculty responding to a Higher Education Research Institute survey indicated they would consider leaving academe, and 28 percent of respondents said that they had recently had other job offers (Lindholm, Szelenyi, Hurtado, and Korn, 2005). People are less likely to remain in a position today than in the past (Gappa, Austin, and Trice, 2007), which is a concern for higher education because faculty are its foremost asset (and its most costly resource). The AAUP, supported by the Sloan Foundation, is conducting the Balancing Academic Career and Family Work initiative, which pushes restructuring the workplace to meet the needs of faculty.

Although the trends discussed in this chapter will likely touch faculty work, they will do so to different degrees and in different ways. Type of institution, discipline, and an abundance of other factors shape the content of an institution's—and faculty's—response to a particular trend. For example, efforts to reform roles and rewards to support multiple forms of scholarship play out very differently by institutional type (O'Meara, 2005a). Ward and Wolf-Wendel (2007) found that the balance of work activities by institutional type causes different kinds of stress on family. Clark's observation (1987) that faculty live in "small worlds, different worlds" has never been more true.

Summary and Implications

Faculty work is typically categorized into three activities: teaching, research, and service. But faculty work also includes numerous tasks that are often unrecognized or unrewarded.

Faculty are increasing the number of hours worked per week, especially at research universities.

Several external forces affect the daily work of faculty, including but not limited to accountability, entrepreneurism, demographic trends, and technology.

The nature of the professoriate's actual work tasks and the knowledge, values, and skills needed to perform them are changing (for example, community engagement requires skills as boundary spanners with nonprofits, teaching with technology requires technology literacy, entrepreneurial environments require developing relationships with foundations and government agencies).

Although faculty satisfaction is high compared with some other professional careers, it is nonetheless declining. Increasing workloads, rising expectations for tenure and promotion, challenges of balancing work and one's personal life, and the decline in a collegial atmosphere at colleges and universities have all been suggested as possible causes. Higher education scholars and practitioners worry that the rising workload and declining satisfaction rates will hinder the recruitment and retaining of faculty, especially women and faculty of color.

It is difficult to discuss faculty work without considering who the faculty are and the kinds of appointments they hold. For example, we may see the faculty appointment structure as contextualizing faculty work. If we view faculty work away from appointment structures, social and cultural issues, and so forth, we see the ideal triumvirate of teaching, research, and service probably in balance. If, however, we contextualize a certain instructor's work—let us say *in* the changing appointment structure that brings many new contingent faculty to campus—we are unlikely to see the triumvirate. If the instructor is herself contingent, we might expect her work, against the backdrop of her temporary appointment, to be focused more on teaching than on research, service, outreach, or other institutional activities. Because the faculty is changing as rapidly as it is, it is hard to talk about faculty work as though the changing appointment structure did not exist. That structure molds the work.

So what does this situation say about faculty growth? We can say that the contexts in which faculty work these days shape or direct faculty work in particular directions and that the work, so constrained, becomes the site of the faculty's learning (Neumann, in press)—and by extension of their growth. For example, the rise in technology and student diversity calls on faculty to organize their work in particular ways, and doing so forces them into substantive learning in an organizational scheme that is new to them. The rise in entrepreneurism calls on faculty to become resourceful in developing relationships with community, social, and business partners in developing projects that bring in funding and are applicable to the real world; faculty learn resourcefulness while engaging as they do with the outside world. Their learning is part of their larger growth as professionals. Regardless of what the contextual change may be (a new appointment structure, new technologies, increased student diversity, expectations for entrepreneurship), it is likely to shift how professors act and interact on the job; their new actions and interactions may spur new thought and new learning—and possibly growth.

Clearly, the changing nature of faculty work requires new intentional kinds of learning; according to Dweck (2006), it requires a "growth mind-set" of scanning the environment for opportunities to learn and practice new skills and to develop new knowledge to work in new contexts. The chaotic and frenetic aspects of faculty work, described in many studies as "overload," seem to be here to stay. So too does the mission creep described by faculty as shifting institutional priorities. As such, this work context requires reflection and a sense of purpose and direction in determining what work is important and what is not, and where an individual's talents lie in responding to myriad calls for contributions.

It appears that we need to think about faculty careers in more complex ways that take into account the traditional faculty career as well as the nontraditional one. At this time, the prevailing image of the academic career continues to be that of a traditional professor. But is this image of the professor—a person working for an institution for decades and conducting research, teaching, and service—a disservice to a better understanding of the realities of the academic career? What does it imply for the way we study and write about faculty careers? What does it imply for how we even define a faculty career in the first place? What types of knowledge, skills, and orientations are needed to effectively engage in the forms of faculty work that are part of this alternate image? These questions have begun to be explored (see Austin, 2002a, 2002b; Austin and McDaniels, 2006; O'Meara, 2008), serving as pathways for future research on academic work.

The call for a new image of faculty work is necessitated by the signs of decreasing faculty satisfaction and disproportionate numbers of women and people of color opting out of a faculty career. It is our belief that research can play a significant role in the development of a new view of faculty work—a view that draws on the ways in which the academic career is changing and the ways in which it is staying the same. What do we know about what faculty themselves are doing about their dissatisfaction? How can we explore and bring awareness to strategies for navigating the current state of faculty work and transforming the future of this work? Recent studies by Rhoades, Kiyama, McCormick, and Quiroz (2008) on "cosmopolitan local" newcomers to the profession; by Huston, Norman, and Ambrose (2007) on how faculty might renew psychological contracts gone bad; and Neumann, Terosky, and Schell (2006) on career-based personal agency offer pathways for future scholarship in this area.

Since their inception, American colleges and universities have drawn some of the world's best and brightest to academic careers. Moving forward, how will the faculty themselves shape this evolving career so that it remains viable for our best and our brightest—for their continued learning? This question is central to American higher education because the fact remains that the best and the brightest—especially those underappreciated, unsupported, and marginalized by the current structures of colleges and universities—will have other professional avenues to pursue to realize their commitments and expertise. They may be lost to higher education—a loss that the field will feel in big ways.

The next chapter examines how higher education institutions acknowledge and reward the work of its faculty, especially in light of new entrants to academic careers and the evolving nature of faculty work.

Recent Reforms of Faculty Reward Systems

Jennifer is walking down the hall with a colleague talking about an oral history archive that the two of them are building in collaboration with members of the local community center. Like many community engagement efforts, the work is time-consuming, but she takes great satisfaction in the opportunities it provides her master's students to carry out interviews on matters of current local import and their historic origins. Together they all are learning about the history of African American women of this community during and after World War II and a quilting business that boosted the local economy while bringing families together. As they learn about the history of this time, they also learn how to use research methods (interviews and analyses of artifacts) to piece together elements of the past. The director of the community center has praised the project in several letters to her department chair and dean. But what most seemed to get their attention was the National Endowment for the Humanities grant she recently received in support of future work on the project. The grant is for $300,000 over five years—which is ironic in that she is on a three-year renewable faculty contract that she hopes will one day be converted to tenure track. To be competitive in a future tenure-track search, she would need to spend a little less time on this community engagement grant project (though it uses research, it seems unlikely to yield research publications) and more on traditional journal publications building off her dissertation. Attending to both the grant project and her *publications is next to impossible, given that her contract is for three high-enrollment courses per semester. Jennifer feels caught between the oral history project that both she and the local community seem to value greatly and the need to publish off her dissertation, which she thinks is fine to do yet far less meaningful. She wonders whether she can find the time to step back and rethink her overall approach to her work but is not sure she has a full enough perspective to make what feels to her like a weighty decision.*

IT IS NOT AN ACCIDENT that so much of the literature on faculty, faculty work, and reward systems has included the phrases "reconsidering," "reforming," and "rethinking." Indeed, many efforts took place during the late 1980s and 1990s—and continue today—to reform faculty reward systems. This chapter reviews research on the nature of reward systems and how they appear to be influencing institutions and their faculties. It considers how women and faculty of color tend to fare in academic reward systems, then reviews research on four efforts to reform faculty reward systems. Before delving into research on reward systems, we pause to consider their meaning in contemporary academic life.

It is interesting to consider the etymology of the word "reward," which the *Merriam-Webster* online dictionary observes is closely related to the word "regard" and has meant "to look back at, regard, care for" (www.merriam-webster.com). Very few stories of tenure-track faculty begin with fond memories of their tenure-track years as a time when faculty were "cared for." Instead tenure-track processes, one form of reward system, have been described as akin to "archery in the dark" (Rice, Sorcinelli, and Austin, 2000), running on a treadmill, and something to get through or survive. The former image captures the ambiguity faculty feel about what they are supposed to be aiming for in the tenure process, while the latter captures the intense feeling of pushing through that period of ambiguity. Many would critique this observation as a privileged problem, given how hard it is to obtain a tenure-track position. Likewise, commentators observe that the tenure track is not unlike entry into many other professions such as the first few years at a law firm, or residency after medical school. Nonetheless it is useful to observe that most faculty feel that this often described aspect of their reward systems is isolating, competitive, and individualistic rather than focused on growth. The Free Dictionary.com defines a reward as "something given or received in recompense for worthy behavior or in retribution for evil acts" and "the return for performance of a desired behavior" (www.thefreedictionary.com/reward). This definition is also consistent with the rhetoric and framing of reward systems in higher education wherein the institution and its major players are like parents to more vulnerable and less powerful faculty, who must win their favor.

Turning to the second part of the often used phrase, "reward system," the same free dictionary observes that a "system" is "a group of interacting or interdependent elements forming a complex whole," with a secondary definition of "the prevailing social order, the establishment" (www.thefreedictionary.com/system). This concept of a system as not just one thing—such as an actual promotion and tenure decision—but rather as a collection of decisions, incentives, disincentives, favor, and disfavor and as both structure and culture seems helpful in considering the broader meaning of reward systems.

We consider these definitions before reviewing research on reward systems and reform in them as a way of opening up the question of what reward systems are and who they are for. What do they accomplish, what might they accomplish? One observation at the onset from review of the research noted in this chapter is that it appears to be framed as more summative than formative or focused on growth. Second, it may overemphasize productivity as a purely output-focused quality of higher education that misses the "craft" and learning inherent "in process"—or at best, it may present an overly narrow view of productivity. Third, not everyone seems to fare equally well in existing reward systems. Fourth and finally, they are actually very important.

At their heart, reward systems are about the valuing of professional work (O'Meara, 2002b). They are a primary way we—the community of faculty and administrators who act as stewards of a place (the establishment)—come together to witness, promote, and assess each other's work. The consequences of such "regard" have lasting impact. Although much faculty motivation is intrinsic, faculty reward systems can facilitate faculty learning and growth, or they can frustrate and damage faculty members' senses of agency to shape their own learning and distinct intellectual and professional careers and work lives.

Sometimes reward systems have little to no influence, as faculty seem to operate outside them. We review below what has been learned about how reward systems influence faculty behavior and how such systems might be reformed to be more equitable—and beyond that to catalyze professional growth.

The chapter's focus is summarized in the case of Jennifer, who weighs the rewards associated with two very different forms of work: on the one hand, community engagement as represented by her involvement in the local oral history project and, on the other hand, traditional publication. Jennifer's experiences of weighing the outcomes of these two very different kinds of work and feeling she must choose one or the other is quite common in twenty-first-century American higher education and is an example of the consequences of our reward systems for the work that we do.

For the purposes of this chapter, we build from the definitions above to consider faculty reward systems broadly as *the many ways in which an institution regards faculty—including but not limited to how it recruits, sustains, assesses, and advances faculty throughout their careers.*

The rest of the chapter breaks down into three main parts. First, a following section considers recent research on how reward systems affect faculty behavior. The next section considers how women and faculty of color are faring in current reward systems. A third section is broken down into four subsections—efforts to create or eliminate tenure, initiating post-tenure review, redefining scholarship, and policies to help academic parents balance work and family. The chapter then turns to discussion of what we have and have not learned from the study of recent reform in reward systems, with implications for both research and practice.

The Influence of Reward Systems on Faculty Behavior

Significant advances have been made over the last two decades in efforts to develop conceptual lenses for understanding how reward systems contribute to the socialization and motivation of faculty and to the coordination, even direction, of their efforts. As early as 1983, Austin and Gamson offered the observation that reward systems can be significant sources of extrinsic motivation. As faculty receive positive reinforcement by way of awards, travel funds, professional development monies, merit pay, and promotion, they are in effect socialized toward the types of behavior the rewards recognize—as legitimate or as desirable. Blackburn and Lawrence (1995) showed how social knowledge about what an institution values, in dynamic interaction with faculty members' self-knowledge (what, as individuals, they do best and what they prefer to do and are drawn personally to do), shapes faculty members' behaviors. These two frameworks suggest that although reward systems are not the only motivating forces worth considering, they are important shapers of faculty work priorities.

Higher education reward systems have historically given research higher priority than teaching, even in primarily teaching-focused four-year institutions, a point underscored by Fairweather's findings (Fairweather 1993, 1996, 2005) that the more faculty members emphasize teaching in their workload, the less they make in salary. This relationship between faculty activity and institutional reward appears to be a powerful incentive for faculty to emphasize research over teaching, despite institutional type.

An important line of inquiry has begun to consider the intersection of appointment type and its associated reward system with different kinds of faculty productivity. Whether because this research is primarily quantitatively focused or recent, we observe that the definitions of productivity emphasized focus on traditional measures of faculty output rather than process-oriented measures of faculty learning, commitment, and accomplishment we advocate for future research. Nonetheless, this research has helped us understand the consequences of different types of appointments that structure in and value one type of work over others. Drawing on an extensive literature review complemented by analyses of the NSOPF:99, Bland and others (2006) identified characteristics of a "productive" department in a research, doctorate-granting institution. Bland and her colleagues classified those characteristics into the individual faculty member, the structure or environment of the faculty member, and the leadership of the organization. Bland and others assert that these domains influence each other and that faculty are likely to be most productive when all features (characteristics) of a given domain are present. Institutional features include rewards, adequate work time, brokered opportunities for professional development, communication networks, mentoring, sufficient size and diversity, positive group climate, a shared culture of research, clear mission and goals that emphasize research, recruitment of driven and research-oriented faculty, and decentralized organization (Bland and others, 2006). This research characterized a productive department as one where faculty contributed to department products such as grants, articles, presentations, and books; achieved tenure and promotion; acted as effective teachers; and overall engaged as committed faculty (Bland and others, 2006). One interesting aspect of this model is that it offers a more nuanced look at all the elements that go into a faculty member's ecosystem that contribute to their work—thus also broadening how we might think about what is and is not in a reward system.

A few researchers have begun to examine how the appointment type itself and the rewards, conditions, and resources associated with it influence faculty productivity, defined most often as "faculty performance and specific outputs" such as use of preferred teaching pedagogies, grant dollars brought in, or research publications produced. As "Faculty Appointments" underscored, this factor is important because more and more institutions are choosing to offer non-tenure-track appointments, rarely with the guidance of forecast data for how they will affect core higher education outcomes—teaching quality, research productivity, faculty commitment, and faculty diversity (Bland and others, 2006). It is also important because each appointment type comes with a different kind of reward system that must be examined for the types of behaviors it promotes.

Finkelstein and Schuster (2001) have conducted a preliminary study of varying kinds of appointment types and different measures of faculty performance. Their report concludes that compared with tenured or tenure-track faculty, faculty in non-tenure-track appointments published fewer articles, worked five fewer hours per week (up to ten fewer at research universities), spent less time out of class with students, and felt less committed to their institutions. Bland, Center, and Finstad's survey (2000) of the University of Minnesota Medical School's full-time faculty indicates that faculty on a clinical scholar track published fewer articles and worked fewer hours per week but were more satisfied than tenure-track or tenured faculty. Likewise, Bland and others (2006) found that in research or doctoral institutions, full-time tenure-appointed faculty were significantly more productive in research and in education, were more committed to staying in academics, and worked more hours per week than their non-tenured colleagues. Particularly stunning was the comparison of newly hired faculty: "newly hired tenure-track faculty spend 5 percent more time on research than newly hired non-tenure faculty members spend, but they are 2.5 times more productive than their non-tenure counterparts" (p. 115). Bland and others (2006) point out that appointment type cannot be said definitively to "cause" these differences; other variables such as recruitment processes mediate influences of performance. Nonetheless, the fact that their study had these findings while holding mission and institutional type constant suggests appointment type and its associated reward system and structure seem to have some influence on faculty work. Bland and others (2006) observe that their findings are consistent with research on other complex organizations showing that systems and conditions of employment, particularly reward systems, significantly affect productivity and satisfaction (Deming, 2000; Senge, 1990). We propose later in this chapter that these conditions also have significant implications for faculty growth.

Likewise, Umbach's research (2007b) on the interaction of appointment type and teaching behaviors suggests that the filter of a tenure system and even of a full-time non-tenure-track system in comparison with primarily part-time faculty has implications for performance in terms of teaching behaviors that research asserts is associated with student learning. Jaeger, Thornton, and Eagan's research (2007) on the intersection of appointment type and retention, finding part-time faculty less effective in promoting retention in gatekeeper courses, likewise points to real connections between appointment type, its associated reward system, and productivity.

Researchers have also explored how some of the factors that differentiate academics and define their "different worlds" (such as institutional type, discipline, career stage, or demographics) interact with reward systems to influence faculty behavior (Clark, 1987). For example, as the arguments for and against post-tenure review revved up, researchers have tried to understand how post-tenure status might influence productivity. Research on faculty performance revealed no significant differences between younger and older faculty (Blackburn and Lawrence, 1995; Bland and Bergquist, 1997; Walker, 2002).

Research suggests that professionals like faculty are more likely to thrive under evaluation systems that provide significant autonomy and freedom (Baldwin, 1990; Blackburn and Lawrence, 1995). Although some studies have noted differences among junior and senior faculty in terms of the kinds of work they produce each year, most of the studies seem to have shown shifts in priorities from one type of academic work to another (more time on teaching or chairing dissertations than writing articles, or more time on books than articles) and a greater emphasis on quality and longer works as faculty age rather than a slow decline by the majority of faculty into "deadwood" feared by some external critics. The key word here seems to be "productivity"; although some types of productivity may diminish with age, others may increase or improve in quality.

Equity for Women Faculty and Faculty of Color

A significant amount of attention in the last decade has gone to the lack of equity between women and men and between faculty of color and white faculty with regard to reward systems and career progression. One major area of research is faculty salary. Before addressing inequity in faculty salary, it is important to contextualize the discussion with two key points.

First, research conducted by the National Education Association (NEA Higher Education Advocate, 2007) shows that the majority of all faculty salaries were stagnant from 2004 to 2007 as faculty salaries did not keep up with inflation. In addition, faculty in private institutions tend to make more than faculty in public institutions (NEA Higher Education Advocate, 2007). In all but one institutional sector (private associate degree institutions), women faculty continue to earn less than men faculty (NEA Higher Education Advocate, 2007, p. 11). The greatest disparity is at doctoral universities, where women's salaries are less than 80 percent of men's salaries and this percentage has not changed over the last five years. Other sectors have shown incremental progress (from 87 to 89 percent among master's colleges, public and private), yet women continue to earn less than male faculty, even when controlling for rank and experience (NEA Higher Education Advocate, 2007, p. 11). Schuster and Finkelstein's longitudinal research (2006) confirms that we have not made steady progress in pay differential by gender over the last twenty to thirty years. Whereas in the early 1970s, women faculty's salaries were at 82.7 percent of men faculty's salaries, by 1990 they were at 79.6 percent (Schuster and Finkelstein, 2006).

The conceptual lens of human capital theory considers how the experiences, knowledge, and skills individuals bring to their jobs influence their experiences. In higher education, this theory suggests that faculty salary is based on an individual's productivity in factors such as educational attainment, experience, research productivity, administrative responsibilities, and supply and demand for a discipline (Perna, 2001a). Several researchers have used human capital theory to explain salary differentials (Nettles, Perna, Bradburn, and Zimbler, 2000; Perna, 2001a; West and Curtis, 2006). Individuals with more human capital are on average expected to earn higher salaries than their peers with less human capital. Theorists argue that when combined with structural factors such as rank and institutional type, much of the difference between any two individuals can be explained. Perna (2001a) and Umbach (2007a) concluded that women earn less than men for a host of reasons, including but not limited to their relative lower position in higher education's rank structure, representation in less prestigious and less well-paid disciplines, emphasis on good citizenship and teaching as opposed to research, time taken off for child rearing, and inability or unwillingness to relocate for higher-paying jobs. Yet an "unexplained gender gap" persists, even after controlling for human capital, structural factors, disciplinary differences, and labor market factors. Some researchers have considered the possibility of blanket discrimination and sexism as a cause of unexplained differences in salary between men and women. Others have continued to strive to break those concepts down operationally into how specific policies or gender-related characteristics may be intervening. For example, Bellas, Ritchey, and Parmer (2001) found that merit pay and across-the-board increases influence women faculty negatively, as women have lower salaries at first appointment. Toutkoushian, Bellas, and Moore (2007) studied the impact of gender, race, and marital status on salaries and found that married women earn 7 percent less than their married counterparts.

Hagedorn's research (1996) on faculty satisfaction suggests that although faculty satisfaction is a cumulative response to many factors, including interactions with students, colleagues, and administrators, nondiscriminatory monetary compensation enhances faculty satisfaction and encourages the retention of female faculty members. Therefore, campuses that conduct gender-equity studies and right unequal salaries as a matter of principle, as MIT did with women scientists (http://web.mit.edu/gep/res.html), will likely find a more satisfied and loyal cadre of women faculty.

Given differences in salaries, it is not surprising that women and men still face differentials in career progression. For example, women do not have the same chances of achieving promotion and tenure. Research conducted as part of the HERI faculty survey suggests that male assistant professors are 23 percent more likely to earn tenure than are females and that for each year after tenure is attained, male professors are 35 percent more likely than female professors to be named full professors (Williams, Alon, and Bornstein, 2006, p. 80).

Perna's research (2001a, 2001b, 2005) has contributed greatly to understanding the interaction of gender and career progression. She has observed that women are not only underrepresented in faculty positions in four-year institutions but also occupy fewer higher-ranking faculty positions than do men. Perna sought to determine whether parental, marital, and employment status was related to tenure and promotion through examination of the NSOPF:99 data. Perna's research (2005) resulted in several conclusions: (1) at the time of her analysis, women held fewer tenured positions than men; (2) fewer than 50 percent of women faculty had at least one dependent (compared with 70 percent of male faculty); (3) a higher proportion of women faculty were divorced or separated; and (4) parental status was more statistically significant for men in terms of tenure and promotion status. Overall, she concluded, women were more likely than men to hold non-tenured, lower-ranking positions. Family ties and academic rank were statistically insignificant for women but significant for men. In other words, men who had children and a partner or spouse benefited from their family status in terms of productivity, salary, and rank on the job. Children did not reduce chances for women's tenure or full-time status; however, Perna (2005) noted that this conclusion is not significant for women in the professoriate, many of whom do not have children anyway. Overall, Perna (2005) asserted that women who have successfully achieved tenure and full-time status are found in less prestigious institutions and in disciplines that are less valued by institutions.

Perna's research (2005) also considers the "why" of the differential salary and career opportunities between men and women in the academy. Academic women seem to be making some career and personal trade-offs: deciding not to have children, limiting the number of children they have, or limiting the positions they are seeking. Social psychologists explain some of the differences in promotion and tenure as the result of implicit bias, cognitive bias, and gender stereotyping (Williams, Alon, and Bornstein, 2006, p. 80), which limit women's careers almost regardless of family choices. Robst, VanGilder, and Polachek (2003) explored whether women faculty are perceived to have fair treatment in the university setting, using NSOPF:93 data and limiting their population to 11,099 full-time tenured or tenure-track faculty members. The survey asked faculty members to rate their perception of female faculty treatment on their campuses; overall, 83.1 percent of men versus 56.9 percent of women agreed that women were treated fairly (Robst, VanGilder, and Polachek, 2003). Interestingly, in all institutional types where women made more money and occupied a greater concentration of higher-level positions, more women reported experiencing fair treatment. Male responses, however, were not statistically significant with pay level or position. Female perceptions of the treatment of women generally were highly influenced by compensation, gender compensation of faculty, and the number of women in positions of power (Robst, VanGilder, and Polachek, 2003). This body of work points out the interconnected nature of reward systems and the importance of context in how they influence faculty work lives. Just as the question of satisfaction as a faculty member is a big one with many potential answers depending on the other part of that sentence (satisfaction with pay, with climate, and with resources), the question of how women and faculty of color fare in a reward system must be viewed in many more local contexts and comparisons in departments and colleges.

Given that professional and career opportunities are connected with issues of institutional type, discipline, and appointment type, researchers have also considered how gender influences careers among these "small worlds, different worlds" (Clark, 1987). The first example relates to recent research on the influence of gender on appointment type. Harper, Baldwin, Gansneder, and Chronister (2001) studied the experience of full-time nontenured women faculty. Using the same NSOPF data from 1993 and data they themselves collected (from large-scale surveys, analysis of personnel policies, and twelve campus visits), they argued that women occupy the majority of nontenured full-time positions and by and large are not happy about it. Although non-tenure-track women were found to report contentment with their jobs despite their non-tenure-track status, clearly the overrepresentation of women in the least-benefited positions in an institution is not equitable and represents a severe limitation to many women's professional career growth, as these positions on campuses where the tenure system is present offer fewer opportunities for promotion, professional development funds, benefits like sabbatical or parental leave, and job security.

Callister, Hult, and Sullivan (2006) examined the experiences of female faculty members in science, engineering, and technology to understand whether women experience a warmer reception across various disciplines. They found that although women have made strides in community colleges and four-year universities, they are still underrepresented in science, engineering, and technology fields in these institutions. They describe the phenomenon as "death by 1,000 paper cuts," whereby women are hurt, indirectly and directly, by actions such as stereotypes, intrinsic prejudice, and operationalized assumptions (women are not serious about their careers after they have children, for example). They interviewed forty-two current and former faculty women in science, engineering, and technology disciplines about their job satisfaction and then interviewed forty of their male colleagues. Although each group reported similar levels (and sources) of job satisfaction, the women were more likely to report negative interactions with colleagues, negative feelings about evaluations and tenure selection, hardships balancing work and family, and overwhelming workloads. Women reported that they spent more time than male colleagues advising students, preparing for classes, and serving on faculty committees. Not coincidentally, these women also felt left out of collaborative research and publishing in their departments.

An important link exists between women's perceptions of their work environment regarding equity in salary and benefits, opportunities for career growth, managing workload, and retention to institution and faculty career. Rosser's analysis (2004) of the NSOPF:99 database reports that perceptions faculty members have of their work life in such areas as workload and other elements of reward systems have a direct and powerful influence on their satisfaction and subsequently their intentions to leave. She further found that female faculty members were less satisfied with their advising and course workload and the quality of their benefits, job security, and salary levels than their male counterparts (p. 304). Although Rosser did not find that being an ethnic minority directly affected faculty members' satisfaction, ethnic minority faculty members were more likely to leave their career or institution than white faculty members were. Clearly additional research is needed to understand why the intention to leave is more prevalent among ethnic minority faculty members (Rosser, 2004).

Four Kinds of Reform of Reward Systems

Just as it has been extremely difficult for researchers to link faculty development activities with faculty growth, it has been difficult to forge an empirical connection between the *reform of faculty roles and rewards* and *outcomes representing intended changes*—for example, in student learning and retention, research products, and shared governance—for several reasons.

First, the reasons some reforms (such as post-tenure review) were created were often ambiguous and based on anecdotal data or bias against academic culture rather than easily observable problems that could be addressed. The lack of well-defined problems creates a conundrum with regard to the identification of potential "solutions." For example, in the 1990s many trustees argued for post-tenure review because they wanted faculty rather than teaching assistants to teach undergraduates at land-grant universities. Some trustees and legislators wanted to see firings of specific faculty, though they lacked specific evidence to justify it. The post-tenure review systems that were put in place were negotiated with faculty unions and senates and, as a result, more often than not tied to teaching evaluations or connected to normed averages for departments for teaching evaluations. Post-tenure review, as negotiated, could not force faculty in research universities to teach more undergraduate courses, especially absent any incentive to do so. The processes that were put in place to "fire" faculty were often based on delinquency in all areas of faculty work rather than one, and only after five or more steps and opportunities for appeal. Thus the policies put in place often responded more generally to the idea of greater accountability than targeting specific outcomes.

Second, it is hard to associate reforms with specific outcomes, because reforms are often at odds with local institutional cultures, thereby inhibiting their implementation. This phenomenon is illustrated well in research on implementation of post-tenure review, parental leave, and "stop-the-clock policies."

Third, as often occurs in studies of complex social settings, higher education institutions among them, it is extremely difficult to explain occurrences, events, or conditions of interest in terms of only two or even three variables. Assessing the impact of a policy often involves taking multiple social factors into account; to reduce representations of policy impacts to two or three factors often obscures the range of local interactions and activities that may be at issue in any change that occurs regarding a newly instituted policy. With few exceptions, studies of policy reform (for example, change in the tenure system and accountability-based budgeting systems) are best documented in case study form; to move then from basic case description to analysis typically requires in-depth longitudinal comparisons of multiple sites over extended time. The next four subsections explore research on reform of reward systems.

Elimination or Creation of Tenure

Much may be learned about reform in tenure systems—key faculty reward structures—from research projects sponsored by the former Forum on Faculty Roles and Rewards and the Harvard Project on Faculty Appointments. Chait (2002) conducted case study research, matching four colleges with tenure systems in place with four peer institutions without tenure. He found that the presence of a tenure system provides a reliable indicator of greater faculty voice in governance. It must be noted, given the limitations of research, that in this study, tenure signaled rather than created these conditions. In institutions without a tenure system, faculty were more likely to express a sense of futility in trying to influence institutional decisions—they felt the president and provost held all power. Chait (2002) cautioned that findings must be viewed in context, as issues of institutional prestige, perceived institutional quality, and financial condition may influence presidential power. Others have indicated that campus cultures may do so as well (Birnbaum, 1988).

Another interestingly designed study by Mallon (2002) involved comparisons of three colleges that moved from a base of contracts for faculty hires to a tenure system with three other colleges that moved from an intact tenure system to a contracts base. Mallon (2002) indicates that all six institutions made their tenure change in large part to enhance faculty quality through evaluation. Mallon's findings (2002) were surprising to proponents and critics of tenure alike: he found that in terms of job security, faculty contracts amount to "de facto tenure." He also found that neither the adoption nor the elimination of a tenure system ensured quality: all six institutions had many of the problems under their new system, whether tenure or contracts. Mallon's findings echo the organizational maxim: one college's ill-defined problem may become another college's ill-defined solution.

Trower (2002) conducted a survey and focus groups with doctoral candidates and faculty members from top departments at sixty-five of the most selective institutions in the United States to identify factors that may mediate faculty members' decisions to pursue tenure-track versus non-tenure-track positions. Trower found that both faculty and doctoral students preferred tenure-track over non-tenure-track positions; however, both would accept a non-tenure-track position under certain conditions. Two quality-of-life issues mattered heavily in the decision: geographic location of the institution and balance of work, specifically teaching and research. As such, it seems to be what tenure signals and what tenure represents to the larger world as much as the thing itself that influences faculty professional lives.

Post-Tenure Review

Overall, research on post-tenure review shows mixed results. Two themes run through it. The first theme relates to outcomes. In two studies administrators and faculty deemed post-tenure review successful after initial implementation if (1) it was not overly intrusive, (2) it encouraged retirement for unproductive faculty qualifying for it, and (3) it was conducted in such a way as to promote faculty development and growth—the latter involved providing resources for it (O'Meara, 2003, 2004a).

A second theme in the post-tenure research relates to the factors influencing faculty response to post-tenure review. A study by Wood and Johnsrud (2005) explored faculty values and beliefs regarding post-tenure review in two public doctoral and research extensive universities in the western United States. Findings suggest that union resistance to post-tenure review influences faculty perceptions of its implementation as does faculty perception of how it will impact the academy overall (Wood and Johnsrud, 2005, p. 413). This research is consistent with Licata and Morreale's finding (1997) that faculty resistance to post-tenure review is often related to a belief that the review can threaten established faculty values and institutional mores. O'Meara (2003, 2004a) explored beliefs held by faculty and administrators about post-tenure review and the factors that influenced beliefs in one public state system. Values of autonomy and collegiality, career stage, institutional history, and other contextual issues were found to influence beliefs about the purposes, processes, and outcomes of post-tenure review. Consistent with Wood and Johnsrud (2005), O'Meara (2004a) found that institutional history and the context of a history of distrust between faculty and administrators influenced beliefs about the purposes and origins of post-tenure review in one higher education system. Bensimon and others (2003) likewise found that post-tenure review did not result in all the outcomes intended by its initiators.

One of the most ironic aspects of post-tenure review, mentioned earlier, is the disconnection between its identified outcomes and those intended by its proponents. Very few of the legislators who pushed for post-tenure review in large state systems are still in office today, and most of their replacements have little sense of what post-tenure review means and what it is for. Very few post-tenure review systems resulted in the firing of faculty. Nor were many post-tenure review systems explicitly linked to faculty members' teaching evaluations or to number of classes taught, both of which were key interests of the legislators who called for tougher reviews of the faculty. Alternatively, little evidence exists of widespread misuse of post-tenure review in ways that threaten the faculty's autonomy, academic freedom, or careers. As such, many campuses appear to have "virtually adopted" post-tenure review as a local reform (Birnbaum, 2000).

Although the external catalyst for post-tenure review may not have been faculty growth, Licata and Morreale (2002) found that campuses that implement post-tenure review in formative ways can provide tenured faculty opportunities for renewal, new career directions, and strengthening of their institutional commitments.

Research on Redefining Scholarship

Another major reform has to do with efforts to redefine scholarship. On the surface it would as though the movement to reform faculty roles and rewards and to broaden definitions of scholarship has had a significant effect on colleges and universities. Just four years after the publication of *Scholarship Reconsidered,* 62 percent of chief academic officers (CAOs) in four-year institutions reported that this slender but important volume had had a role in campus discussions of faculty roles and rewards (Glassick, Huber, and Maeroff, 1997). The Institute for Scientific Information's citation database reveals that *Scholarship Reconsidered* is one of the most frequently cited education publications in the last decade (Braxton, Luckey, and Helland, 2006).

Yet the impact of *Scholarship Reconsidered,* in terms of "real reform" instituted, is largely unknown. This area of study is growing as scholars and academic leaders try to understand the extent of reform in faculty roles and rewards prompted by *Scholarship Reconsidered* (Berberet, 1999; Braxton, Luckey, and Helland, 2006; Huber, 2002; O'Meara, 2002a; O'Meara and Rice, 2005). Braxton, Luckey, and Helland (2006) have explored faculty professional performance to understand the degree to which faculty in four disciplines institutionalized the four domains of scholarship in their everyday work. The authors found that (1) all four domains of scholarship had attained the most basic (or structural) level of institutionalization; (2) the scholarships of discovery and teaching had attained procedural institutionalization (wherein the activity is a regular part of workload); and (3) only the scholarship of discovery had achieved incorporation at the highest level of institutionalization (wherein faculty values and assumptions support the activity). O'Meara (2002a, 2002b) conducted case studies at four colleges and universities to assess the extent to which community engagement was considered a form of scholarship for promotion and tenure. She found that each of the four campuses had reformed their promotion and tenure policies and were experiencing slight improvements in balance across reward systems, faculty involvement in alternative forms of scholarship, and faculty satisfaction with institutional work life. The Carnegie Foundation's national survey of college and university faculty in 1997 explored the emphasis institutional reward systems put on different forms of scholarship over the previous five years. It found that nearly half of faculty at research universities said greater emphasis was being placed on teaching by their reward systems than five years before (Huber, 2002).

O'Meara and Rice (2005) conducted a three-year study that included a national survey of chief academic officers at four-year institutions, regional focus groups with CAOs, and demonstration projects with nine campuses all amending their reward systems as suggested by Boyer (1990). CAOs from reform institutions where changes were made (in the previous five to ten years) to acknowledge, support, and reward multiple forms of scholarship were significantly more likely than CAOs at institutions that had not made similar reforms to observe that at their institutions innovation was encouraged and rewarded, the primary interests of new faculty hires match the institution's primary goals and direction, and that over the previous ten years their institutions had found a greater balance in the faculty evaluation process, that is, research was not rewarded over teaching and service for promotion and tenure (O'Meara, 2005a). In contrast, CAOs at nonreform institutions were significantly more likely to report that the institutions found it hard to initiate innovations that do not conform to norms at peer institutions and that faculty at their institutions wanted strategic decisions to make the institution more like peer institutions. Likewise, survey research found CAOs at reform institutions were more likely than those at nonreform institutions to say that they had seen faculty involvement in the scholarships of teaching, integration, and engagement increase and to report that the impact of scholarship on the local community or state, the institution, students, the mission of the institution, and the priorities of the academic unit influenced promotion and tenure decisions. And CAOs at reform institutions reported a higher percentage of tenure and promotion cases that emphasized their work in teaching and engagement scholarship. They were more likely as well to report that chances of achieving tenure and promotion based on teaching or engagement increased over the previous decade (O'Meara, 2005a).

Both the Braxton, Luckey, and Helland (2006) and O'Meara (2005a) studies drew on representative samples of four-year institutions, and they complement each other in that the former explored institutionalization of Boyer's conceptions of scholarship from the perspective of faculty and the latter from the perspective of CAOs. Braxton, Luckey, and Helland's study (2006) also contributed significantly to the literature by creating measurable constructs to measure faculty work activity in each of the areas of scholarship. A limitation of these constructs is that some forms of the scholarship of teaching, application, and integration fall outside the list of published outcomes. Likewise, O'Meara and Rice's (2005) study asked CAOs for their bird's-eye view of change over time, which is important because of CAOs' role in overseeing promotion and tenure. Those perceptions, however, were at a distance from where the initial promotion and tenure decisions were made in departments. An interesting complement to these two studies is Huber's in-depth anthropological exploration (2004) of faculty crafting careers around the scholarship of teaching. This study examines the nature of faculty teaching scholarship and how it has played in reward systems.

By 2010, the Boyer report will be twenty years old. The research reviewed above represents first steps. At this time, more research is needed to understand the lasting influence of the historic movement to redefine scholarship in American higher education. Such studies will need to take place at both micro and macro levels. At the micro level, one might ask whether reconceptualizations of scholarship reached graduate school so that new entrants to the professoriate believe that they can craft careers emphasizing the scholarships of teaching or engagement. Do faculty feel as though revised personnel policies provide the cultural and political armor advocates hoped they would provide? Does the work that has been done by the National Clearinghouse for Engagement and The Carnegie Foundation for the Advancement of Teaching, which define and create criteria and standards for high-quality work in teaching and engagement scholarship, help faculty across disciplines and institutional types? One recent ASHE conference session was titled "Can Women Survive Entrepreneurialism?" A related question for further research is whether the redefinition of scholarship can survive new pressures for entrepreneurialism. How will women and faculty of color, who report great interest in teaching and engagement, be supported by new definitions of scholarship in reward systems? What has this framework and efforts at related reform offered community colleges? Future research is needed to explore these questions and their implications for faculty work.

Research on Tenure Reform to Balance Work and Family

Of the remaining types of reform of tenure systems in the late 1990s and early 2000s accomplished to date, perhaps the most popular has involved efforts to create *balance of work and family.* This issue and the reform efforts around it are powerful reminders of the differences that still exist in gender roles and the powerful effects of external social forces on academe. Many would argue that in an ideal world, men and women would have equal opportunities to balance work and family issues in ways that allow them to compose meaningful personal and professional lives. In this idealized world, society would not expect women to shoulder a disproportionate share of family care. Rather men and women would share equally in family care. Workplace policies would be put in place to guarantee the potential for such parity in family life, including policies that give women and men options for parental leave, part-time faculty appointments, stop-the-clock options for child-rearing built into tenure policies, and other policies ensuring the perpetuation of family-friendly workplaces. In fact, several foundations have been promoting such initiatives by supporting a variety of policy reforms and research initiatives, many of them carried out over the past ten years by academic administrators and higher education scholars (Colbeck and Drago, 2005; Erskine and Spalter-Roth, 2005; Williams, Alon, and Bornstein, 2006).

A major theme in research to date on parental leave policy reform is that even when institutions put parental leave policies in place, the local institutional culture may not facilitate faculty taking adequate advantage of them. For example, a survey of Ohio State University assistant professors reported that one in three women and one in five men were interested in reducing their working hours to create more time for family and personal needs, but only twenty-three out of three thousand had ever taken advantage of a part-time policy established in 1996 for that very reason (Williams, Alon, and Bornstein, 2006). Similarly Williams, Alon, and Bornstein (2006) found that between 1992 and 1999, more than five hundred faculty members at Pennsylvania State University became new parents, yet Penn State records indicate that only seven formally filed for parental leaves. And none of them were by men (p. 84).

Research suggests that one explanation for the low rate of use of such policies is the concern, by faculty members needing these leaves, that doing so may harm their relative strength as they come up for promotion, tenure, and the like. Several studies suggest that women are less likely to take advantage of parental leave policies if they have not reached certain career benchmarks, including amassing certain quantities or kinds of publications, grants, and prestigious fellowships. For example, Erskine and Spalter-Roth (2005) examined use of family and work policies in higher education, focusing on female faculty members' adoption of flexible work life policies. They initiated a cohort study of new Ph.D.s in 1996 and resurveyed the cohort in 2003. They found that women faculty, the majority of whom were junior and unpublished, made little use of such policies. The women indicated that they were afraid to use the policies, despite the fact that they were encouraged to do so. Women believed that their career progression, including chances for tenure and promotion, would be negatively affected by their taking time off from work for child bearing. Interestingly, the number of published, peer-reviewed articles completed by women increased the likelihood of their using the policies by 9 percent. In addition, the more courses the professor taught, the less likely she was to use family-friendly policies (Erskine and Spalter-Roth, 2005). These findings are alarming because it is unlikely that many academic women of child-bearing age (in their late twenties and thirties) will have achieved all the career goals they feel they should by the time they want to have children. Fear of inflicting damage on one's career and absence of the sense that there are clear openings to take advantage of policies without doing so appear to prevent these women from doing so.

A second related explanation for underused parental leave policies relates to an attempt to avoid blanket discrimination. Williams, Alon, and Bornstein (2006) cite a Cornell University study finding that given two identical resumes, 84 percent of employer participants would hire the childless woman job applicant but that only 47 percent would hire the mother (p. 83). By taking advantage of parental leave policies, women and men draw attention to themselves as parents as opposed to purely as scholars and teachers, an attention few feel is advantageous in the workplace.

Armenti's interview-based study (2004a) of nineteen Canadian women at varying stages of a tenure-track career and representing a variety of disciplines provides an interesting picture of how related each of the preceding issues is to the composition of satisfying work lives. Armenti (2004b) used Bensimon and Marshall's Female Critical Policy Analysis Model (1997) to analyze her interviews. She found that when her subjects took advantage of stop-the-clock policies and parental leave, they felt the enormous pressure of backlogged work, lost research grant opportunities, and stigma from coworkers. Women without children but considering having children tended to report that they wanted to give birth in early summer or late spring so as to avoid having to take maternity leave. By and large, the most significant influence on young professors was older tenured women professors who often advised younger, untenured professors to delay having children until their tenure was secure. Doing so, however, could compromise a woman's ability to bear children altogether.

Women in Armenti's study (2004a) felt pressure from a career time crunch, feeling they must achieve tenure and develop a solid research reputation before having children. Women in this study felt that having children and completing research were incompatible with one another and that their gender and personal desires interfered with their academic success. An academic life friendly to their preferences—to the creation of a woman- and family-oriented workplace where taking a leave in accordance with stop-the clock policies— had to be put aside as women complied with male-dominated visions of what it meant to live a professorial life. Armenti (2004b) asserted that such obstacles—more cultural and symbolic than instrumental—resulted in women settling into less prestigious placements than otherwise they might, sacrificing balanced family and work lives, and readjusting their expectations with regard to the acquisition of tenure and the crafting of research careers. Women report feeling torn and stressed and as having to settle into less than desirable work positions or family situations (Armenti, 2004b).

Local institutional and cultural blocks to women considering the activation of stop-the-clock and other family-oriented policies represent but one set of barriers to individuals desiring to create a balance between work and family. It must be realized that larger social norms (well beyond the institutional) can interact with the local, slowing efforts to make academic workplaces more equitable than historically they have been. For example, research has shown that marriage seems to work against career progression for academic women. Academic women who marry men of equal professional background tend to opt out of the tenure track at higher rates than do women who are not married. These women are more likely than their male partners to move to follow their partner's job offers (Morrison, Rudd, Nerad, and Picciano, 2007).

Whereas the initiation of parental leave and stop-the-clock policies was a significant step forward in ensuring family-friendly campus environments and in improving workplace equity for women faculty, researchers are urged to pursue studies of institutional and professional factors that may enhance or detract from women's inclinations to activate such policies on their own behalf and of men's participation (Colbeck and Drago, 2005). Feminist frameworks are particularly helpful in the design of research that questions images of the "ideal worker" in academe and in consideration of workplace-design options existing outside current practice (Bracken, Allen, and Dean, 2006). For example, part-time tenure-track positions have been unpopular in colleges where faculty have unionized (out of fear of exploitation), yet researchers who have studied balances between personal and professional life view this possibility positively. A systematic look at the relative advantages and disadvantages of this policy option would be worthwhile. Likewise, it will be worth exploring further the "ethic of competitive individualism" (Creamer, 1998) that appears to pervade many academic cultures, with attention to how it is manifest in women's and men's work lives, as well as how it shapes decisions about the balance between work and family life.

Analysis Across Reforms in Reward Systems

The four examples provided in this chapter of major reforms in reward systems illustrate some of the strengths and limitations of research on faculty reward systems in higher education. Some insights and recommendations follow.

First, given contextual differences (including the multiple varying factors that may influence quality of work life in diverse institutions), it is very difficult to compare reforms and thereby to assess their varying effects across campuses. As a result, efforts to link presumed changes—to institutional strategies, operations, or cultures—must be undertaken cautiously, and claims that assert such links must be fully qualified. That said, it is possible to design studies around key features known to influence reform (for example, institutions of similar prestige, public versus private status, and so on), thereby garnering some insight on potentially workable reforms. This approach, however, requires lines of research that will in fact identify institutional and other features likely to shape the outcomes of key reform efforts; though this kind of cross-field coordinated effort is all too rare, its outcomes are likely to be useful in advancing useful research designs for the study of college and university change.

Second, regardless of whether we look at a reform that is aimed at instituting post-tenure review, revising approaches to scholarship, improving balances between work and family life, or something else, *reform* and *its unfolding effects* need to be studied longitudinally, experientially, and in light of the local dynamics of the specific social and cultural context at issue. It should further be studied across multiple and mixed faculty cohorts, that is, varying relative to discipline and field, institutional type, career stage, and so on, and configured so as to represent the full population of contemporary faculty in terms of age, racial and ethnic diversity, gender and sexual orientation, disability, and so on. This point merits special attention.

These and potentially other factors relating to faculty diversity need to be kept in mind in rethinking reward structures and faculty work lives in general, preferably at the ground level or in the trenches where faculty do their daily work: in academic programs, departments, institutes, and relationships with colleagues. In a study of forty university professors in an early post-tenure career, Neumann (in press) found that faculty members' abilities to engage in scholarly learning were influenced greatly by the quality of their day-to-day colleagueship in programs and departments; women were vocal in describing negative effects, while males emphasized positive colleague relations or said little about this topic. Porter (2007), Bland and others (2006), and others have called for research on faculty work life that looks closely at the department as the unit of analysis for research on faculty productivity and satisfaction. This point is especially relevant for the study of how reward systems in departments promote faculty growth or stunt it.

In reviewing the literature on institutional efforts to accommodate to the needs of increasingly diverse faculty, we also note the paucity of writing on the openness of academe to faculty representing diverse sexual orientations—gay, lesbian, bisexual, and transgender. Though acknowledged as meriting the attention of institutional leaders and policymakers, not enough is known, and not enough has been done to date, to open up lines of research and policy consideration on the workplace needs of gay, lesbian, bisexual, and transgender faculty in the American professoriate. We discuss this and related topics and their implications for understanding the faculty and faculty work in the next chapter.

Third, each policy reform will interact not only with institutional contexts and internal norms but also with external forces bearing on its potential outcomes, which must be considered in research design. Examples of these external forces include pressures on an institution to strive toward prestige, changes in the diversity of the students and faculty, and decreased funding from state, federal, or private sources.

Summary and Implications

In summary, we know the following points from research on academic appointments and reward systems over the last two decades:

After a decade of critique, the tenure system seems to have survived for a shrinking (proportionately speaking) strand of academics—namely, those in tenure-track positions—though with certain modifications: the institution of post-tenure reviews, broadening of the definition of scholarship, implementation of family- and personally-oriented parental leave and stop-the clock policies.

These three modifications to traditional tenure seem to work more at the edges than at the center of reward systems, and each seems to be inhibited by academic traditions, cultural norms, and external (disciplinary, social) forces. For example, redefining scholarship reforms works against dominant disciplinary norms around peer review, expertise, and quality; post-tenure review pricks at norms around autonomy, collegiality, and academic freedom; and stop-the-clock and parental leave work against an ideal worker norm.

Each of these reforms appears to have taken hold to some extent, despite barriers. Research suggests campuses that have redefined scholarship have shown improved recognition of newer forms of scholarship in reward systems. Some campuses that have initiated post-tenure review have found ways to facilitate opportunities for professional growth, and some campuses that have created stop-the-clock policies have assisted faculty, especially women, in balancing work and family.

Outcomes of reform in faculty roles and rewards, however, differ greatly by institutional type, discipline, career stage, and individual characteristics.

Traditional tenure systems reflect vestiges of past discriminatory practice; specifically, women and faculty of color are less likely to be retained in tenure-track positions and then move through the upper faculty ranks than white male faculty members.

The interaction of faculty members' *appointments* (tenure track, non-tenure-track, full time, part time) and *faculty work productivity* (active participation or contribution in research, teaching, outreach, and service) remains something of a puzzle. Research does indicate associations between these two variables in that faculty in tenure-track positions exhibit "more" or "better" desirable activities and products (for example, teaching behaviors that promote active learning, production of research articles and books, positive grant activity) than do faculty in temporary (contingent) appointments. Even when part-time faculty are eliminated from comparisons, thereby focusing data analysis only on full-time faculty (tenure-track versus non-tenure-track), notable performance differences remain. What is unclear and what requires in-depth follow-up is understanding the nature of the association: its directionality (does appointment structure contribute to differential productivity, or do faculty inclined to particular forms of productivity tend to assume certain appointments?) and also its experiential features (invisible or hard-to-articulate dimensions of the non-tenure-track job that pose "invisible" barriers to the incumbent's productivity, differential barriers across the two sets of faculty, and so on).

The reforms discussed in this chapter and the concrete suggestions for remaking academic environments so as to highlight equity, academic freedom and autonomy, flexibility, professional growth, and collegiality as five essential elements of academic work (Gappa, Austin, and Trice, 2007), offer significant potential for composing academic environments that support the development and expression of diverse faculty talents. To extend this conversation, we present below several observations about past research and possible future research directions focused on reward systems.

First, this chapter discussed many different structural aspects of reward systems, including promotion and tenure and contract renewal, merit pay, salary, resources, and professional development funds. It also reviewed research that considered aspects of reward systems that are less easy to measure, including the equity of the system among faculty, distribution of work in a department, favor given to some forms of scholarship over others, and politics. As researchers and administrators who support faculty, we need to remain open to broader definitions of what reward systems are, how their different strands connect, and to whose perhaps unfair advantage. The same is true of both conceptions and measures of productivity that are often used in research on reward systems.

Second, research reviewed here shows that reforms to reward systems face powerful cultural norms with the potential to inhibit their implementation. In the academy, as in many organizations, extant visions of who the ideal worker is and what that person does or does not do, typically in a competitive environment, define how researchers have traditionally framed, studied, and understood faculty careers. External forces, usually in the form of societal expectations about women's roles and more insidiously in the form of outright sexism and racism, invade and pervade the academy even as many of its members strive to change policy and practice.

The legacy of prior discriminatory practice is hard to eradicate; traces of its past exist, open at times, more quietly at others. Ignoring it is problematic for authentic reform, as its sources may be the wellspring from which many barriers to reform arise. That noted, very little has been said in research on higher education on extant features of institutional cultures, also silent or invisible, that may facilitate workplace reforms aimed at enhanced equity. For example, a culture that values regular faculty gatherings of the "town meeting" variety can use this cultural practice to introduce discussion of workplace reform rather than introducing it through more bureaucratic means.

Third, much of the research on faculty and reward systems positions faculty as subject to inhibiting cultural norms in colleges and universities—as opposed to featuring them as potentially empowered, as making choices consciously about which norms to adopt, ignore, and transform. We need theoretical frameworks and research designs that reveal faculty who pave their own distinct paths, often against the grain of long-entrenched reward systems so that these navigation skills, these sets of confidences in oneself and the importance of self-defined work are more visible. One example of faculty who enact such agency, to choose and do from their own sense of direction and desire, are the scores of faculty currently involved in community engagement despite institutional reward systems that do not acknowledge or support this work (Boyte, 2008; O'Meara, 2008). Faculty repeatedly say they "had to do this work" and were willing to row against the tide in countercultural, albeit politically savvy, ways. We need frameworks that help us better understand these faculty, where their sense of agency comes from, and how they turn it into "real action." Life and career histories of faculty who have become pathfinders in teaching and community engagement have been and will be helpful in tracing the origins of creativity, sense of agency, and commitment (Boyte, 2004; Colby and Damon, 1992; Daloz, Keen, Keen, and Parks, 1996; Gumport, 2002; Huber, 2004; Neumann and Peterson, 1997). Terosky's (2005) research on faculty who take teaching seriously in research universities provides an example of such inquiry, as do recent writings on faculty career construction post-tenure when both choice and constraint loom visibly before them (Neumann, in press; Neumann and Terosky, 2007; Neumann, Terosky, and Schell, 2006). We turn to recommendations for development of the concept of agency as a feature of the academic life in the next chapter in discussing promising directions for future conceptualizations of the faculty career.

In addition, research discourses on this topic should continue to consider equity—but perhaps we need to assert greater expectations as well. Basic fairness and equity assume that women and faculty of color—their contributions and their desires for equity and balance in work and life—will be accommodated, though not necessarily embraced. Rather than aiming to stem the departure of pretenure women and faculty of color from tenure-track positions—for example, as a result of challenges in balancing work and family or because of the inability to spend time on meaningful community service that will count in tenure reviews—perhaps institutions, and especially their leaders, should look hard at campuses themselves, striving to turn their colleges and universities into "hospitable academic homes" (Sandmann, Saltmarsh, and O'Meara, 2008), that is, into places the faculty's intellectual and professional pursuits will be both scrutinized and valued, reviewed constructively, and honored in meaningful ways. Likewise, instead of asking how reward systems can create satisfied customers, we might perhaps elevate the question, pondering how reward systems aimed at recruiting, supporting, and retaining faculty promote that faculty's learning as well. What networks, opportunities, or webs of support might colleagues and leaders create to engender faculty growth through the probationary period? The next chapter turns to theories and frameworks that may help address such questions in future research, thereby moving extant discussions of faculty roles and rewards—and faculty development—from mere basic goal achievement to a spirit of "greater expectation."

Perspectives Guiding Studies of Faculty Toward an Era of "Greater Expectations"

Justin sits back and considers the letter from the dean in front of him. The letter informs him of his impending post-tenure review. He is fifty-eight years old and has had a successful career at Striving University, including having won an award from his disciplinary association for his research and having always had good relationships with students and colleagues. He is considering refusing to go through post-tenure review, however, and taking early retirement.

Justin knows if he does take retirement, one administrator or another will likely characterize him as yet another "deadwood faculty" whose post-tenure review effectively threatened him into retirement, regardless of his record of productivity. But Justin believes he has earned the professional right to determine his own academic priorities and looks more to colleagues outside his institution for guidance in his research and other work than he does to colleagues on campus. He is concerned that certain junior faculty (possibly abetted by some senior colleagues) might try to use his "peer evaluation" to push his research in a direction that is close to their own. Whereas Justin respects his colleagues' agendas, he has his own clear interests. Moreover, he has been asked to consider running for president of his disciplinary association, becoming a program officer for a local foundation that has funded his research, and pursuing several fellowship offers to travel and write abroad. Despite what his local colleagues think of his research and other professional undertakings, he takes these invitations as signs that his work speaks well to various communities beyond the campus. Yet he does feel the campus press to change his work, a press that is exacerbated by his impending post-tenure review. Early retirement would allow him to accept some or all of the invitations at hand and let go the institutional struggles that he saw on the horizon.

Sitting in Washington, D.C., six months later, Susan, a higher education research policy analyst, reviews some of the output of the large database she has recently accessed. The database includes survey responses from more than five thousand faculty who have recently decided to retire, one of whom is Justin. Survey questions ask why faculty have decided to retire, inventories their productivity, accesses their professional values and beliefs, and probes for their experiences in community and with local colleagues. Susan considers several data patterns, the story lines they suggest, and the theories that shaped the survey questions in the first place and that will doubtless shape the findings that her analysis will eventually yield as well as the interpretations that will follow.

She pauses to reflect on the theories behind the questions that survey respondents addressed. The theories are diverse and multidisciplinary; they intersect in fascinating ways, yet each theory in itself seems incomplete. For example, market theories suggest several economic reasons for fifty-eight-year-old faculty like Justin to choose retirement. Might they capture a portion of Justin's reasoning to take retirement now? On the other hand, a variety of social-organizational theories suggest that retirement may be framed as turnover resulting from individuals' declining commitment to their university—for example, the invocation of policies that make them feel devalued and less "free" to follow their intellectual passions. Feeling valued and feeling free to inquire and create are both important to faculty like Justin. Susan then wanders in her thinking to political theory: some faculty may take early retirement for political reasons. They may have recently lost allies, or they may feel distanced from the work of their local colleagues, as their own work differs from the interests of a new and growing majority. On to career developmental theory, and Susan acknowledges too that a faculty member may feel there is little more for him to do at the institution: he has made his major contribution; he is no longer feeling challenged; there is little left to grow into. Puzzled, Susan awakens to the realization that though useful, her data may mask a variety of stories—and thereby a variety of careers—and a multitude of reasons for entering the academic career, staying with it, or choosing to leave.

THE FOUR PREVIOUS CHAPTERS reviewed recent research on specific areas of faculty work life (demographics, appointment types, faculty work, and reward systems). This chapter examines and discusses the *perspectives*[1]—disciplinary and interdisciplinary—that higher education scholars have used to study faculty in postsecondary institutions. Why include this discussion? Studying higher education and its faculty in particular is a complex endeavor requiring multiple lenses. Rather than relying on a single theory, higher education benefits from "epistemological diversity" (Pallas, 2001).

As such we begin with an assumption that higher education researchers and scholars may study the faculty from many different disciplinary vantage points. Yet rarely do these researchers compare and contrast those vantage points relative to what they reveal and obscure about their targets of study: the faculty. Rarely do those researchers consider the implications of using one disciplinary or interdisciplinary vantage point as opposed to another—what they may gain in choosing one over others and what they stand to lose (or set aside) in so doing.

In addition, as we showed in earlier chapters, much about the faculty is changing: who the faculty are, the appointment contexts of their work, what faculty do on the job, and how they do it. The contexts of the faculty's work are changing as well, motivated in good part by forces such as entrepreneurism, pressures for community engagement, and globalism. Yet even amid this extensive change, continuity is evident, including the tendency of individuals to choose the academic life as an expression of their personal commitments to pursuits of knowledge.

With this mixture of change and continuity in mind, we argue that the perspectives we use to study faculty and their work need to be thought through carefully: How applicable are our traditional theories of faculty work and career development to contemporary professors and instructors? What modifications in how we think about the faculty should we be considering? What new lenses might be brought to bear on the "new realities" that faculty today face? With these questions in mind, we examine in this chapter the disciplinary and inter-disciplinary perspectives that undergird contemporary research on the faculty, noting the distinctive offerings and limitations of those theories. We work from the assumption that an analysis of the weaknesses and strengths of the theory underlying research on faculty will unveil weaknesses and strengths in what we do and do not know about the faculty.

Given the quantity of research now available, we do not attempt to cata-logue every theory or perspective ever used to study the faculty. Instead, hav-ing analyzed recent research on this expansive topic area, we pause. In this "pause," or moment of reflection, we consider a select set of theoretical "bundles"—we call them *perspectives*—that guide the ways we ask questions, make assumptions, frame studies, and interpret findings about faculty work. We selected the perspectives based on their repeated appearance in the body of literature we reviewed (these perspectives are well known) or their promise for contribution (they exist though are less well known and used). After reviewing the perspectives, we lay out several recommendations for future development of perspectives on faculty growth.

Perspectives

We turn next to a discussion of perspectives that in recent years have framed much of the research on college and university faculty. We refer to these frames as:

- Historic shift
- Cultural
- Social-organizational
- Political
- Market
- Career development
- Epistemic

For each perspective, we identify a focus, note disciplinary origins, provide examples of faculty studies, and note distinct strengths and weaknesses.

Historic Shift

A historic-shift perspective considers how individuals, institutions, communities, and society have developed over time. Scholars who use this perspective may study the evolution of the faculty career, for example, by analyzing pivotal events that shaped the academic profession since its beginnings (the founding of the AAUP, for example). From this perspective, faculty behavior and work life are examined in the context of time and space, typically with attention to societal norms and historical turning points that shape the faculty's work or social identities as well as institutional missions, goals, and aspirations. As its name indicates, this perspective draws theories and modes of thought primarily from the discipline of history, though as the following discussion shows, it may draw as well from complementary social science disciplines (for example, sociology).

With this definition in mind, we turn to a few studies that make use of the historic-shift perspective. A primary example is the work of the historian of higher education, Martin Finkelstein. In Finkelstein's *From Tutor to Specialized Scholar,* (2007) he reviews the history of the faculty career by tracing faculty roles from the first Harvard tutors to contemporary research university professors. Finkelstein discusses shifts in the faculty's identities and aspirations relative to changes in campus missions, institutional structures, and academic roles and careers.

In addition to using the historic-shift perspective to frame large-scale, chronological change, higher education scholars have used it to guide studies that are narrower in scope—such as studies of specific social trends as they shape faculty careers. For example, applying a generational lens, Finnegan (1996) studied a historic shift toward creation of research-oriented faculties. She analyzed the hiring practices of comprehensive universities over three time periods, finding that institutions were replacing retiring faculty with research-oriented early-career faculty. By using a generational lens and by drawing also on an analysis of market conditions, Finnegan concluded that the more research-oriented the faculty, the greater the institutional push toward prestige measured in terms of research productivity. Finnegan's and others' research helps to explain a key feature of American higher education today: diverse institutions' strivings for prestige (Finnegan, 1996; Finnegan and Gamson, 1996).

Scholars using the historic-shift perspective also have been intrigued by trends toward specialization in the faculty's knowledge and disciplinary ties. Jencks and Riesman (1968), both renown sociologists, coined the phrase "the academic revolution" to describe the faculty's tendencies over time to become increasingly specialized in their scholarly knowledge and research. Finkelstein (2007) and Geiger (2004) have since chronicled this shift. The academic revolution yielded two prominent results: it positioned graduate education as a central feature of higher education, and it positioned specialized disciplinary knowledge as a desired attribute of "star faculty" at premier institutions. Collectively, historians such as Jencks, Riesman, Finkelstein, and Geiger draw a picture of specialization and disciplinary connection as shaping faculty careers over the past century. Such change appears to have influenced tenure and promotion structures, curriculum decision making, and other features of institutional governance (Geiger, 2004).

Historic-shift approaches are powerful tools for studying faculty in that they surface interconnections among higher education actors such as faculty, institutions, and society. They also highlight conceptual links among more intangible yet equally powerful features of the higher education enterprise: among various social norms, among patterns of opportunity or possibility (resource availability) and constraint (resource scarcity, loss). Though highlighting a variety of such intersections, the historic-shift perspective also can trace time-based fluctuations in those intersections—for example, tendencies at times for universities to distance themselves from their surrounding communities (minimal interconnection) yet over time to draw far closer out of desires to serve those communities, to be valued by them, or to make a case for resources from them (maximum interconnection). Historic-shift frameworks thus make clear that few features of contemporary higher education reality have "fallen from the skies fully formed"—they have developed over time. The historic-shift perspective also indicates that though continuity has been a significant feature of higher education, little about the enterprise truly stands still. Much is in flux though often bearing some relationship to what existed in the past.

The historic-shift perspective, like all perspectives, has its limitations. Studies that employ it typically focus on faculty as members of groups rather than as separate individuals with distinctive life experiences. Unless an explicit psychological dimension enters historical consideration (as in some historical biography), the person in history—and the person's experience of historical change—may well be lost. Although many higher education historians do rely on faculty members' personal letters, diaries, instructional materials, and other primary documents for data, they use them primarily to shed light on larger social trends or events. This approach contrasts with using faculty members' personal documents to study individuals' first-hand experiences with a situation. In this alternative view, the human experience of trends and events, whether unique or shared, matter more than the trends or events themselves—which are not unimportant but not front and center in researchers' attention either. Historic-shift frames spotlight faculty more as products of their times and of their social contexts and less as individuals with commitments and passions that may occasionally set them apart from those times and social contexts.

Cultural

A cultural perspective focuses on how values, beliefs, and norms are developed, maintained, and passed on through socialization, ritual, language, and symbolic actions (Aguirre, 2000; Bergquist, 1992; Clark, 1987; Tierney and Bensimon, 1996; Weidman, Twale, and Stein, 2001). Scholars of the faculty career have extensively used this perspective, drawing heavily from anthropological views, though they are often linked to theories drawn from sociology, organizational studies, history, and other fields. For example, studies of graduate student and faculty socialization and acculturation build on work from organizational-cultural theories as well as from anthropology (Austin, 2002b; Schein, 1985; Senge, 1990; Weidman, Twale, and Stein, 2001). Perhaps best-known are Clark's characterization (1987) of the "small worlds, different worlds" of faculty, Tierney and Bensimon's account (1996) of the rites of passage in graduate and faculty socialization, and Becher's look (1989) at and Biglan's examination (1973) of the differences in epistemology and work goals of different disciplines. Writings in higher education also include focused analyses of cultural practices, among them Tierney and Bensimon's discussion

(1996) of "smile work and mom work" (p. 83) in academe, an example of faculty's being asked and agreeing for political reasons to carry out significant maintenance work in academic programs and departments for little recognition or other rewards. Such maintenance work includes committee service, mentoring, and other forms of low-level institutional administration. A prominent cultural perspective is apparent as well in O'Meara's exploration (2002b) of the values and beliefs influencing assessment of community engagement as scholarship and in her exploration of the values and beliefs influencing implementation of post-tenure review (2003).

In considering the advantages of the cultural perspective, several higher education scholars have observed that the higher education system is strongly value laden (Birnbaum, 1988; Clark, 1987; Kezar, 2001). Studies guided by a cultural perspective have revealed some of these values, among them academic freedom, including the freedom to teach and research what one considers important, shared governance, and specialization (Clark, 1987; Kezar, 2001). Likewise, cultural perspectives have illuminated the values that women faculty report bringing to their work and leadership, for example, favoring collaboration (Astin and Leland, 1991; Kezar, 2001; Neumann, 1999b). A shortcoming of the cultural approach is that it may be viewed as nongeneralizable in that cultural scholars often focus on "n-of-1" studies or small-sample research at best. Yet this criticism is debatable in the view of case-study researchers, who speak to such studies' abilities to "generalize to theory" (Glaser and Strauss, 1967) and to serve as starting points for comparative work that seeks to refine their initial conceptual findings (Erickson, 1986; Yin, 2003). Culturally attuned studies also tend to focus on the values, beliefs, and norms of groups, thereby differentiating what counts as legitimate knowledge from what does not, which ideas are central to particular communities and which are less than central, and which individuals or groups are cultural insiders and which are not. As such, a cultural perspective may err in overemphasizing a culture's current features and concerns without adequate attention to change in the culture over time and to the malleability of culture itself.

Finally, a cultural perspective, typically associated with the discipline of anthropology, may work best when infused with other disciplinary perspectives. The exclusion of extradisciplinary views may narrow the anthropological vision. For example, historical neglect in cultural studies may narrow views of that culture to what it is in a specific moment rather than what it represents over time. Similarly, sociological neglect may block out attention to the larger hand of society and social structure in the workings of a setting under study. Psychological neglect in research on community-based tradition, beliefs, or rituals may obscure the role of personal motivation, agency, commitment, and need growing perhaps from smaller units in community or separated from it (for example, families, dyadic relationships, separatist groups).

Social Organizational

We define the social-organizational perspective as taking seriously the workings of human society and social organization as they bear on higher education as the primary locale of professors' work and career development. Though we use the words "social" and "organizational" together in naming this perspective, we acknowledge that at times one or the other term may be more appropriate and that one, the other, or both may be further framed by other disciplinary views (for example, psychology, social psychology, philosophy, history). As the following discussion bears out, however, we define this perspective as framed primarily by theories drawn from the discipline of sociology.

Cast sociologically, the social-organizational perspective attends to the status, positioning, and experiences of individuals or groups in society or social institutions, including how and why societies and institutions are organized as they are, with attention to the benefits and constraints that their members' positioning may yield for their lives and efforts. This perspective includes microlevel studies (such as the study of contact among a very small number of people) and macrolevel studies (such as global-social processes). Some social-organizational theories operate between the micro and macro, for example, considering how macroforces shape the life experiences of individuals in institutions, organizations, and society (Bronfenbrenner, 1979) and conversely how individuals exert agency to adjust their own and others' experiences of the multiple contexts in which lives are cast (Pallas, 2007). Studies guided by this perspective consider the social-professional dynamics at play in the institutions, communities, and societies in which faculty work (see Clark, 1987), with attention to implications for those faculty members' access to valued resources (voice, opportunity to learn, helpful colleagues, finances, and so on). Studies guided by a social-organizational perspective also consider diverse societal trends and forces that influence the faculty career and access to it, for example, by virtue of academic aspirants' racial, gender, religious, and other identities and the "receiving communities'" openness to difference and commitments to tolerance and equity (see, for example, Antonio, 2002; Kanter, 1977; Turner, Myers, and Creswell, 1999).

Over the last few decades, scholars of higher education have increasingly applied selected facets of the social-organizational perspective to studies of faculty identity and faculty work life. For example, a sociological construct commonly applied by higher education scholars is the American "ideal worker" (Bailyn, 1993; Whyte, 1956; Williams, 1999). Higher education scholars study how expectations about ideal workers operate in higher education culture, including the ramifications of these expectations for the divide between workplace and home, a topic central to research on the sociology of work and family as well (Hochschild, 1997). In higher education, expectations about ideal workers typically run up head to head with the desires of many faculty to achieve improved balances between work and family life, between personal and professional existence (Gappa, Austin, and Trice, 2007; Ward and Wolf-Wendel, 2007). This body of work spotlights a growing professional concern in the field: the extent to which the traditional academic career ladder (and especially pursuit of tenure) follows a model derived from men's normative life paths rather than women's (Gappa, Austin, and Trice, 2007; Ward and Wolf-Wendel, 2003; see "Recent Reforms of Faculty Reward Systems" for further discussion).

Another common sociological theme addressed by scholars who use the social-organizational perspective is inequality. Writers who draw on sociological theory to frame inequality in the work and work life of college and university faculty consider degrees of work and workplace satisfaction and dissatisfaction among women and faculty of color (Gappa, Austin, and Trice, 2007; Wolfinger, Mason, and Goulden, 2004). Scholars writing in this vein also have contributed to understanding the reproduction of privilege in faculty careers. This body of work includes explorations of the concept of cumulative advantage or disadvantage: the accumulation of resources and opportunities in relation to peers and of social capital toward career advancement (Clark and Corcoran, 1986).

The sociology of the life course represents a promising collection of theories for research on college and university faculty, especially for explorations of learning and career-identity construction (for a comprehensive discussion of the sociology of the life course and its applicability to education broadly, see Pallas, 2007). Studies conducted in this specialized sociological domain consider how social factors (including historical contexts) interact with individuals' resources and limitations to shape those individuals' life trajectories (Baltes and Baltes, 1990; Clausen, 1986). The life course frame draws on four key ideas: faculty lives are embedded in historical contexts; faculty construct their life trajectories through their choices and actions; the various facets of a faculty member's life (such as work, family, and background) are intertwined; and the developmental impact of a transition in life depends on when it occurs in a person's life (Giele and Elder, 1998). Neumann's *Professing to Learn: Creating Tenured Lives and Careers in the American Research University* (in press) provides insights into how life-course theories may be used in studies of the faculty. In *Professing to Learn,* Neumann analyzes role transition from untenured (probationary) status to full-fledged tenured status in the academic community, institution, and, to some extent, society. That transition bears implications for professors' professional and personal identities cast in the shifting social-institutional contexts of their changing professional and personal lives. Drawing on experiential perspectives, Neumann notes that although the transition from untenured to tenured status is desirable, it implies increased institutional and collegial responsibilities, pressures, and tensions because the pre- to post-tenure transition is more than a career shift; it is also a workplace shift in that it involves change in the relationship between worker and workplace. Faculty may expect to feel freer after tenure than they did before, but their employing organization often asks more of them. Expecting freedom, they learn they must exert agency to have it and exercise it. How faculty respond to such shifts in professional contexts and the extent to which they exert agency (a significant construct in the sociology of the life course) in so doing appear to frame professors' future identities as learners and possibly their scholarly learning (Neumann, in press; Neumann, Terosky, and Schell, 2006). Further, Neumann and Terosky (2007) apply life course considerations in their analysis of how service responsibilities change through career stages along with the role transitions such changes imply.

In addition to the ideal worker, inequality, and life course frames, research on higher education faculty has also been greatly influenced by the sociology of organizations and by still broader institutional theories. Although we focus in this book on faculty rather than on larger campus-based and extracampus higher education phenomena, we recognize that faculty work, think, learn, and develop—as faculty—largely in their employing organizations (their colleges and universities) and in related professional communities (their disciplines and fields, the professional organizations that formalize them). Institutional theory posits that an organization's survival is closely tied to its members' self-perceptions of legitimacy (DiMaggio and Powell, 1983). Organizations in fields like higher education, where goals are hard to measure, technology is unclear, and the organization is highly professionalized, are highly susceptible to challenges to legitimacy through pressures to mimic prestigious institutions' behaviors (DiMaggio and Powell, 1983; Morphew and Huisman, 2002). DiMaggio and Powell (1983) found that institutions are compelled to emulate the most prestigious institutions by coercive, mimetic, and normative forces. In higher education, images of institutional isomorphism suggest that the greater the professionalization of the faculty, including the more that faculty look outside their own communities (campuses and disciplines) for norms and directions for their work, the more likely it is that the faculty and the communities at issue (including higher education organizations) will follow priorities that do not originate, organically, in them (for examples, see DiMaggio and Powell, 1983; Morphew and Huisman, 2002).

Writing in a different but not unrelated tradition, Blackburn and Lawrence (1995) have demonstrated the influence of organization on faculty motivation. Their research shows that faculty are compelled toward certain behaviors (such as emphasizing teaching or research) based on a complex interaction of their own graduate school socialization and an institutional (employment) reward system that sends consistent messages about what is desired (for example, that they emphasize teaching or research). Institutional theory, including constructs such as institutional isomorphism, elucidates how individuals such as faculty come to be shaped by their participation in the organizations where they spend their careers and lives. Rhoades (2007) presents future directions for sociologically informed higher education research as emphasizing several concepts, themes, and vantage points: managed professionals and the balance between professional autonomy and managerial discretion; emergent positions in the organization of academic labor; and feminism, marketization, and globalization (p. 139).

Finally, in the field of higher education, the social-organizational perspective includes as well considerations of the faculty that are perhaps less sociological in content than more purely organizational. Drawn from the field of organizational careers psychology (Katz and Kahn, 1978) and to some extent management studies (Kast and Rosenzweig, 1985), those studies are anchored in open-systems theories that conceptualize social organizations, including colleges and universities, as amoeba-like macroscopic organisms protected by more or less permeable membranes ("boundaries") that separate an organization's internal workings ("throughput") from external forces ("environment") but on which the organizations at issue rely on critical life resources ("input") and to which they contribute ("output"). The now classic organizational cycle of input, throughput, and output (Katz and Kahn, 1978; Scott, 1987) portrays higher education organizations as resource dependent and more broadly as environmentally dependent related to other social organizations (collaboratively or competitively) and as caught up in simultaneous struggles to maintain their functionality, responsiveness, and social identities (Bensimon, Neumann, and Birnbaum, 1989; Chaffee, 1984; Pfeffer and Salancik, 1978; Scott, 1987). Though the logic of this perspective leads naturally to discussions of institutional leadership (Bensimon and Neumann, 1993; Birnbaum, 1988, 1992), its implications for conceptualization of the faculty role and for faculty sense making and identity work (Bensimon, 1991; Neumann, 1995; Weick, 1979) cannot be underplayed. Though presented as being "in service" to larger visions of institutional survival and growth, defined as leadership concerns, a fair amount of this writing also considers the implications for faculty understanding, agency, and vitality (Bensimon, 1991; Neumann, 1995). As previously indicated, the latter are framed from alternative perspectives: human learning and cognition, phenomenological study, symbolist theories.

Like the other perspectives discussed herein, the social-organizational perspective on faculty work reflects both strengths and shortcomings. Social-organizational perspectives reveal faculty behaviors and experiences in institutions and across diverse networks, and thus they speak to how the collectivity can shape faculty work. Though alternative theories—in particular, those drawn from agency studies in the sociology of the life course—emphasize individuals' own powers to shape the contexts of their work and development (and thereby their own work and development), such theories have just recently begun to enter higher education research. Further, selected social-organizational perspectives, especially those drawn from the discipline of sociology, illuminate social privilege and its reproduction and maintenance in higher education. The perspective thus helps to frame dynamics of racism, sexism, and inequity as they influence the faculty, their work and workplace identities, and their opportunity structures. Though some social-organizational theories do consider individuals' experiences in structures of work and power, such views continue to be all too rare, which suggests, of course, a need to couple the social-organizational view with other perspectives that mine personal experience more intentionally, especially so in studies that emphasize faculty learning and growth.

Political

We define the political perspective as focusing on power in college and university decision making and governance (Birnbaum, 1988) and, by extension, in the design of academic work and careers. Political scientists typically associate resource scarcity with power acquisition in higher education and other organizations. A political perspective usually considers how change evolves through agenda setting, networking and coalition building, and bargaining and negotiation (Birnbaum, 1988; Pfeffer and Salancik, 1978). In some cases, it may also speak to issues of strategy aimed less at adaptation than at social identity construction as a power-directed activity—for individuals as much as for organizations (for organization-level discussions of strategy, see Peterson, Dill, and Mets, 1997; for strategy making in faculty careers, see Neumann, in press; Neumann, Terosky, and Schell, 2006). Though both views "count," we emphasize individual strategy making in discussion of this perspective, though we consider as well individuals' experiences of organization-level strategy making. As the name of this perspective suggests, the field of political science drives it, even as organizational, psychological, and policy perspectives help shape its content.

In higher education research, political perspectives have been applied to study power and its implications for faculty behavior and work. Studies examine how power operates in academic departments, colleges, and universities and how power agents (interest groups, government) use advocacy, persuasion, negotiation, and mediation strategies to influence faculty roles, rewards, and values (Hearn, 1999; Kezar, 2001). A widely studied higher education phenomenon related to power is the growing tension between administrators and faculty as institutions engage in reorganization around faculty work expectations, faculty governance, and faculty reward systems (Gumport and Pusser, 1999; Rhoades, 1998). Political perspectives shed light on faculty and institutional decision making, both formal and informal.

Political perspectives are particularly relevant in bringing power to light in decision making, with academic cultures characterized as highly political even if consensus driven (Kezar, 2001). A political perspective illuminates how and why individuals seek out power, including whether and how such persons align themselves with its sources, for example, as they seek out allies or engage in the complexities of negotiation and bargaining (consider the special case of collective bargaining). Though expansive in scope, the political perspective, like the other perspectives herein described, has its limitations. Like the others, it focuses on a few key ideas such as power and resources, thereby presenting a valuable though partial picture of the complexities of higher education institutions. We suspect that a political perspective will be very important in future studies of non-tenure-track faculty members' efforts to negotiate for resources, given concerns about scarce resources and power that this topic also brings into play. A political perspective promises to guide studies of temporary and other non-tenure-track faculty members' considerations of options to form unions or to explore self-advocacy strategies that will advance their causes without harming prior gains toward professionalization of their work. Likewise, a political perspective is likely to be helpful in explorations of the status and strategies of women academic pioneers—especially in medicine, science, and other male-dominated fields—who, though cast as "tokens" of accomplishment, nonetheless strive to strengthen their own and other women's positions by creating powerful networks and professional development programs (Fitzpatrick and Sloma, 2007; Glazer-Raymo, 2008; Gumport, 1990). Other than framing how faculty can successfully negotiate professional advancement—for example, accession to intellectual and organizational leadership—political perspectives are less helpful in framing how faculty learn and grow. They say little about the human development aspect of careers.

Market

A market perspective considers how the behaviors of faculty (individuals and groups) and institutions may be framed by forces of supply and demand and by competition in higher education markets. A market perspective considers how both tangible and intangible resources such as salaries, prestige, or quality are exchanged as currency among faculty members and groups, among institutions, and between faculty and institutions and how such exchanges constitute or otherwise shape faculty work. A key consideration of the market perspective is how environmental forces (demand, competition), public opinion, and other contexts (including internal processes such as budgeting) shape faculty work. Clearly the discipline of economics drives the market perspective, though as coordinated with social, political, and organizational views emphasizing institutional strategy, management, and finance.

Higher education faculty scholars have used market frames to analyze how tangible and intangible resources shape faculty (and institutional) behavior. For example, Clotfelter (1996) compared costs across humanities, social sciences, and sciences departments at three leading research universities with those of a leading liberal arts college between 1976–1977 and 1991–1992. He concluded that higher education costs are rising because colleges and universities are paying high salaries to "star" faculty and providing generous financial aid packages to high-ability students. Clotfelter describes these practices as efforts to increase the quality and the prestige of the faculty and student body. From the perspective of individual faculty, employment turnover may be viewed as an individual's efforts to "trade up"—leaving one position for another in search of greater prestige (an intangible resource) or increases in compensation (a tangible resource). Viewed through a lens of job satisfaction, the market perspective suggests that a professor's or instructor's job satisfaction depends in part on the range of employment, salary, and benefit options available to that person by virtue of what she or he brings to the table (contributions) and relative to what institutional leaders view their institution as needing—hence the local value of a faculty member's contribution to his or her institution.

Academic capitalism also falls in the market perspective. In this view, higher education is driven more by the marketplace and less so by aspirations for the "public good." In *Academic Capitalism,* Slaughter and Leslie (1997) explain that scarce resources and threats of financial reduction (declining federal support for higher education that leads to thinning of institutional budgets) relate closely to academic decision making based on economic viability that gives little attention to the social or intellectual good. For example, academic leaders may withdraw faculty lines from programs that promise little direct payoff to institutions or departments (for example, liberal arts programs) while favoring those with more obvious financial payoff (for example, lucrative applied science programs). Budget decisions that hinge primarily on financial viability rather than substantive value may erode historically valued features of an institution's curriculum, identity, and societal offerings. An institution's social mission may become caught in an intractable tension: between aims for financial success and pursuits of academic value. The two only rarely align (Chaffee, 1984; Gumport, 2000).

Administrators and policymakers may favor a market perspective in that it forces attention to what its name emphasizes: marketplace realities, the public's demands, the public's willingness to pay for particular services but not others. The perspective cannot be ignored, for it asks faculty to justify the relevance, social meaning, and value of their work, especially so in times when public support for the faculty's work is dwindling. Yet the market perspective is limited, obscuring personal, value-driven motivations for faculty engagement in academic work. For example, a market perspective may mask a professor's intense personal and political commitment to provide substantive advice to an environmental protection group. The market perspective also may cover up the aesthetic passions that drive artists and scientists alike in pursuit of creativity on the one hand and discovery on the other (Neumann, 2006). It may further hide a professor's personal commitments and unrewarded efforts to right gender inequities on campus.

Career Development

A career-development perspective illuminates individuals' growth and development across the life span, with attention to how adults reframe their identities, needs, and aspirations over time. Drawing primarily from the field of psychology (human development emphasis), this perspective incorporates the framing work of theorists such as Erikson (1993), Levinson with Levinson (1996), and Neugarten (1968) to name but a few, but it draws as well from fields with related interests, notably sociology (socialization studies), anthropology (acculturation studies), and organizational psychology. This work typically views individual lives as unfolding across generalized developmental stages, typically coordinated with social-cultural and physical shifts that are often linked by periods of transition. Classical human development theories emphasize child and adolescent development, stopping short of adulthood, though recent theories have attended increasingly to development in the middle and later years of life (Levinson with Levinson, 1996; Neugarten, 1968).

In higher education, scholars have applied a variety of life-stage or developmental theories to conceptualize stages of the faculty career. For example, Baldwin (1979) and Baldwin (1990) ground their tristage theory of the faculty career (early career, midcareer, and late career) in life stage and human development theory. Baldwin, Lunceford, and VanderLinden (2005) likewise use this body of theory to examine midcareer experiences.

As an alternative to life-stage and human developmental theories, other higher education scholars have connected psychological theories that consider self-knowledge and social knowledge to the career experiences of the faculty (Blackburn and Lawrence, 1995). *Self-knowledge* refers to a faculty member's sense of his or her interests, talents, and capacities; *social knowledge* refers to a faculty member's sense of what is valued in her or his professional or workplace environment. Blackburn and Lawrence (1995) found that a dynamic interaction of self-knowledge and social knowledge influences faculty members' views of the work that they construe as important and that many pursue. Faculty are likely to pursue work if they find the work interesting, if they perceive themselves as able to competently perform the work, and if they perceive their work will have concrete outcomes.

Scholars who rely on a career developmental perspective to conduct research on faculty work and careers often draw on psychological theories informing workplace and human resource issues: such theories emphasize faculty members' personal and professional development and their relationship to organizational structures (Alderfer, 1972; Herzberg, 1966). Recent research on the changing faculty workplace draws extensively on this perspective, comprehensively documented in recent research by Gappa, Austin, and Trice (2007). Hagedorn (2000) applies psychological theories central to this perspective in analyses of contemporary faculty members' job satisfaction. In particular, she uses Herzberg's theory of job satisfaction factors (1966)—achievement, recognition, the work itself, responsibility, the possibility of advancement or growth, and salary and status—to consider how gender, ethnicity, institutional type, academic discipline, and environmental conditions (such as faculty relationships with colleagues, students, administrators, and institutional climate or culture) influence job satisfaction. Drawing on other psychological studies suggesting that major life events can serve as triggers influencing satisfaction (Latack, 1984; Waskel and Owens, 1991), Hagedorn (2000) identifies six potential triggers for the faculty's satisfaction: change in life stage, change in family-related or personal circumstances, change in rank or tenure, transfer to a new institution, change in perceived justice, and change in mood or emotional state. Hagedorn suggests that these factors will shape job satisfaction along a continuum from disengagement to acceptance or tolerance of job to appreciation or engagement in work. Daly and Dee (2006) and Johnsrud and Rosser (2002) likewise emphasize psychological variables such as morale, commitment to institution, and satisfaction in exploring faculty turnover.

Though rooted in the long history of developmental psychology, the career-developmental perspective continues to be of significant interest to researchers who seek to understand faculty workplaces with an eye toward their improvement in ways that will enhance the faculty's adult and professional development. Given massive contemporary changes in faculty work processes, workplaces, and appointment structures (Gappa, Austin, and Trice, 2007; Schuster and Finkelstein, 2006), the perspective is likely to remain central in the work of researchers who explore the shifting nature of the faculty career. For example, research on how academics as professionals can derive senses of achievement, recognition, and opportunities for advancement—all of which are central to the career-developmental perspective—will be crucial in future efforts to design faculty appointment structures outside the traditional tenure system. A strength of the career-developmental perspective is that it focuses on individuals' needs, skills, and relationships as bases for institutionally sponsored faculty development efforts aimed at academic work enhancement. This perspective has been criticized, however, for its lack of sociological and anthropological sensibilities emphasizing context, belonging, and insider-outsiderness.

Epistemic

We conceptualize the epistemic perspective (emphasizing individual and collective knowledge construction) as encompassing several branches of theory: theories of organizational cognition, sociocultural theories, and standpoint theories (feminist and black feminist thought). Collectively these theoretic branches consider how individuals come to know what they know along with the implications of what they know for their daily work and lives. Yet focus often differs among particular groupings of epistemic theory (indicated by the "branches") such that what each theoretic grouping (branch) lets the theorist "see"—about epistemic issues—differs from what another lets her see. We group the theories then according to their focus and concern, though recognizing that each branch (or theoretical grouping) reflects substantial internal variance as well. The first group, *theories of organizational cognition,* focuses on how individuals know and learn individually and organizationally, with attention to how they "interpret their world and reconstruct reality on an ongoing basis" (Kezar, 2001, p. 47). *Sociocultural theories* emphasize an individual's learning as dependent on the social context in which the person exists and the fact that features of context infuse the content of learning (Bronfenbrenner, 1979; Wertsch, 1985). *Standpoint theories* attend to how individuals' positionings in structures of power (typically social but also broadly organizational and community) influence the content of what they know and how they know it (Harding, 1986, 1991; Hill Collins, 1990; Ladson-Billings, 1997; Smith, 1987). Given this thematic variation as evidenced by these three theoretical branches, the epistemic perspective encompasses many of the previously reviewed perspectives, especially the cultural, social-organizational, and political. Its disciplinary roots cross multiple fields: cognitive and cultural psychology, management theories, sociology of knowledge, and philosophy (epistemology).

Theories of organizational cognition emphasize sense making and knowledge construction as the bases of college and university "realities." Organizational sense making (Weick, 1979) has long been used in higher education studies, though in the past they focused on leaders' symbolic (meaning-making) actions (Birnbaum, 1988) and occasionally on faculty members' understandings and images of the social realities that their institutional leaders construct (Bensimon, 1991; Bensimon and Neumann, 1993; Neumann, 1995). Yet a sense-making lens may apply as well to explorations of faculty work life. In this view, sense making refers to the ways in which professors and instructors make meaning of their campus environments and what is happening in them. Theories of organizational sense making posit that an individual's efforts to know, or to make sense, are grounded in identity construction, retrospective, enactive of sensible environments, social, ongoing, focused on and by extracted cues, and driven by plausibility rather than accuracy (Weick, 1995, p. 15).

Sense making as a theory has been used to explore a variety of topics bearing on faculty work life: graduate student socialization in entrepreneurial departments (Mendoza, 2007), faculty experiences of post-tenure review (O'Meara, 2003, 2004a), academic unit reorganization (Mills, Bettis, Miller, and Nolan, 2005), faculty responses to presidential succession (Bensimon, 1991), faculty understandings of and reactions to financial stress (Neumann, 1995), among others. Mills, Bettis, Miller, and Nolan (2005) used sense making and social identity theory to understand faculty members' experiences of academic unit reorganization, finding that the meaning that faculty made of campus change was influenced by the language used to describe the change (through changes in policies and changes in academic departments) and the connection faculty felt personally to a new or old department. Similarly, Bean (1998) and Weick (1995) focus on the role language plays in producing change in organizations, noting that language creates legitimacy for chosen images (Bean, 1998). Swartzman (1987) stresses that "meetings are sense makers" (p. 288) in which people exchange and negotiate views and perceptions and come to mutual understandings (see also Birnbaum, 1988). Weick (1995) observes that when a significant amount of environmental uncertainty, ambiguity, complexity, turbulence, information overload, or lack of information is involved, sense-making activity increases. In these cases, actors engage in sense making to "structure the unknown" (Waterman, 1990, p. 41) and develop "cognitive maps of their environment" (Ring and Rands, 1989, p. 342). Therefore, sense making holds much promise for understanding faculty responses to new, unfamiliar, or otherwise complex situations—for example, early career challenges, unheralded increases in administrative and service responsibilities after achieving tenure, ambiguity in the course of organizational change or during times of financial stress, and the challenges of open discourse and struggles to understand amid incidents of campus racism, sexism, or other forms of discrimination.

The theme of social cognition also encompasses expectancy theories, which strive to explain the processes whereby beliefs influence behavior (Blackburn and Lawrence, 1995; Kezar and Eckel, 2002; Mills, Bettis, Miller, and Nolan, 2005; Weick, 1995). Expectancy theories posit that individuals are motivated to action when they expect that their efforts will "lead to desired outcomes, and when they value work activities" (Blackburn and Lawrence, 1995, p. 22; Vroom, 1964). O'Meara (2004a) used expectancy theory to frame a study of post-tenure review implementation in a large state system, positing that a faculty member would undertake professional development as part of her post-tenure review if she believed (hence, expected) that the effort expended in updating her knowledge and skills would bring her to a level of desirable competence or accomplishment. Alternatively—and as was the case in O'Meara's study—when faculty do not expect that the professional development that departmental colleagues recommend for them will be useful to them, they are unlikely to undertake it. Likewise, colleagues on personnel committees are not likely to offer such advice, expecting it will not be appreciated. Weick (1995) observes that expectations influence what a person notices, what she infers, what she remembers, and what she does. Thus expectations often become self-fulfilling prophesies (Weick, 1995; for selected higher education applications, see Birnbaum, 1988).

Sociocultural theories have also been used to explore the nature of faculty work and work life. Sociocultural lenses build heavily on the work of Lev Vygotsky and colleagues who argued that an individual's learning depends heavily on the social context in which the person exists (Wertsch, 1985). To understand an individual's learning is then to understand how her mental processes and relevant social settings interact (Creamer & Lattuca, 2005; Lattuca, 2001). In her studies of interdisciplinary faculty collaboration in teaching and research, Lattuca (2001; Creamer and Lattuca, 2005) used sociocultural and cultural history theories to explore the many local contexts in which faculty carry out their work. Likewise, Amey and Brown (2005) used a sociocultural framework to guide their eighteen-month study of a university-community partnership, articulating its utility in conceptualizing the skills required by leaders and participants in interdisciplinary collaboration. They found that interdisciplinary learning requires "cultivating dialogue, developing shared language and understandings, reflection and deep learning" (p. 31). This work further positions team leaders as needing to see issues and events from multiple perspectives. Leaders, say these authors, must be cognitively complex thinkers themselves (Amey, 2002; Amey and Brown, 2005).

Standpoint theories argue that processes of coming to know—regardless of what they are called (learning, sense making, expectancy realization)—are conditioned by knowers' situatedness in structures of power that are framed socially, culturally, and, indeed, epistemically. "Contexts" in this view are always stratified and by virtue of status differentials power-infused— influencing how individuals understand reality relative to the distribution of power in it. Individuals may be fully aware about power differentials in the worlds they live in, or they may be but semiconscious of them. They may use their positioning strategically to gain knowledge-related benefits, or they may act in and in response to hierarchically defined knowledge structures. Standpoint theories also state that the views or vantage points for knowledge construction of persons and groups in superordinate positions tend to be legitimated as "official knowledge" in societies, whereas the knowledge of those in subordinate positions is cast typically as deficient, flawed, undeveloped, or otherwise rudimentary (Harding, 1986, 1991). For our purposes, the key messages of standpoint theory are that both of these locations for knowledge construction—the super- and subordinate—are partial and incomplete (Haraway, 1988) and that individuals of lower social stature, mastering "the view from below," typically develop facility in understanding the knowledge-making dynamics of those who create, espouse, and legitimate knowledge "from above." Their view then may be more complex in its orientation.

Who are the key creating subjects of standpoint theory? In gender studies, women are typically cast as creating knowledge on lower rungs of the social-power hierarchy, whereas majority males are cast as creating it from upper, "ruling" positions that to access, women must master, often in a language and from a perspective that is at odds with their native knowing. In this view, women's knowing is largely excluded from elite sites of knowledge construction (often created historically by males), notably research in academic institutions (Harding, 1986, 1991; Smith, 1987). In studies of racialized knowledge construction, ethnic minorities, notably people of color and often religious minorities, are viewed as engaged in knowledge construction on lower rungs of the social power hierarchy and as struggling for legitimation among dominant (typically white) populations who espouse knowledge that grows from the privileged views of the upper rungs. The partiality of both views (offered by persons and communities on lower and upper social rungs) is rarely acknowledged, however; occupants of any one social rung become committed to specialized knowledge construction modes, that is, unique images of reality. In brief, deficiencies in dominant (legitimated) views are typically exempt from questioning or critique; the distinct contributions of visions "from below" are rarely acknowledged. Exemplary standpoint theoreticians include Dorothy Smith (1987) and Sandra Harding (1986, 1991) for feminist studies and Patricia Hill Collins (1990) and Gloria Ladson-Billings (1997) for black feminist thought as a forerunner of contemporary critical race theory.

In standpoint theories, the views (understandings, experiences, knowledge construction) of women and of racial or ethnic minorities are cast as deserving of voice amid other long-legitimated views. In this spirit, educational scholar and anthropologist Gloria Ladson-Billings draws on the writings of sociologist Patricia Hill Collins to articulate her own educational research methodology and, by extrapolation, her approach to the framing of educational realities, including those of higher education. Ladson-Billings presents several propositions: "(1) concrete experience as a criterion of meaning, (2) the use of dialogue in assessing knowledge claims, (3) the ethic of caring, and (4) the ethic of personal accountability" (1997, p. 62). In this view, with others that have grown alongside it, the grounded experience of knowing in one's day-to-day life is a primary criterion of authenticity. Faculty lives and learning, like all human lives and their learning, emerge from lived experiences (Neumann and Peterson, 1997).

Researchers in higher education and beyond whose work espouses a standpoint sensibility applicable to academic settings include Estela Bensimon (1992) and Susan Talburt (2000), who document the lived experiences of lesbian professors and scholars making their way in academic worlds that largely fail to understand their identities and knowledge pursuits; Mary Romero and Abigail Stewart (1999), who assemble documentaries of diverse women's silences as sources of their stories of strength, struggle, and survival; Anna Neumann and Penelope Peterson (1997), who collect diverse women's representations of their research experiences and narratives of the sources of their educational subjects of study; Ruth Behar (1993) and Dorinne Kondo (1990), whose analyses of self in research reveal the personal and cultural sources of their anthropological contributions, among others. A distinctive contribution to this literature is the research of Gregory Anderson (2002), who, in drawing out the case of change in South African higher education, raises concerns about the power of institutional and social policy to "zone" educational opportunities in ways that sequester oppressed people's attempts to know and learn through the courses of their lives. Such zoning, an artifact of governmental and intellectual apartheid, may be viewed as "locking in" standpoints for knowing self and world—in effect, "locking out" opportunities for individuals to learn freely and, likewise, for historically oppressed communities to offer their knowledge as legitimate sources of academic knowledge work.

Writing in the spirit of epistemic predecessors—notably Harding and Hill Collins—a new generation of scholars has surfaced to explore the positions of power and constraint in which academic women and people of color have crafted intellectual careers and persisted in the construction of academic knowledge. In the case of women, feminist scholars have explored both the manifold "ceilings" and barriers that women striving for academic lives and careers encounter (Glazer-Raymo, 2008; Guinier, Fine, and Balin, 1997; Shaw, Leder, and Harris, 2007) and occasionally the hidden "doorways" or "connections" that provide some women with surprising opportunity (Gumport, 1990; Romero and Stewart, 1999). The contributions of scholars of color to standpoint-anchored analysis in higher education have persisted with great force, notably in the work of legal experts who have moved epistemological critique (previously applied broadly to social texts) to analysis of the legal doctrines governing the workings of American society. Scholarship in this tradition, often referred to as "critical race theory," offers views of both the everyday lived experiences of people of color in American society and its institutions (Berry and Mizelle, 2006) and legal critiques directed at the advancement of racial justice (Delgado, 1995; Williams, 1991), in the United States and worldwide (Wing, 2000). Writers in the field of higher education who have used this and related lenses to explore the experiences of faculty of color in the academic workplace include Antonio (2002); Turner, Myers, and Creswell (1999); and Howell and Tuitt (2003).

Summary and Implications

As the preceding examples suggest, the epistemic approach may be manifest in multiple ways, yielding diverse theories to explain faculty members' access to and engagement in opportunities for learning and growth. Those theories vary in their strengths and weaknesses, in what they offer or lack.

The strength of theories of organizational cognition is that they strive to get inside the thinking and knowing of professors. The weakness of these theories is that typically they do not go far enough to acknowledge the role of context in framing what faculty learn, how they learn it, and the implications of these experiences for what they know and do not know.

The strength of sociocultural theories is that they take account of the immediate contexts of faculty members' learning but often without differentiating features of context that are local from those that are broader and more social or global (though manifest in the local). This absence makes consideration of the effects of large-scale social movements and of broad policy initiatives hard to trace at the level of "lived experience." Sociocultural theories in their current formulation also fail to take dynamics of social power into account in opportunities to learn (see prior definition of "standpoint").

The strength of standpoint theories is that they focus on knowledge construction and on knowers' positioning in structures of power as the primary contexts of their work; further, they emphasize the authenticity of knowing at diverse levels of social power hierarchies. Their weakness is their tendency to critique the partiality of elite or superordinate views without adequately acknowledging the related partiality of views from lower levels of the social power structure (even though "views from below" may at times be more complex than those "from above"). That said, we need improved understandings of how the views from below may be brought more fully into public arenas. We also need improved understanding of how epistemic conversations may be thoughtfully framed among individuals who live and work on diverse rungs of various social hierarchies. In this spirit, it must be recognized that differences in the gender- and race-based positioning of both the researchers and the researched are critical concerns for educational research today. Yet so are the professional and occupational positions of those individuals whose ideas define the diverse realities in higher education. For example, faculty and administrators occupy very different standpoints for their making sense of organizational and intellectual realities. To create generative environments for learning, their ways of knowing too must be brought into productive conversation with one another (Neumann, in press).

Though broad-ranging and diverse, the epistemic perspective as a newcomer to theory in higher education and education more broadly holds great promise for framing connections between knowledge about the larger worlds in which education occurs and the knowing in which individuals engage daily—as they teach, learn, and lead educational institutions. Yet more must be done in this vein of work, including developing "epistemic locations" for scrutinizing potential links between governing or policy-based views and those arising from lived experience.

"We should understand our goal of enhancing the theory base for research on faculty work as on ongoing dialogue" (Creamer and Lattuca, 2005, p. 19). This statement recognizes the importance of reflecting on the perspectives that frame extant research on higher education faculty and continuing to question them over time, especially as the faculty career itself changes. In the spirit of the statement, we conclude with the following observations and recommendations.

As we look across the current and forecast state of the American professoriate, we view the perspectives presented in this chapter as extremely helpful in conceptualizing some areas of faculty work and careers but as ignoring or deemphasizing others. We have noted already that our analysis of more than one thousand pieces of scholarship on college and university faculty reveals a vacuum on the topic of faculty growth—and so does our assessment of perspectives that might usefully frame research on growth-anchored topics: professors' learning, development, creativity, generativity, and intellectual and professional energy. For example, as of 2008 we have a much better understanding of factors that promote faculty satisfaction than we do of their learning—especially their learning of the subjects they teach and study, what Neumann (in press) refers to as "scholarly learning." We know a great deal about the means whereby department cultures exclude women and faculty of color but not yet enough about how professional relationships support their intellectual and professional development. We know more about how reward systems inhibit faculty involvement in scholarly activities they deem important than how some faculty assume agency (defined here as a "life course" issue) to reshape reward systems so as to value what they personally believe is important. How can these absences be explained? We suggest that at least some of the absences grow from failures to pause for reflection on theories in use—and disuse—in higher education research. What kinds of views might be missing?

A quick review of this chapter reveals that most theories in use in the study of higher education faculty derive from the social sciences. We suggest that the subject of faculty growth and related topics like faculty learning would benefit from infusion of perspectives from the arts and humanities and potentially of various interdisciplinary views. Such perspectives are already in use in higher education research. For example, Terosky (2005) used the philosophical construct of vocation to study professors who take their teaching seriously; Neumann (2006, in press) has used aesthetic perspectives to study tenured university professors' "passionate thought" about their subjects of study and teaching. Combining a humanistic and arts-based perspective with perspectives drawn from the social sciences may promote fresh (if not surprising) views of the faculty career. In line with this view, we suggest that other cross- or interdisciplinary perspectives be developed to explore professors' work and careers, including some drawn from seemingly unlikely fields like the sciences (for an example, see Neumann, 1999a). By calling for an interdisciplinary perspective that considers faculty growth and learning as central to faculty careers and work lives, we do not by any means advocate for the dissolution of faculty studies anchored in political, social, organizational, or economic theory. Rather we urge that at least some portion of the higher education research community be more intentional and systematic than in the past to draw interdisciplinary views on growth and learning to the forefront of research considerations. We believe that doing so will shape the questions we ask and the research methods we use. For example, studies of faculty involvement in research, teaching, service, or community engagement would ask not only about incentives and reward systems (aimed at organizational improvement) but also and just as often about human learning, moral courage, personal and collective agency, commitment, passion, and care (aimed at professional and personal-intellectual development). Studies such as these promise to introduce considerations of personal desire and will, intellectual learning, moral responsibility, personal investment, and professionalism into plans for development of future faculty in higher education. We urge as well that the findings of studies anchored conceptually in a faculty learning and growth perspective then be brought into conversation with those anchored in a broader policy or organizational- and societal-development perspective. We urge then a standpoint-informed conversation as a frame for future research on faculty and higher education broadly.

This chapter focuses on the perspectives guiding research on college and university faculty. We note that the perspectives we have discussed emphasize some research methodologies over others (Kuntz, 2005). As we look for new theoretical frameworks to guide future research on the faculty, we are likely to look as well for fresh approaches to learning about the faculty, including new methods for conducting research. The concluding chapter discusses current narratives of faculty work and suggests an alternative perspective grounded in images of faculty growth.

Designing a New Narrative

It is a cold November day, and Daniel has just entered a coffee shop to do some writing before heading over to the university to teach his evening class. It is his first semester on the tenure track and he has high hopes for his career. As he waits for his soup, he overhears a colleague from another department having lunch with a young man, obviously a former undergraduate who must have once sat in the colleague's classes. The colleague appears to be advising the former student about graduate school and job searches. Sitting up straight, tense and serious, the young man shares that he has not received much advice from his family, has been out of college for two years, and is feeling rather lost.

Redirecting his attention, Daniel writes for two and a half hours. Preparing to leave, he realizes that his colleague is just now finishing his discussion with the former student. The young man is now smiling, seemingly more at ease and engaged than earlier. Daniel had heard, in hallways and over lunches, that this colleague of his showed unusual commitment toward his students, current and former alike. He heard too just how much his students appreciate his direction and caring. Daniel contemplates this special sense of commitment and what it must contribute to campus life: in Daniel's view, the colleague provides something of a touchstone to the college's students, someone they can count on to be there long past graduation. Daniel considers the invisible strings that connect some students and their former professors after graduation. He wonders where the forging of those strings and their maintenance fit into the job description of an academic. Given that his university's formal reward system will not acknowledge the time this colleague has just spent with his former student, Daniel is all the more impressed. This choice, he observes, flows against most campus norms of which he is aware. As Daniel leaves the coffee shop, heading toward his office (to send a brief e-mail to his research collaborator), he wonders what norms he himself will have to navigate, reject, or transform to make the professional contributions that he finds most important—and what he will learn in the process of so doing.

T HIS CHAPTER CONSIDERS THE OVERRIDING NARRATIVE(S) and underlying assumptions that have undergirded research on faculty over the last two decades. We critique this narrative with regard to what it emphasizes—what it lets us see, think about, and act on. We critique it also in terms of what it obscures—what it masks about growth for current and future faculty.

Our goal then in this chapter is to suggest a "counternarrative," one that has begun in some recent research on faculty, which we think holds the most promise for both studying and promoting faculty growth—especially in ways that are centered on learning in faculty work and that better understand and facilitate faculty agency, professional relationships, and faculty commitments to important higher education arenas.

The Power of Narrative

We use the word "narrative" as others have—as the general term for telling a story (Birnbaum, 2000; Postman, 1995). Historians of higher education have a tradition of providing and critiquing narratives of higher education. For example, Johnson (2007) observes the common historical narrative regarding the origins of land-grant colleges, observing that when they were first created, many were not primarily agricultural but provided liberal arts studies. Nor did the original land-grant institutions open wide the doors of higher education to a group of students ready to engage. At the point these institutions were founded, collegiate enrollment was low (the American system of K–12 public education was still in the making). Those who went to college were a relatively privileged group vis-á-vis their peers. Most land-grant schools grew into their present missions to emphasize applied fields alongside arts and sciences and to address a broadly public-educated student body (Johnson, 2007).

The concept of narrative as a common organizing story is fairly familiar in higher education. For the purposes of this chapter, we draw on the word to consider the story lines that the extant research creates and that researchers and higher education leaders typically espouse. Three components of narrative seem especially relevant to our task: the way in which narrative shapes our expectations and the very questions we ask, the way in which narrative provides a context for interpreting study findings and how narrative helps to contextualize study findings in practice, and the extent to which narrative represents unfinished work, that is, texts in progress.

We begin with the observation that narrative focuses researchers' attention and then provides the language and context within which findings will be made meaningful. Postman (1995) talks about the power of narrative in education to tell a story, but, he notes, "not any kind of story but one that tells of origins and envisions a future, a story that constructs ideals, prescribes rules of conduct, provides a source of authority, and above all, gives a sense of continuity and purpose" (pp. 5–6). Postman advocates the importance of narrative in constructing the goals of educational institutions and the means to achieve those goals. Much like literature on sense making wherein individuals receive cues from their environment that focus their attention, narratives focus our attention in ways that connect us and our work to a common story: "Our genius lies in our capacity to make meaning through the creation of narratives that give point to our labors, exalt our history, elucidate the present, and give direction to our future. To do their work, such narratives do not have to be true in a scientific sense. . . . The measure of a narrative's truth or falsity is in its consequences: Does it provide people with a sense of personal identity, a sense of community life, a basis for moral conduct, explanations of that which cannot be known?" (Postman, 1995, p. 7). As such, narrative cues our attention and helps us to make sense of what we see. For example, Kuntz (2005) observes that narratives on faculty reveal power dynamics in social structures. Rhoades, Kiyama, McCormick, and Quiroz (2008) observe that the prevailing model of the professional in the academy is one that assumes academics must distance themselves from practitioners and from communities of origin to move up in the academic hierarchy. As narratives become popular and are read and reread (or told and retold, acted and reenacted), they become normative: they come to represent the discourses whereby we understand what and how things are. Thus narratives about faculty have real power in the reproduction of hierarchical structures of power in higher education and in society at large (Kuntz, 2005).

Another key element of narrative is its living and unfinished nature (Peters, 2006). As previously indicated, historians constantly revise extant narratives about particular time periods, narratives developed by a combination of fact, myth, culture, tradition, and perhaps attention. Peters (2006) has been exploring the scholarship of faculty employed in colleges of agriculture and life sciences and how they foster partnerships with community organizations. Peters (2006) notes that the history of land-grant faculty is filled with a metanarrative of faculty providing technical expertise to local farmers, which paints faculty as technical (and powerful) saviors and farmers as thankful recipients of the knowledge that the scholars dispense. Peters (2006) observes as well an opposing and parallel metanarrative positioning farmers as victims and faculty as distant professionals. In this alternative view, the distanced faculty use their professional expertise and power to exploit less-resourced communities.

Peters (2006) observes that both metanarratives are "incomplete, misleading and in some ways untrue" (p. 10). He draws then on historical evidence to propose a "prophetic counternarrative" that could come to replace the other two, thereby spurring the development of new kinds of micronarratives—new modes of enacting the faculty role. Peters's proposed counternarrative does not project faculty as villains or as saviors but as imperfect partners who can both give and receive knowledge in collaborative relationships between university and community.

As illustrated by Peters (2006), research on faculty has the power to "script," "place," or "locate" faculty in a particular role when in fact they may understand themselves to be playing a different role or multiple roles. In their narratives of student life histories and career choices, Rhoades, Kiyama,

McCormick, and Quiroz (2008) described students who may easily have been scripted as weighed down by family obligations that slow or altogether stop their accession of careers. These students, in fact, felt they were exercising something akin to "critical agency," wherein they were making contributions that were personally and professional meaningful (Baez, 2000). By scripting these students as victims of professional norms, we strip them of agency that they have to make decisions that are personally and professionally meaningful. This scripting has implications for the kinds of options others following in their career path may see for themselves.

How we think, write, and talk about faculty also has implications for policy. Giroux (1993) observes that colleges and universities "produce a particular selection and ordering of narratives and subjectivities" (p. 90). Yet acknowledging and critiquing the dominant social narrative about higher education faculty overall is a valuable and underused practice. Bensimon and Marshall (1997), through feminist policy analysis, and Allan (2003), through discourse analysis of women's commission reports, have critiqued dominant narratives regarding women in higher education, showing us that the story we tell matters. The very questions researchers ask about faculty can either reproduce the dominant social narrative or serve as a catalyst for transformation about the way we view faculty and faculty work.

Given this overview of the concept of narrative, we look across the research reviewed in this monograph to name a dominant story line that, in our assessment, has preoccupied higher education scholars concerned with faculty careers, work, and workplaces. Building on the description provided in the first chapter, we outline what we mean by a narrative of constraint. Second, we discuss seven aspects of this narrative, considering what each aspect both reveals and obscures about faculty.

The Narrative of Constraint

As mentioned in the first chapter, our literature review has caused us to see a dominant narrative in faculty literature on constraints. By "constraints," we mean barriers in the structure and culture of workplaces that prevent faculty from doing their work or being all that they can be. The tag line for this narrative is "he or she can't because. . . ." As faculty, we have consistently heard of doctoral students who are scared away from a faculty career because of the myriad constraints facing academics, especially after taking a class that reviews research on the academic profession. As regular attendees of the annual conferences of the Association for the Study of Higher Education and American Educational Research Association, among others, where research on faculty is presented, we observe that many presentations have focused explicitly on faculty members' treading water, surviving, and just making it through the constraints of present challenges—to academic work and higher education broadly. This narrative of constraints in part evolves from research on real barriers that faculty face in their career workplaces and reward systems that may not function as expected. Whether the study focuses on reward systems that fail to acknowledge a broad enough definition of scholarship or workplaces that promote the ideal worker as a norm or examples of discrimination faced by women and faculty of color, the tale is often bleak.

Moreover, studies report that faculty purposefully decide to have fewer children than they might have preferred because of the rigors and expectations of their career, that their scholarship choices are skewed toward fulfilling rigid departmental expectations, or that faculty cannot find the collegial relationships they desire in their workplaces. The image of the faculty member staggering to the finish line of tenure and then constrained by expectations for post-tenure service is a common part of the tenure-track story. This narrative of constraints emphasizes the ways in which the faculty career perhaps does not measure up to what faculty and potential faculty expected upon entering their academic careers.

Rhoades, Kiyama, McCormick, and Quiroz (2008) observe similarly that much of the literature on faculty concentrates on obstacles, challenges, and discrimination, particularly for women and faculty of color. Although such critique is important, they observe that it focuses on assuming newcomers must navigate current institutions instead of transform them, that is, more about how to "make it than how to remake it" (p. 215).

In critiquing the narrative of constraint, we do not suggest that research that reveals constraints ought to be avoided. We strongly believe that research along this line is important in revealing problems and potential solutions. We believe, however, that it is equally important to analyze the narrative of constraint in light of what it might obscure: namely, realities of accomplishment and growth existing occasionally (at times frequently) alongside constraint and loss. By focusing only on constraints faced by faculty, might we fail to see and study achievements? Might we fail to see faculty overcoming barriers toward growth and learning? Just as in history it is easy to focus on the constraints women and faculty of color faced in gaining access to higher education and their struggles in that endeavor (rather than their authentic accomplishments once enrolled and after college), we posit that the emphasis on constraints can obscure the very point of the struggle—these women's achievements of particular ends through accession to higher education and through deployment of the new knowledge they gained there. We say all this of course with an emphasis on balance: even in discussing women's and minority faculty members' accomplishments, we must acknowledge their struggles and losses in "getting there," struggles and losses that others may not experience as blatantly as they have. The emphasis on constraints in the American story of the professoriate at times can also feed into the public critique of higher education faculty as privileged and as not appreciating how privileged they are with regard to the work and constraints on individuals in other occupations in the United States or in other countries, including what it may mean to be an academic in a more constraining national culture.

Features of the Prevailing Narrative of Constraint in Faculty Studies

Based on the preceding discussion, we ponder what an alternative narrative for the faculty career might look like. Although we view the formation of that narrative as a major goal for future higher education scholars, we pause, first, to draw our thoughts together about the major features of the existent narrative constraint. In doing so, we hope to position ourselves to articulate what the community of scholars of higher education has missed and what it may wish to pursue in a reconstructed framing of the faculty career. But first we return to a discussion of seven features of the narrative constraint: a persistent image of certain faculty as victims; the image of the academic as a lone ranger, limited by isolation; preoccupation with faculty productivity; measures of faculty satisfaction in terms of turnover and whether faculty would again choose to pursue an academic career; conceptualization of faculty as a dependent variable; images of faculty as disinterested intellectuals disengaged from the real world; and views of the faculty professional and of faculty work as the accrual of resources, prestige, and standing.

Image of Faculty as Victims as Opposed to Agents. Allan's examination (2003) of women's commission reports (through the lens of discourse analysis) revealed how well-meaning advocates for women in higher education unintentionally presented women as vulnerable, weak, in need, dominated by stronger forces at play, and in general at the mercy of the discrimination and biases they faced. We suggest here that in an effort to point out discrimination faced by women and faculty of color as well as challenges faced by faculty throughout their careers, the literature runs a continuous headline of "what isn't working." Faculty are positioned as victims of chilly climates, departments with a lack of mentoring and support, and reward systems that deemphasize teaching and community engagement or are overtly political and unsupportive. Although much research on faculty has been conducted in research universities, the general image of victimization spills over into other institutional contexts. Although we have learned a great deal about the challenges of the faculty's "academic homes" from this particular focus, we learn little about how faculty use what Baez (2000) refers to as critical agency to overcome challenge, what Neumann (in press) refers to as newly tenured professors' "agency for learning" with "strategies" toward realization, and what Rhoades, Kiyama, McCormick, and Quiroz (2008) allude to in their study of students' efforts to remake organizations and professional standards in the face of contentious circumstances. Research that focuses on the victim reveals a fair amount about barriers to all kinds of "entrances" into academe: becoming a Ph.D., acquiring a tenure-track position, becoming a full professor. Yet it provides little insight into how faculty may navigate requirements, acquire organizational resources, and make meaningful contributions once in the particular door they are accessing. In a word, little has been said about it what takes to "activate" resources and opportunities gained.

Image of the Academic as a Lone Ranger, Limited by Isolation. Traces of this narrative abound: the "lone ranger," the "sage on the stage," the "solo artist," and so forth. Interestingly, this narrative, alive in everyday academic life, also is infused with a fair amount of higher education research. We are surprised by how many studies echo the existent discourses of practice in higher education, for example, by assuming conceptual frameworks that position faculty members as untouched by context or simply as working alone, as opposed to viewing them as parts of larger relationships, communities, or networks. Clearly, we have studies that intentionally explore the social bases of faculty careers and lives, among them studies of faculty kinship (Daly and Dee, 2006), colleagueship (Aguirre, 2000; Hagedorn, 2000), interdisciplinary collaboration (Creamer and Lattuca, 2005), faculty learning communities (O'Meara, 2005b), women's professional support groups (Dickens and Sagaria, 1997), and academic women's connectedness in civic, religious, familial, and other communities as sources of their scholarship (Neumann and Peterson, 1997).

The lone ranger narrative may well derive from the view of faculty as cosmopolitan—and thereby connected to an invisible college of colleagues who live and work elsewhere rather than being committed to their local campus and the colleagues in it (Gouldner, 1960; Rhoades, Kiyama, McCormick, and Quiroz, 2008). That narrative is consistent with observations about faculty as individual entrepreneurs and autonomous workers (Jencks and Riesman, 1968). Whereas the lone ranger narrative may well support scholarship on research universities and on higher education at large (given its consistency with the solo norms of these institutions), it inhibits research on the dynamics of campuses that count on more collaboration, interaction, and other relational activity amid day-to-day work life. Such campuses include community colleges, liberal arts colleges, historically black colleges and universities, and religiously affiliated institutions. One line of research indicates that lone ranger narratives conflict with what a good number of doctoral students and junior faculty say they want in their careers (Austin, 2002a, 2002b; Rice, Sorcinelli, and Austin, 2000). It also negates the commitments to community building that many scholars of color and other first-generation faculty have made and wish to maintain (Rhoades, Kiyama, McCormick, and Quiroz, 2008).

As we review the body of research on faculty, we see more portraits of faculty as individuals than as participants in webs or networks. This focus on the person minus surrounding persons and minus a full display of key themes of the surrounding social context limits our understanding of how professors and college instructors learn and grow in relationship with or through others—and possibly because of others. We noted in the previous chapter that researchers need to explore more thoroughly than they have before the broad range of contexts in which faculty work (personal, dyadic, group and community, social, cultural, economic, historical, and so on). But perhaps more important, they need to identify what it is about these contexts that serve as resources and constraints on what they know, think, and learn.

Preoccupation with Faculty Productivity. This narrative focuses on what faculty accomplish in terms of measurable output—teaching and advising loads, number of publications, awards and grant dollars—as well as assessments of whether each stream is enough. The rhetoric behind this narrative line is all too familiar: from fears of what "deadwood" faculty are doing to higher education to prompts for beginning faculty to "hit the ground running" to worries about some faculty members' overloaded plates and others' underuse. The literature of the late 1980s through the 1990s reflects the multiple management fads that institutional leaders and policymakers sought to measure and otherwise quantify as they created "data" in response to the demands of this narrative (Birnbaum, 2000).

The narrative of faculty performance and productivity is important to rethink if we hope to communicate the value of postsecondary education to the various publics for which higher education exists and to which the enterprise turns for support. The productivity narrative, however, represents a disconnect between measures-in-use (like countable classes, quantity of advisement sessions, and number of publications) and measures that, we believe, matter more such as the quality of teaching, the effectiveness of advising, and the relevance of research undertaken. We suggest that the narrative of faculty performance and productivity—or as we have come to refer to it, the narrative of "how much?"—obscures the yet more important narrative of "how meaningful?" It may well overemphasize cosmopolitan views such that local contributions disappear from sight—contributions that could, however, be broadly (in fact, generally) replicated and shared.

Measures of Faculty Satisfaction. This measure gauges faculty satisfaction in terms of turnover and whether faculty would again choose to pursue an academic career. A tag line for this narrative might be "how does it feel to you?" Given the significant investment that institutions make in hiring, developing, and reviewing faculty—and given the centrality of faculty to institutional missions—analysis of faculty satisfaction and reasons for turnover are critical (see Daly and Dee, 2006; Rosser, 2004, 2005a; Hagedorn, 1996). Although we noted earlier that many studies indicate decreases in faculty satisfaction, surveys conducted over the past twenty-five years have consistently shown high satisfaction among faculty compared with persons in other careers (Gappa, Austin, and Trice, 2007, p. 104). Perhaps the greatest contribution of this line of inquiry is that it highlights differences in the experiences, including the satisfaction of women and faculty of color, and of faculty at diverse career stages. Such data have the potential to guide institutional and departmental change bearing on campus climates and cultures. This body of research indicates that what matters to individuals does differ and that how institutions forge psychological contracts with their faculty does matter (Huston, Norman, and Ambrose, 2007); this work also explores the consequences of faculty beliefs that those contracts have not been fulfilled. But research on faculty satisfaction is complex in that faculty work and the faculty's feelings about their work are complex; for example, faculty may be deeply satisfied with one work role and dissatisfied with another. Further issues of personal satisfaction may mask issues surrounding the quality of work produced: satisfaction with or about what, and questions about the sources of satisfaction are rarely asked. Further, no efforts have been made to date to distinguish contentment, as a form of satisfaction, from the kind of passion that drives professors' scholarly learning (Neumann, 2006) or forms of commitment to vocation that lead some professors to "take their teaching seriously" (Terosky, 2005), possibly at risk of sanctions.

Conceptualization of Faculty as a Dependent Variable and of Faculty Development as a Way to Redirect Faculty Toward the Institution's Goals. Another dominant narrative in faculty development research is one of faculty as a dependent variable or the idea that if we do X to faculty, then we will get Y out of faculty (Neumann, in press; Terosky, 2005). Many dissertations and large research studies have explored factors that influence faculty behavior; some of these studies even attempt to predict faculty behavior based on factors external to themselves. Still other studies consider interactions of internal and external factors: intrinsic and extrinsic motivations (Austin and Gamson, 1983), self-knowledge and social knowledge (Blackburn and Lawrence, 1995), appointment type and productivity (Bland and others, 2006), and type of faculty work emphasized and salary (Fairweather, 1993, 2005). These studies build on Clark's work (1987) in that they show faculty experiences are highly dependent on factors such as discipline and institutional type.

Like students, faculty are influenced by environmental norms and changes therein; they may shift their behavior to respond to cues in priorities and reward systems. As previously noted, this line of research suggests that cumulative advantage and disadvantage (Clark and Corcoran, 1986) are alive and well among the faculty. The discourse that this research yields may be summarized as follows: academic culture and norms are so strong that graduate education is the main place to look to influence career success, including work patterns. This narrative reveals the complexity of factors that influence faculty work and that may aid leaders and faculty development specialists to "develop" the faculty through programs and policies by that name.

What might the narrative of faculty as dependent variables obscure? Our response, for one, is faculty growth. This line of work focuses on the influence of factors on faculty work, not faculty growth. Further, this body of research tends to position the faculty in a deterministic manner, as products of the systems around them—systems that administrators and their technical staffs can manipulate, thereby "reshaping faculty" in objectifying ways. In positioning faculty as manipulatable, we strip research of the possibility of exploring faculty agency as foundational to their learning, to their own direction of their growth, and, just as important, to the construction (and reconstruction) of the organizations and reward systems (including promotion and tenure) in which they frame their knowledge, careers, and lives.

We acknowledge that recent research on graduate students and early-career faculty socialization (through promotion and tenure systems) is critical to our understanding of how academic cultures come to be reproduced; we believe, however, that the story has more to it. This story is of faculty who remake their environments, who act in countercultural ways, who resist accommodation. Such a counternarrative is present in the work of Rhoades, Kiyama,

McCormick, and Quiroz's discussion (2008) of local cosmopolitans, Terosky's (2005) analysis of teacher-scholars, and Baez's conception (2000) of critical agency. We discuss this issue more deeply in the next subsection. For now, we emphasize that though it is important to understand how various factors shape the content and form of faculty work, a narrative that positions faculty as the sum of invasive forces strips researchers of the potential to explore images of them with the potential for choice, intention, confidence, agency, and self-designed strategy—and thus the distinct stamp that individuals as "agents of learning" (Neumann, Terosky, and Schell, 2006) can put on their work.

Images of Faculty as Disinterested Intellectuals Disengaged from the Real World. A dominant narrative in the history of faculty work since World War II has emphasized faculty as disinterested intellectuals who are disengaged from "the real world" where nonacademic workers (including practitioners) engage in front-line efforts. In this view, faculty exist in an ivory tower aloof from everyday (real) life. In part, this narrative articulates the value of singular views of "objectivity in scholarship" and of beliefs that research requires researchers to pursue their inquiries apart from worldly contexts and constraints (Rice, 1996). As may be inferred, "insider views on research"—namely, epistemological analyses of the research process across multiple disciplines—question this stance, especially so in the social sciences, for example, by positioning the researcher as inescapably the instrument of research and to some extent its target (Haraway, 1988).

Moreover, this narrative paints a view of faculty and their work values as requiring the suppression of emotion, bias, commitment, or passion. It is embedded in what Rice (1996) refers to as notions of the "assumptive world of the academic professional," developed around World War II. In this view, "the distinctive task of the academic professional is the pursuit of cognitive truth." This narrative line also portrays faculty as comfortable in "silos" of academic study, where they carry out work presumed to be important and that advances their disciplines and fields. When things go awry (for example, during times of general economic distress), political, entrepreneurial, community, fiscal, or other forces are likely to invade the "siloed" spaces in efforts to shape and reshape faculty priorities so as to align them with "external realities."

One strength of this narrative is that it highlights key aspects of faculty work, including academic freedom and independent thought. At times, however, it obscures the benefits of external forces that might enrich faculty work, for example, by making faculty work relevant to specific communities and social issues through engaged scholarship (Colbeck and Janke, 2006; Jaeger and Thornton, 2006; O'Meara, 2008; Ward, 2003). The narrative of objectivity and ivory tower scholarship can do a disservice to growing understandings of the ways in which autobiography—personal lives—inescapably influences faculty work and careers (Neumann and Peterson, 1997). Mills (1959) wrote in *The Sociological Imagination* of the importance of linking such autobiography to understandings of individuals in organizations and society: "no social study that does not come back to the problems of biography, of history, and of their intersections [in] a society has completed its intellectual journey" (p. 6).

This narrative of distance and disinterest tends to constrain faculty by withholding their emotional involvement in their studies—a false imagery all too rarely discussed in higher education (Neumann, 2006). Likewise, the narrative assumes that professional success is found in distancing oneself from communities of origin and the issues important to them, acting as the detached expert as opposed to the interested, invested scholar, and, indeed, advocate (Rhoades, Kiyama, McCormick, and Quiroz, 2008). To summarize, this narrative line may obscure the very important role the personal has in professional and intellectual (even scientific) endeavor.

Views of the Faculty Professional and of Faculty Work as the Accrual of Resources, Prestige, and Standing. This narrative may have emerged in light of how competitive it has become in recent years to obtain a tenure-track position. This story of faculty work life prizes autonomy, expertise, and highly individualistic ways of working. This line of thinking has brought significant critique to other professions such as the clergy, doctors, and lawyers (Sullivan, 2005) and given birth to diatribes on the sins of the professoriate. One example is Sykes's claim (1988) that faculty, especially in research universities, pursue their own selfish interests (usually grant funding and prestigious journal appointments) to the neglect of undergraduates and good teaching (p. 5). Rhetoric surrounding this narrative focuses on excessive individualism and elitism, which is problematic for many reasons but perhaps mostly because it obscures the service component and ethic of responsibility embedded in the academic career. Having presented seven features of a narrative of constraint, we now turn to a discussion of our proposed counternarrative.

Toward a Counternarrative about and for Faculty Growth

With the various narratives previously presented in mind, we now turn to a counternarrative that we believe will help to advance research-based understanding of faculty growth. If the proposed counternarrative had a headline, it would be something to the effect of *Faculty: Living, Learning, Acting, and Committing Their Professional Lives to the Distinct Goals of Higher Learning.* This narrative promotes the idea that the faculty—the very people responsible for teaching, research, and service in a college or university—are also central players in the design of the developmental supports they themselves require to grow as individuals, scholars, teachers, and members of multiple communities. Thus in this view, professors' and instructors' development, learning, and growth—their activation—is self-reflexive: it looks in on itself, taking a hand in its own shaping. Faculty in effect choose or invent their own developmental supports for growth that they themselves craft, typically in interaction with a variety of others in their lives. Such growth may or may not be facilitated by institutions and by disciplines or fields, though clearly we believe it should. We make the point that regardless of institutional and other forms of support, faculty themselves must be actors, and preferably leading partners, in the design of their own developmental trajectories. This view is foundational to visions of faculty agency sociologically defined (Neumann, in press; Pallas, 2007). In the new narrative, the focus is on faculty contributions to their own growth. The narrative also highlights ways in which the faculty evolve and grow toward new and deeper understandings of their work.

Our counternarrative of placing faculty at the center of their career is supported by several key ideas:

- Learning is at the center of faculty work and their contributions.
- Faculty have and can develop a sense of agency to navigate barriers and put effort, will, intent, and talent into their work.

- Faculty learn, grow, and make contributions through professional relationships embedded in communities.
- Who a faculty member is—her history, identity, and experiences—shapes what and how she learns, the types and quality of contributions she makes to academe, and the ways in which she makes them.
- Faculty are professionals with capacities for deep commitment and vocation.

The following five subsections describe these five aspects of our emerging counternarrative of faculty growth. We explore these key ideas through a three-pronged approach: new directions for research on faculty, new directions for faculty development and organizational support for faculty, and new approaches to presenting faculty work to the public.

Learning Is at the Center of Faculty Work and Their Contributions

The new narrative assumes that learning is at the center of faculty growth, work, and careers; it assumes we need to take faculty learning seriously (Neumann, in press). We build on Neumann's observation (2006) that we cannot study learning without understanding what is being learned. Research on flow and passion in faculty scholarship shows a strong relationship between *learning* and the nature of the *content* being learned, suggesting we need to understand what in particular is being learned to design appropriate ways to support the faculty in their learning of it (Neumann, 2006). Building on this point, we next explore ways in which research, professional development, and public discourses about the faculty could be broadened to incorporate faculty learning as a central (but typically underdiscussed) aspect of what it means to be a professor or instructor in American higher education today.

Despite decades of theories about adult learning, human development, and life span and recent work on social-cognition and sense making to draw on, researchers studying learning as a central feature of faculty work face a formidable challenge. The field of higher education still knows relatively little about how social context, demographics, career stage, and organizational contexts influence faculty learning. For clarification, we illustrate how one common topic of research—appointment type—could be approached from learning as central narrative. The extant research presents the impact of different appointment structures on career opportunities or power in shared governance as well as the advantages or disadvantages of creating specialized roles for faculty (such as teaching and research appointments). By turning to a narrative that places faculty learning at the center of attention, researchers can analyze ways in which different appointments enrich or hinder a faculty member's growth in teaching or research or foster or discourage a faculty member's capacity to make long-term commitments to specific areas of higher education—commitments that provide for deep learning. A narrative around learning and appointment structures can ask, for example, what the impact of "unbundled" faculty positions (positions that emphasize only one of the three roles—teaching, research, service) will be on the quality and texture of the work in which they are engaged. What are the advantages and disadvantages of the "integrated professional" model (Colbeck, 1998) containing all three roles versus the unbundled role, and how do they differ for different types of faculty work? Similar contrasts could be made shifting current foci—for example, on satisfaction, quantifiable productivity, or other features of the previously discussed narrative of constraint—toward faculty learning as a central framework for research on contingent appointments.

Turning to the issue of professional development and organizational support, we acknowledge that over the years, numerous efforts have been launched to place faculty learning at the center of reform. Examples include the Lilly teaching program, which creates an early-career peer mentoring and learning community around teaching issues, and other peer or mutual mentoring programs that emphasize faculty as persons connecting with peers in nonhierarchical ways (Sorcinelli, Austin, Eddy, and Beach, 2005). Clearly, research on faculty learning communities represents a promising base for understanding how and why faculty learn through professional relationships with others. We suggest, however, that this literature could be further advanced by specifically highlighting the question of *what it is* that faculty learn in these relationships and then assessing the extent to which that content is what the learner sought to pursue—and if not, what got left out (or added), why, and with what consequences to whom. In brief, discussions of learning processes, relationships, and other locational or process-oriented issues can move off target if not explicitly connected, by way of research design, to the *what* of what is learned" (Neumann, in press). We qualify this statement by saying that under no circumstances do we view the faculty's learning as isolated from other learning that goes on in higher education, most especially the learning of students. Yet as significant research in K–12 education and in educational psychology has shown, researchers have a long way to go in conceptualizing the nature of the possible connections that may (and may not) exist between the teacher's learning and her teaching and the learning of the individuals in her or his classroom. Higher education scholars would do well to join other researchers at the forefront of research on this and related topics.

With regard to the public, a new narrative that emphasizes faculty as learners themselves represents faculty to the public in new and thought-provoking ways. First, it reveals the faculty as people. The typical face of the faculty member has been one of expert—an expert who is certain, all-knowing, and somewhat fixed in his views. In contrast, the face of a learner is of someone who comes to the table with knowledge but does not know everything, admits it, and is able to learn more. A narrative of faculty as learners positions faculty as master learners (Neumann, in press) who purposefully open themselves to learning more than they know already. In this view, the faculty become "learners in motion" as opposed to fixed experts or dispensers of static knowledge. We urge that faculty come to be known as moving forward on a continuum of what Alexander (2008), among others, discusses as "fragile competence," wherein one is learning continuously and thus subject to growing toward knowing still more. A narrative focused on faculty as learners also shifts accountability from the constraining narrative of "how much do our faculty know?" to "how fully and richly are they able to continue learning and sharing both the content of their learning and their ways of learning it with others?" The revised narrative asks faculty to demonstrate what they learn and also to reflect on how they arrived there, then to translate those processes for colleagues and students as colleagues.

We believe that it is essential that higher education researchers and professional development staff find new ways to define learning as it shows up in the numerous roles of faculty, including teacher, researcher, mentor, advisor, community partner, entrepreneur, and administrative leader (see Neumann, in press, for examples and discussion of the forms it may take). Under a narrative of learning at the center, research and practice could then draw on theories and methodologies that enrich our understanding of how learning can be initiated and how it evolves over time.

Faculty Possess and Can Develop a Sense of Agency to Sustain Their Work

Amid the louder noise of faculty relenting to dominant norms and constrained by forces outside their control, we suggest a counternarrative of faculty leading a professional and personal life in ways they value. We envision faculty pushing their campuses to expand notions of legitimate professional contributions, to navigate barriers, and to put effort, will, and talent toward their work.

For research on higher education faculty, we believe that a narrative of faculty agency fills gaps produced by the narrative of constraint. Research reviewed in "Faculty Work" reminds us that faculty often do not feel in control of their work; rather, they feel that work choices and priorities are being chosen for them—sometimes by pressures resulting from career stage (Baldwin, Lunceford, and VanderLinden, 2005; Neumann, Terosky, and Schell, 2006), by pressures and expectations influenced by gender or race (Aguirre, 2000; Rosser, 2004, 2005b), or by reward systems that value work that is different from what they want to pursue (O'Meara and Rice, 2005).

Although reward systems vary by institutional type, by the nature of faculty work, and by discipline, changes now occurring in faculty roles and rewards across these academic locations suggest that there was never a better time to position faculty as leading actors in—as well as authors, directors, and producers of—their own stories. As Generation X and Y faculty join colleges and universities, they will no doubt question certain structures, casting them as antiquated (Cook, 2008). They will no doubt look into themselves as sources of ideas for how to transform their cultures into improved places to work. Just as research on inequity among female scientists at MIT galvanized many women faculty to push their campuses to examine gender bias in pay and reward systems, these new faculty will need strategies to imagine careers that go against the current (Boyte, 2008), whether toward interdisciplinary work, toward taking time out for parenting, toward engagement in multiple forms of scholarship, or toward opening their programs to community partners. We are encouraged by research on faculty taking action, including Gumport's study (2002) of the development of women's studies programs; Colbeck and Drago's study (2005) of faculty resisting bias against family caregiving; Neumann, Terosky, and Schell's research (2006) on post-tenure faculty determining their own work priorities and taking strategic action; and Kuntz's research (2005) on faculty taking positions on controversial political issues. Such examples are not merely inspirational. They offer evidence of alternative strategies for shaping academic careers. Tools for creating new career paths may become evident as these strategies are invoked, revised, and refashioned persistently. Such examples have implications for the shaping of institutional policy so as to scaffold and facilitate the faculty's activation of their agency and their own shaping of their career paths. We strongly encourage other researchers to build on this view, of agency as a key feature of the faculty career, in considering how gender, race and ethnicity, faculty perception of their own marketability, or networks of support influence faculty efforts to craft their careers in meaningful ways.

From the perspective of organizational and professional development, institutions best support faculty by fostering agency throughout the academic career (Neumann, Terosky, and Schell, 2006). Policies that intentionally subvert the norm of ideal worker in favor of supporting new pathways with political cover support faculty agency (Colbeck and Drago, 2005). Additionally, faculty unions facilitate agency by supporting faculty in discriminatory or hostile work environments, advocating for policies that provide choices and flexibility for family care and providing opportunities for faculty to develop skills in advocating for themselves, their students, and their institutions.

In the public view, faculty often are cast as self-interested and self-protecting. We need a different public image—of faculty members actively making sound, responsible, and creative decisions and pursuing work that draws on their expertise for the benefit of others but doing so by drawing on their own best motivations, choosing work that is guided by the compass of their passions (Neumann, 2006) intertwined with their moral draw to attend to the growth of others (Hansen, 1995). As this statement suggests, doing for self and doing for others is not clear-cut; the relationship is circular and joined, and neither can be cut fully out of the picture. In this spirit, we urge researchers to document and analyze a variety of meaning-laden forms of contemporary faculty work, including forging university-community partnerships that offer the potential to improve people's lives (O'Meara, 2008), taking teaching seriously (Terosky, 2005), and mentoring and helping women and faculty of color to advance in the sciences and other fields (Austin, Connolly, and Colbeck, 2008). A variety of other directions might be imagined. Contrary to the now legendary narrative of *Profscam* (Sykes, 1988)—of faculty "getting away with whatever they can"—the new narrative of agency draws connections between the invaluable autonomy central to academic careers and the contributions those careers can make to society.

Faculty Learn, Grow, and Make Contributions Through Professional Relationships Embedded in Communities

Professional relationships are rarely a major focus of study in faculty careers. Yet professional relationships are an undercurrent—both text and subtext—in much of the research reviewed in this monograph. In earlier chapters we highlighted research on women, faculty of color, and part-time faculty as feeling isolated, as lacking in the kinds of professional relationships they desired. "Faculty Work" discussed professional relationships as critical to all kinds of faculty work, while "Recent Reforms of Faculty Reward Systems" discussed the fact that many faculty feel that they cannot be rewarded, recognized, or promoted without such relationships.

Though present in the background of many studies, professional relationships for and among faculty have not, for the most part, been an explicit focus of study in higher education. Rather, most research considers what faculty report as missing: satisfaction, opportunities for advancement (especially for members of minority groups), mentoring through the tenure process, adequate recognition for "invisible work," and so on. Because the process of developing collaborative relationships and webs of support and learning are rarely the primary focus of studies of faculty, the field of higher education knows little about how to facilitate this aspect of faculty growth. Some important exceptions exist to this observation, especially in recent work. Research on faculty learning communities and their positive impact on teaching, especially in STEM disciplines (O'Meara, 2005b, 2007b), and research on interorganizational relationships between faculty and community partners have explored the motivation and commitment faculty derive from professional relationships (Sandmann and Weertz, 2007). Likewise, Kadar (2005) and Neumann (in press) have studied the role of peer mentoring and colleagueship and the learning and support that they may provide tenure-track faculty at research universities. Additionally, feminist scholarship has a long history of exploring the support provided between women academics (Dickens and Sagaria, 1997; Gumport, 2002).

Given that the boundaries of faculty work keep expanding and the skills and knowledge sets needed to help students succeed keep changing, it is important for faculty research to take faculty professional relationships, on and off campus, increasingly seriously. We need to ask ourselves which perspectives, fields of study, lenses, and research methods will facilitate understanding professional relationships more fully than the typical "snapshots" offered through relationship-building programs such as formal mentoring and learning community programs. A role may be available for major national surveys of faculty such as the one done by the HERI or the NSOPF in gaining a national perspective on the extent of and types of faculty engagement in professional relationships. To understand how and why such relationships grow and how they feed faculty work, however, we need longitudinal and qualitative studies of relationships and webs of faculty working together. We need to understand when relationships go bad and how to foster generative, supportive relationships for and among faculty.

In summary, we need theories and research designs that reveal how faculty learn in communities and webs of people in communication with one another. We need to understand how this learning feeds back into teaching, research, administration, and community engagement. For example, how do faculty use invisible colleges or networks of scholars in their disciplines to mentor their graduate students? In what ways do the relationships that community college faculty develop with local industry help them in teaching students vital work skills? Asking such questions will yield insight into approaches for supporting faculty in developing their expertise beyond the baseline knowledge that they bring to their jobs when they first enter them.

As we begin to learn about relationship building for faculty, we can apply that knowledge to professional development. A direct implication of fostering professional relationships is the debunking of the "one mentor" or "lone ranger" myth. By broadening webs of colleagues, faculty can learn that different people can provide support for different needs. We suggest then multiple mentors for professional development and growth. Another implication is that such mentoring relationships can be reciprocal: peers can learn from one another as well as from others' work (Kadar, 2005). With these implications in mind, it is imperative that institutions of higher education provide opportunities for all faculty, tenure track and non-tenure-track, full time and part time, to build relationships with colleagues, whether on campus or beyond.

In framing faculty work in terms of the counternarrative of professional relationships, we heighten opportunities to educate the public about faculty work—casting it as a complex and unfolding human endeavor. This view reminds the public that faculty work is (and should be) imprecise and time-consuming; it is further embedded in the lives of academics who are as human as the next person and who themselves need to nurture their humanness even as many do so for others. This view also proposes that faculty work may, for some faculty, be heightened by collaboration—even as we acknowledge that virtually no scholar works on his or her own, that academic labor and learning itself are interactive and shared to the core.

Who a Faculty Member Is Shapes His or Her Learning, Commitments, and Contributions

Faculty work is rarely depicted in a personal manner, perhaps because of a fear that depicting faculty work in this way will make it appear unscientific (Neumann, 2006; Neumann and Peterson, 1997), unprofessional (Rhoades, Kiyama, McCormick, and Quiroz, 2008), or irrelevant to public concerns, institutional missions, or disciplinary agendas (Neumann, 2006; Rice, 1996). On the research front, a gap remains in research on faculty work as personal endeavor—what professional work feels like personally, why scholars pursue it, and its meaning in their lives (for an excellent discussion of this topic, see Hansen, 1995). We do, however, have a growing body of knowledge on the converse—how professional responsibility can reach into personal lives

(Ward and Wolf-Wendel, 2007)—though this branch of the literature would benefit from expansion. Our emphasis in this section, however, is on the former: the personal dimensions of the professional and intellectual endeavor in which faculty engage.

We are encouraged by a movement to include frameworks capable of exploring personal themes in faculty work. For example, Kuntz (2005) explores how (self-defined) faculty may advance social transformation through the course of their own daily activities such as in teaching political reasoning skills in class, advocating for issues as part of shared governance, or combining their disciplinary expertise with political advocacy to influence public issues outside academe. This research is beginning to ask questions about how faculty members' political passions interact with their work. Another example of embedding research in a personal framework can be observed in the writings of Neumann (in press) and Neumann and Terosky (2007) on post-tenure faculty work and learning. Interviews with post-tenure professors and their work reveal highly personal, contextual, and relational creative moments—instances of what Neumann refers to as "passionate thought"—in their scholarship. Neumann (2006) further observes that despite the overriding narrative of "research as preeminent" in research on higher education, including attempts to separate emotion from objective research, neuroscientists have begun to establish links between human emotion and thought; the two may be naturally interconnected, requiring one another, even in research. O'Meara's research (2008) on exemplars in community engagement and the ways in which identity and life history interact is another example. Finally, Rhoades, Kiyama, McCormick, and Quiroz (2008) explore the contributions of personal identity and values of family connectedness to career decisions and mobility. The field would benefit from additional research highlighting the person behind and in the professional role (Hansen, 1995), including how individuals' accumulated experiences, personal and professional, shape their growth trajectories and work.

Many faculty enter the academic profession because they are drawn to a subject of study and the desire to share their knowledge or passion of a subject matter; they may then be drawn to the very "stuff" they teach and study (Neumann, in press). Ironically, professional development programs rarely capitalize on such interests and passions. Rather than faculty feeling that they need to hide the origins of their deepest convictions and passions, faculty professional development could create programs that invite them in, for example, by framing their content so as to make room for autobiographical reflection.

The truth behind faculty work is that it is personal, whether explicitly or implicitly so, in that it is the creation of persons—often individuals who devote their lives closely to what they do. By creating a fabricated boundary between the professor as an academic and the professor as a person, the current narrative presents an oversimplified picture of faculty to the public and to future professors. We suggest communicating the full picture of faculty life, including its personal sides filled with interests and passions, to the public so that the fullness of who professors are and what they strive for can be better understood. Without fully knowing what motivates faculty, the public cannot make appropriate decisions or judgments of the effectiveness of today's professoriate.

Faculty Are Professionals with the Capacity for Deep Commitment

The current narrative on faculty work stresses prestige, rankings, and "climbing the academic ladder" rather than stressing the intrinsic purposes of higher education and ways in which faculty contribute to the public good. Sullivan (2005) argues in *Work and Integrity* that this situation is not unique to the academic enterprise but is in fact part of the larger landscape of the discourse around the "professions," where autonomy and individualism are emphasized. Sullivan (2005) argues for a renewal of the "intrinsic purposes of the professional enterprise," a pledge professionals have traditionally made to "deploy their technical expertise and judgment not only skillfully but for public-regarding ends and in a public-regarding way" (p. 180). Sullivan (2005) and Peters (2006) warn that if faculty are to regain the confidence of the public, they will gain that confidence on the basis of their contributions to public life. Sullivan's work (2005) has great importance for the study of professional lives, as it reminds us that to whom much is given, much is expected. Faculty have a responsibility to communicate to the public what they do with the relative autonomy granted to them in their teaching, research, and institutional lives;

they have a responsibility to use that autonomy wisely, toward creation of "the good," as amorphous as that concept may be. Likewise, Rhoades, Kiyama, McCormick, and Quiroz (2008) critique the assumption developed in common notions of professionalism that to be a professional means to separate oneself from other groups. Given that research shows commitments form in community—and that commitments often relate to desires to advocate for those communities—we need a renewed sense of professionalism. Such a new vision of professionalism envisions faculty as professionals who can be rooted and competent, rigorous and systematic while focused on the needs of specific groups for whom they are also advocates.

Rarely has research tried to examine faculty from a longitudinal perspective in terms of their *commitments.* The concept of commitment in faculty work in particular is largely undertheorized. Research on passion in academic work (Neumann, 2006) and on the nature of vocation (Braskamp, Trautvetter, and Ward, 2006; Hansen, 1995) edges close to what we refer to as commitment as part of faculty growth. Given that psychological and other social science research has indicated benefits to individuals and to society of professionals making deep commitments over time to specific problems (Daloz, Keen, Keen, and Parks, 1996), it is incumbent on higher education researchers to explore how faculty commitment develops, how and why it changes over one's life span, how it relates to identity and autobiography, and how it influences faculty contributions. One might ask, for example, how faculty commitment to teaching is viewed as a major part of the academic's life work and shaped as a function of personal experiences, world views, interests, politics, and discipline.

Research on commitment in faculty work is vitally important given the trends depicted in this monograph. Research reviewed in the third chapter on demographics suggests that identity and demographics influence the kinds of work contributions that faculty make in various job areas, but it does not completely explain why they strive to contribute in such ways. Research presented in the fourth chapter raises concerns about the extent to which length of appointment and job security influence faculty members' capacities to make meaningful contributions through their work. The consequences of increases in part-time and non-tenure-track positions over the last two decades, relative to issues of professional commitment, have yet to be fully explored. In relieving faculty of research responsibilities, to what extent and under what conditions might non-tenure-track appointments open up these faculty to commit to teaching and student mentoring? And to what extent might it (surprisingly) diminish commitment to a teaching career? How will the work of research centers that connect with communities in urban centers be influenced by decreases in full-time faculty, as communities depend on such centers and enclaves for ongoing long-term partnerships? The relationships between faculty commitments and appointment structure are largely untapped territory. Research presented in "Faculty Work" explored the different understandings and skills necessary to be effective in different areas of faculty work. "Recent Reforms of Faculty Reward Systems" presented research on how reward systems seem to reward some types of work over others and how faculty employment and workload policies do and do not shape faculty priorities. We hear about faculty work but rarely in ways that elucidate the emotions, passions, strengths of conviction, and personal or professional identities that accompany long-term commitments to specific kinds of work—that is the person inside the work, the person coming through the work.

More recent research, however, has given us glimpses of faculty commitments. Braskamp, Trautvetter, and Ward's *Putting Students First* (2005), explored how faculty in religiously affiliated institutions frame their work; the study reveals significant commitments to liberal arts goals, to fostering civic engagement in students, and to encouraging students' spiritual development. Additionally, through critical discourse and narrative analysis of transcripts from individual and focus group interviews of faculty involved in community engagement, Peters and Alter (2006) conceptualize faculty motivation as an expression of civic professionalism. The engaged land-grant faculty that Peters and Alter studied conceived of their work as enactments of their personal, professional, and political commitments to civic issues. As such, these faculty constructed their classes, research questions, and approaches to learning in "public-regarding ways" (Sullivan, 2005, p. 10). We need more narrative work and stories of commitments—both as inspiration for graduate students and junior faculty and their career development and as pictures for the public of what faculty work entails. These narratives would show evolving growth and understandings as faculty fall deeper and deeper into commitments to specific groups of students, intellectual pursuits, and partnerships.

Turning to the issue of professional development, we consider what happens when faculty self-organize not by department or identity or career stage but by passion. We recall the faculty member in one institution who said that she wanted to go to brown-bag lunches where service learning was being discussed because she knew that was where all the great teachers on campus collected and she wanted to be a part of that group (Bloomgarden and O'Meara, 2007). Leadership literature tells us that a big part of leading is "bringing followers into their better selves" (Burns, 1978). When deans, department chairs, senior faculty, and other academic leaders know—and understand—the deep personal commitments, reasons for entering academe, and scholarly interests of their faculty, they can bring people together in various configurations so as to meaningfully support and challenge one other. Rarely these days do we talk about organizing in this way. What might it mean to use passion as an organizing theme in higher education?

A narrative focused on faculty commitments gives the public—and especially parents, alumni, and citizens—credit for caring about more than rankings and prestige. This new narrative assumes that the public does not just want to hear about how faculty prestige will help a child get a good job or how it will energize the economy. Such a narrative assumes that the public wants to have a more complex understanding about what faculty put first at *this institution* and why, what it is that faculty actually do when they are not teaching, and how it is that commitment, individual and shared, can move an institution forward.

A New Narrative in Summary

This new narrative for faculty is one that assumes that their primary work, personally and professionally, is to learn and grow. It assumes that faculty face a set of constraints in approaching their work and learning but that they can find ways to work through these barriers to make distinct contributions to teaching and mentoring, to commitments to discovery (or construction) of new knowledge, to the shared governance of their institutions, and to community and broader public engagement. Available to them as major sources of learning and growth are professional relationships and webs of community, interdisciplinary and disciplinary, among faculty and with practitioners and community members inside and outside the academy. Faculty work takes place on and off campus, online, and more often face to face. It is important to remember, however, that in all the work faculty do—whether in choosing research questions, mentoring students, crafting pedagogies, or designing community outreach—they involve themselves; they must "be there" and "be in it" to do it. Increasingly, their work must be judged, both by disciplinary norms and by local community members, regardless of who those members are: students struggling to learn, local citizens, colleagues, regional industry, citizens in other parts of the country, people around the world. Faculty learn and grow through professional relationships that at their best enrich their work in multiple ways, at multiple levels, and over many years. Although, as in every profession there are those who "phone it in," there are perhaps more who become invested, often passionate and biased toward one aspect of their work. And at that point, they make distinct contributions. These commitments take effort, will, and the activation of agency coupled with commitment.

We close with a wish: that alongside the staunch "realism" of past research that has painted—albeit helpfully—visions of barriers and constraint in higher education, we begin to paint an alternative vision, an alternative narrative of research and practice that emphasizes growth, learning, and, with an eye to the future, generativity.

Summary

This volume reviews recent research on faculty demographics, appointment types, work life, and reward systems. It also analyzes major theoretical perspectives that researchers have repeatedly used in the study of faculty work, careers, and professional development. This analysis, as well as our own professional experiences as faculty working with doctoral students and with national initiatives on faculty work, suggests that a major part of the national conversation on faculty has been missing: namely, an explicit focus on faculty growth. We therefore considered in the first and second chapters what we meant by faculty growth and defined four of its embedded elements: learning, agency, professional relationships, and commitments. These elements emerged from our analysis of the entire body of research on faculty. It points out the details of those features of growth that we see in the research conversation about faculty as lacking at this time. Thus in writing our findings for this volume, we chose to position the concept of faculty growth and its four elements upfront and to use them throughout the monograph as touchstones around which we synthesized key points, drawing attention to themes present and absent. That is, we presented the narrative as it has been written in each area of faculty research (the main findings from research on faculty demographics, appointments, work life, and reward systems), but then we invited the concept of faculty growth (and its four embedded concepts) into the discussion. We have likewise used the perspectives for study of the faculty as lenses for assessment of the conceptual bases of prior research and lucrative future directions—paths that may illuminate options and opportunities for growth in the faculty career.

We organized the volume this way for several reasons. First, given recent (and indeed sweeping) analytic reviews and trend studies focused on the faculty and their work, we felt that the distinct contribution this volume could make was less pure synthesis in search of focus than synthesis directed at a focus that was based on our own prior research, which we view to be of special value. We also sought to present the literature on faculty, their work, and their careers (notably recent contributions by Schuster and Finkelstein, 2006, and by Gappa, Austin, and Trice, 2007) in ways that would generate questions and fresh thought amid a larger continuing conversation. Second, we wanted to focus readers' attention on what we believe is the next challenge for higher education research, professional development, and public knowledge about the faculty and their work: articulating the relationship between research on faculty and between developing thoughts about the goals of higher education. Framing research on faculty and about faculty growth inevitably raises an important question: Faculty growth toward what? Or for what? We believe that is one place where research needs to be strengthened—to understand how faculty learning relates to concomitant faculty contributions to teaching and learning, discovery of knowledge, engagement and transformation of institutions as key goals of the higher education enterprise overall.

Third, and importantly, we decided to orient our synthesis of research on faculty toward considerations of faculty growth, because the context of faculty as professionals requires it. As researchers, it is in our best interest to recognize and study the professional nature of this work—at the heart of which exist a myriad of important learning experiences, relationships, practices, and commitments. By considering recent research on faculty in higher education in this way, we hope to advance views as well of the faculty's work as simultaneously professional and personal, as parts of their careers and lives—and as parts of the lives of the many communities of which they are a part.

Note

1. We use the word *perspective* to denote disciplinary and cross-disciplinary themes that "hold together" several related (sometimes disciplinarily diverse) theories, thereby allowing us to view a larger intellectual territory than we could were we using only single disciplines or single interdisciplinary lenses to do so. Though we qualify perspectives as disciplinary, we acknowledge too that no one discipline "owns" a perspective and that members of different disciplines may share perspectives shared by members of different disciplines. One or more disciplines may "lead" in a perspective, but others may contribute in significant ways as well. We approached the creation of perspectives as an exercise in categorization: we bundled theories, concepts, frameworks, and so on, from a variety of disciplines and fields into thematic groupings (for a related approach, see Birnbaum, 1988, and Bolman and Deal, 1997).

References

Addams, A. N. (2008). Doctorate recipients from United States Universities: Summary Report 2004. *On Campus with Women, 35*(1). Retrieved August 27, 2008, from http://www.aacu.org/ocww/volume35_1/data.cfm.

Advocate. (2007). *Advocate online special issue.* Retrieved July 7, 2008, from www2.nea.org/he/advoc07/special/index.html.

Aguirre, A., Jr. (2000). *Women and minority faculty in the workplace: Recruitment, retention, and academic culture.* ASHE-ERIC higher education report, no. 27. Washington, DC: Association for the Study of Higher Education.

Alderfer, C. P. (1972). *Existence, relatedness and growth: Human needs in organizational settings.* New York: Free Press.

Alexander, P. A. (2008). Yes. . .but: Footnotes to sage advice. *Educational Psychology Review. 20,* 71–77.

Allan, E. (2003). Constructing women's status: Policy discourses of university women's commission reports. *Harvard Educational Review, 73*(1), 44–72.

Altbach, P. (2003). *Decline of the guru: The academic profession in developing and middle-income countries.* New York: Palgrave McMillan.

American Association of University Professors. (n.d.) *What do faculty do?.* Retrieved July 1, 2007, from http://www.aaup.org/AAUP/issuesed/facwork/facultydolist.htm.

American Association of University Professors. (1999). *Post-tenure review: An AAUP response.* Retrieved July 7, 2008, from http://www.aaup.org/AAUP/pubsres/policydocs/contents/PTR.htm.

Amey, M. J. (2002). Evaluating outreach performance. In C. L. Colbeck (Ed.), *Evaluating faculty performance.* New directions for institutional research, no. 114 (pp. 33–42). San Francisco: Jossey-Bass.

Amey, M. J., and Brown, D. F. (2005). Interdisciplinary collaboration and academic work: A case study of a university-community partnership. In E. G. Creamer and L. R. Lattuca (Eds.), *Advancing faculty learning through interdisciplinary collaboration.* New directions for teaching and learning, no. 102 (pp. 23–36). San Francisco: Jossey-Bass.

Anderson, G. M. (2002). *Building a people's university in South Africa: Race, compensatory education, and the limits of democratic reform.* New York: Peter Lang.

Angelo, T. A., and Cross, P. K. (1993). *Classroom assessment techniques: A handbook for college teachers.* San Francisco: Jossey-Bass.

Antonio, A. L. (2002). Faculty of color reconsidered: Reassessing contributions to scholarship. *Journal of Higher Education, 73*(5), 582–602.

Antonio, A. L. (2003). Diverse student bodies, diverse faculties. *Academe, 89*(6), 14–17.

Antony, J., and Valadez, J. (2002). Exploring the satisfaction of part-time college faculty in the United States. *Review of Higher Education, 26*(1), 41–56.

Aper, J., and Fry, J. (2003). Post-tenure review at graduate institutions in the United States: Recommendations and reality. *Journal of Higher Education, 74*(3), 241–260.

Argyris, C. (1964). *Integrating the individual and the organization.* New York: Wiley.

Armenti, C. (2004a). Gender as a barrier for women with children in academe. *Canadian Journal of Higher Education, 34*(1), 1–26.

Armenti, C. (2004b). Women faculty seeking tenure and parenthood: Lessons from previous generations. *Cambridge Journal of Education, 34*(1), 65–83.

Astin, H. S. (1997). *Race and ethnicity in the American professoriate.* Los Angeles: University of Los Angeles Higher Education Research Institute.

Astin, H. S., and Davis, D. E. (1993). Research productivity across the life and career cycles: Facilitators and barriers for women. In J. S. Glazer, E. M. Bensimon, and B. K. Townsend (Eds.), *Women in higher education: A feminist perspective.* Needham Heights, MA: Ginn.

Astin, H. S., and Leland, C. (1991). *Women of influence, women of vision: A cross generational study of leaders and social change.* San Francisco: Jossey-Bass.

Austin, A. E. (2002a). Creating a bridge to the future: Preparing new faculty to face changing expectations in a shifting context. *Review of Higher Education, 26*(2), 119–144.

Austin, A. E. (2002b). Preparing the next generation of faculty: Graduate school as socialization to the academic career. *Journal of Higher Education, 73*(1), 94–122.

Austin, A. E., Connolly, M. R., and Colbeck, C. L. (2008). Strategies for preparing integrated faculty: The center for the integration of research, teaching and learning. In C. L. Colbeck, K. O'Meara, and A. Austin (Eds.), *Educating integrated professionals: Theory and practice on preparation for the professoriate.* New directions for teaching and learning, no. 113 (pp. 69–82). San Francisco: Jossey-Bass.

Austin, A. E., and Gamson, Z. F. (1983). *Academic workplace: New demands, heightened tensions.* ASHE-ERIC higher education research report, no. 10. Washington, DC: Association for the Study of Higher Education.

Austin, A. E., and McDaniels, M. (2006). Using doctoral education to prepare faculty to work within Boyer's four domains of scholarship. In J. M. Braxton (Ed.), *Analyzing faculty work and rewards using Boyer's four domains of scholarship.* New directions for institutional research, no. 129 (pp. 51–65). San Francisco: Jossey-Bass.

Baez, B. (2000). Race-related service and faculty of color: Conceptualizing critical agency in academe. *Higher Education, 39*(3), 363–391.

Bailyn, L. (1993). *Breaking the mold: Women, men, and time in the new corporate world.* New York: The Free Press.

Baldwin, R. L. (1979). The faculty career process—continuity and change: A study of college professors at five stages of the academic career. Unpublished doctoral dissertation, University of Michigan, Ann Arbor.

Baldwin, R. G. (1990). Faculty career stages and implications for professional development. In J. H. Schuster and D. W. Wheeler and Associates (Eds.), *Enhancing faculty careers: Strategies for development and renewal* (pp. 20–40). San Francisco: Jossey-Bass.

Baldwin, R. G., and Chang, D. (2005). Reinforcing our keystone faculty. *Liberal Education, 92*(4), 28–35.

Baldwin, R. G., and Chronister, J. (2001). *Teaching without tenure: Practices and policies for a new era.* Baltimore: Johns Hopkins University Press.

Baldwin, R. G., Lunceford, C. J., and VanderLinden, K. E. (2005). Faculty in the middle years: Illuminating an overlooked phase of academic life. *Review of Higher Education, 29*(1), 97–118.

Baltes, P. B., and Baltes, M. M. (1990). Psychological perspectives on successful aging: The model of selective optimization with compensation. In P. B. Baltes and M. M. Baltes (Eds.), *Successful aging: Perspectives from the behavioral sciences* (pp. 1–34). New York: Cambridge University Press.

Banerji, S. (2006). AAUP: Women professors lag in tenure, salary. *Diverse Issues in Higher Education, 23*(20), 16.

Barr, R. B., and Tagg, J. (1995). From teaching to learning: A new paradigm for undergraduate education. *Change, 27*(6), 12–25.

Bass, R. (2005). *Making learning visible: Technology and teaching for understanding.* Retrieved July 7, 2008, from http://www.wlap.org/wl-browser/browser.php?ID=20050511-umwlap001–03-bass.

Bean, J. P. (1998). Alternative models of professional roles. *Journal of Higher Education, 69,* 496–512.

Becher, T. (1989). *Academic tribes and territories.* Milton Keynes, U.K.: Open University Press.

Behar, R. (1993). *Translated woman: Crossing the border with Esperanza's story.* Boston: Beacon.

Bellas, M. L., Ritchey, P. N., and Parmer, P. (2001). Gender differences in the salaries and salary growth rates of university faculty: An exploratory study. *Sociological Perspectives, 44*(2), 163–187.

Benjamin, E. (2002). How over-reliance on contingent appointments diminishes faculty involvement in student learning. *Peer Review, 5*(1), 4–10.

Bensimon, E. M. (1991). The social processes through which faculty shape the image of a new president. *Review of Higher Education, 62*(6), 637–660.

Bensimon, E. M. (1992). Lesbian existence and the challenge to normative constructions of the academy. *Journal of Education, 174,* 98–113.

Bensimon, E. M., Bauman, G., Bleza, M., Oliverez, P., Patriquin, L., Polkinghorne, D., and Soto, P. (2003). Post-tenure review: The disparity between intent and implementation. *Review of Higher Education, 26*(3), 275–297.

Bensimon, E. M., and Marshall, C. (1997). Policy analysis for postsecondary education: Feminist and critical perspectives. In C. Marshall (Ed.), *Feminist critical policy analysis II: A perspective from post-secondary education* (pp. 1–21). London: Falmer Press.

Bensimon, E. M., and Neumann, A. (1993). *Redesigning collegiate leadership: Teams and teamwork in higher education.* Baltimore: Johns Hopkins University Press.

Bensimon, E. M., Neumann, A., and Birnbaum, R. (1989). *Making sense of administrative leadership: The "L" word in higher education, vol. 1.* Washington, DC: School of Education and Human Development, The George Washington University.

Berberet, J. (1999). The professoriate and institutional citizenship toward a scholarship of service. *Liberal Education, 85*(4), 33–39.

Bergquist, W. H. (1992). *The four cultures of the academy: Insights and strategies for improving leadership in collegiate organizations.* San Francisco: Jossey-Bass.

Berry, T. R., and Mizelle, N. (Eds.). (2006). *From oppression to grace: Women of color and their dilemmas within the academy.* Sterling, VA: Stylus Publishing, LLC.

Bieber, J. P., and Worley, L. K. (2006). Conceptualizing the academic life: Graduate students' perspectives. *Journal of Higher Education, 77*(6), 1009–1035.

Biglan, A. (1973). Relationships between subject matter area characteristic and output of university departments. *Journal of Applied Psychology, 57,* 204–213.

Birnbaum, R. (1988). *How colleges work: The cybernetics of academic organization and leadership.* San Francisco: Jossey-Bass.

Birnbaum, R. (1992). *How academic leadership works: Understanding success and failure in the college presidency.* San Francisco: Jossey-Bass.

Birnbaum, R. (2000). The life cycle of academic management fads. *The Journal of Higher Education, 71*(1), 1–16.

Blackburn, R. T., and Lawrence, J. H. (1995). *Faculty at work: Motivation, expectation, satisfaction.* Baltimore: Johns Hopkins University Press.

Bland, C. (2004, November 5). *The impact of appointment type on the productivity and commitment of full-time faculty in research/doctoral institutions.* Paper presented at the Annual Conference for the Association for the Study of Higher Education, Kansas City, MO.

Bland, C. J., and Bergquist, W. H. (1997). *The vitality of senior faculty members: Snow on the roof—fire in the furnace.* ASHE-ERIC higher education report, no. 25. Washington, DC: The George Washington University Graduate School of Education and Human Development.

Bland, C. J., Center, B., and Finstad, D. (2000). *Medical school faculty's perception of presence or absence of features that facilitate productivity and high morale: An in-house report.* Minneapolis: University of Minnesota Medical School, Office of the Dean.

Bland, C., Center, B., Finstad, D., Risbey, K., and Staples, J. (2006). The impact of appointment type on the productivity and commitment of full-time faculty in research and doctoral institutions. *Journal of Higher Education, 77*(1), 89–123.

Blau, P. M. (1964). *Exchange and power in social life.* New York: Wiley.

Bloomgarden, A., and O'Meara, K. (2007). Harmony or cacophony? Faculty role integration and community engagement. *Michigan Journal of Community Service Learning, 13*(2), 5–18.

Boice, R. (1992). *The new faculty member.* San Francisco: Jossey-Bass.

Boice, R. (1993). New faculty involvement for women and minorities. *Research in Higher Education, 34*(3), 291–341.

Bolman, L. G., and Deal, T. E. (1997). *Reframing organizations: Artistry, choice, and leadership* (2nd ed.). San Franscico: Jossey-Bass.

Bowen, H. R. (1977). *Investment in learning: The individual and social value of American higher education.* San Francisco: Jossey-Bass.

Bowen, H. R., and Schuster, J. H. (1986). *American professors: A national resource imperiled.* New York: Oxford University Press.

Boyer, E. (1990). *Scholarship reconsidered.* Princeton, NJ: Carnegie Foundation for the Advancement of Teaching.

Boyte, H. C. (2004). *Going public: Academics and public life.* Dayton, OH: Kettering Foundation.

Boyte, H. C. (2008). Against the current: Developing the civic agency of students. *Change, 40*(3), 8–15.

Bracken, S. J., Allen, J. K., and Dean, D. R. (2006). *The balancing act: Gendered perspectives in faculty roles and work lives.* Sterling, VA: Stylus Publishing.

Braskamp, L. A., and Ory, J. C. (1994). *Assessing faculty work: Enhancing institutional and individual performance.* San Francisco: Jossey-Bass.

Braskamp, L. A., Trautvetter, L. C., and Ward, K. (2006). *Putting students first: How colleges develop students purposefully.* Bolton, MA: Anker.

Braxton, J. M., and Bayer, A. E. (1999). *Faculty misconduct in college teaching.* Baltimore: Johns Hopkins University Press.

Braxton, J. M., Luckey, W. T., and Helland, P. A. (2006). Ideal and actual value patterns toward domains of scholarship in three types of colleges and universities. In J. M. Braxton (Ed.), *Analyzing faculty work and rewards: Using Boyer's four domains of scholarship.* New directions for institutional research, no. 129, 67–76.

Breneman, D. W., and Youn, T. K. (1988). *Academic labor markets and careers.* New York: Falmer Press.

Bronfenbrenner, U. (1979). *The ecology of human development: Experiments by nature and design.* Cambridge, MA: Harvard University Press.

Brown, A., Benson, B., and Uhde, A. (2004). You're doing what with technology? *College Teaching, 52*(3), 100–104.

Burgess, L. A., and Samuels, C. (1999). Impact of full-time versus part-time instructor status on college student retention and academic performance in sequential courses. *Community College Journal of Research and Practice, 23*(5), 487–98.

Burns, G. M. (1978). *Leadership.* New York: Harper and Row.

Callister, R., Hult, C., and Sullivan, K. (2006). Is there a global warming toward women in academia? *Liberal Education, 91*(3), 50–57.

Carlin, J. F. (1999, November 5). Restoring sanity to an academic world gone mad. *Chronicle of Higher Education,* A76.

Centra, J. (1979). *Determining faculty effectiveness: Assessing teaching, research, and service for personnel decisions and improvement.* San Francisco: Jossey-Bass.

Chaffee, E. E. (1984). Successful strategic management in small private colleges. *Review of Higher Education, 55,* 212–241.

Chait, R. (2002). *Why tenure? Why now? Questions of tenure.* Cambridge, MA: Harvard University Press.

Chang, Y. (2000). Evaluation of outreach for promotion and tenure considerations: Views from university faculty. *Journal of Continuing Higher Education, 48*(3), 5–13.

Checkoway, B. (1997). Reinventing the research university for public service. *Journal of Planning Literature, 11*(3), 307–319.

Chism, N.V.N. (2006). Teaching awards: What do they award? *Journal of Higher Education, 77*(4), 589–617.

Chism, N.V.N. (2007). *Peer review of teaching* (2nd ed.). Bolton, MA: Anker.

Chronicle of Higher Education. (2007). *2006–2007 almanac, 53*(1), 28. Retrieved June 1, 2007, from http://chronicle.com. [Chronicle source for statistics is: The American College Teacher: National Norms for the 2004–2005 HERI Faculty Survey, published by the University of California at Los Angeles Higher Education Research Institute]

Clark, B. R. (1987). *The academic life: Small worlds, different worlds.* Princeton, NJ: Carnegie Foundation for the Advancement of Teaching.

Clark, S., and Corcoran, M. (1986). Perspectives on the professional socialization of women faculty: A case of accumulative disadvantage? *Journal of Higher Education, 57,* 20–43.

Clausen, J. A. (1986). *The life course: A sociological perspective.* Englewood Cliffs, NJ: Prentice-Hall.

Clotfelter, C. T. (1996). *Buying the best. Cost escalation in elite higher education.* Princeton, NJ: Princeton University Press.

Colbeck, C. L. (1998). Merging in a seamless blend: How faculty integrate teaching and research. *Journal of Higher Education, 69*(6), 647–671.

Colbeck, C. L. (2002a). *Integration: Evaluating faculty work as a whole.* New directions for institutional research, no. 114. San Francisco: Jossey-Bass.

Colbeck, C. L. (2002b). State policies to improve undergraduate teaching: Administrator and faculty responses. *Journal of Higher Education, 73*(1), 3–25.

Colbeck, C. L. (2004, April). *Managing multiple roles: Time drain or creating energy.* Paper presented at the Meeting of the American Association for Higher Education, San Diego, CA.

Colbeck, C. L. (2008). *Professional identity development theory and doctoral education.* New Directions for Teaching and Learning, no. 113, 9–16.

Colbeck, C. L., and Drago, R. (2005). Accept, avoid, resist. *Change, 37*(6), 10–17.

Colbeck, C. L., and Janke, E. (2006, November 4). *If not for the rewards. . .Why? Theory-based research about what motivates faculty to engage in public scholarship.* Symposium presentation at the Annual Conference of the Association for the Study of Higher Education, Anaheim, CA.

Colbeck, C. L., and Michael, P. (2006). Individual and organizational influences on faculty members' engagement in public scholarship. In R. A. Eberly and J. R. Cohen (Eds.), *Public scholarship* (pp. 17–26). San Francisco: Jossey-Bass.

Colby, A., and Damon, W. (1992). *Some do care: Contemporary lives of moral commitment.* New York: The Free Press.

Cole, S., and Barber, E. (2003). *Increasing faculty diversity: The occupational choices of high-achieving minority students.* Cambridge, MA: Harvard University Press.

Collins, J., Hubball, H., and Pratt, D. (2005). Enhancing reflective teaching practices: Implications for faculty development programs. *Canadian Journal of Higher Education, 35*(3), 57–81.

Conley, V. M. (2006). Demographics and motives affecting faculty retirement. In D. W. Leslie and V. M. Conley (Eds.), *New ways to phase into retirement: Options for faculty and institutions.* New directions for higher education, no. 132 (pp. 9–30). San Francisco: Jossey-Bass.

Conley, V. M., and Leslie, D. W. (2002). Part-time instructional faculty and staff: Who they are, what they do, and what they think. *Education Statistics Quarterly, 4*(2), 97–103.

Connelly, C. E., and Gallager, D. G. (2004). Emerging trends in contingent work research. *Journal of Management, 30*(6), 959–983.

Cook, S. G. (2008). *A perfect storm: Generation X and today's academic culture.* Retrieved July 7, 2008, from www.wihe.com/displayNews.jsp?id=16593.

Cooner, D., and Tochterman, S. (2004). Life inside a professional development school: What experienced teachers learn. *The Teacher Educator, 39*(3) 184–195.

Cooper, J. E., and Stevens, D. D. (2002). *Tenure in the sacred grove: Issues and strategies for women and minority faculty.* Albany: State University of New York Press.

Cowan, J., and Westwood, J. (2006). Collaborative and reflective professional development. *Active Learning in Higher Education, 7*(1), 63–71.

Creamer, E. G. (1998). *Assessing faculty publication productivity: Issues of equity.* ASHE-ERIC higher education report, no. 26(2). Washington, DC: George Washington University Graduate School of Education and Human Development.

Creamer, E. G., and Lattuca, L. R. (2005). *Advancing faculty learning through interdisciplinary collaboration.* New directions for teaching and learning, no. 102. San Francisco: Jossey-Bass.

Curtis, J. (2005). Inequalities persist for women and non-tenure-track faculty. *Academe, 91*(2), 21–30.

Daloz, L. A., Keen, C. H., Keen, J. P., and Parks, S. D. (1996). *Common fire: Lives of commitment in a complex world.* Boston: Beacon Press.

Daly, C., and Dee, J. (2006). Greener pastures: Faculty turnover intent in urban public universities. *Journal of Higher Education, 77*(5), 776–803.

Davis, S., Jones, A., and Price, J. (2004). Preparing future faculty: A new approach at North Carolina State University. *Teaching Sociology, 32*(3), 264–275.

De la Luz Reyes, M., and Halcon, J. J. (1991). Practices of the academy: Barriers to access for Chicano academics. In P. G. Altbach and K. Lomotey (Eds.), *The racial crisis in American higher education.* Albany: State University of New York Press.

Delgado, R. (Ed.). (1995). *Critical race theory: The cutting edge.* Philadelphia: Temple University Press.

Deming, W. E. (2000). *Out of the crisis*. Cambridge: MIT Press.

De Simone, C., Ives, C., and McWhaw, K. (2005). Reflections of researchers involved in the evaluation of pedagogical technological innovations in a university setting. *Canadian Journal of Higher Education, 35*(1), 61–84.

Diamond, R. (1999). *Aligning faculty rewards with institutional mission*. Bolton, MA: Anker.

Dickens, C. S., and Sagaria, M. D. (1997). *Feminists at work: Collaborative relationships among women faculty*. Retrieved June 5, 2007, from http://muse.jhu.edu/journals/review_of_higher_education/v021/21.1dickens.html.

DiMaggio, P., and Powell, W. (1983). The iron cage revisited: Institutional isomorphism and collective rationality in organizational fields. *American Sociological Review, 48,* 147–160.

Dowd, K., and Kaplan, D. (2005). The career life of academics: Boundaried or boundaryless? *Human Relations, 58*(6), 699–721.

Dweck, C. (2006). *Mindset: The new psychology of success*. New York: Random House.

Ehrenberg, R., and Rizzo, M. (2004). Financial forces and the future of American higher education. *Academe, 90*(4), 28–31.

Ehrenberg, R., and Zhang, L. (2005). Do tenured and tenure-track faculty matter? *Journal of Human Resources, 40*(4), 647–659.

Elder, G. H. (1994). Time, human agency, and social change: Perspectives on the life course. *Social Psychology Quarterly, 57*(1), 4–15.

Elder, G. H. (1997). The life course and human development. In W. Damon and R. M. Lerner (Eds.), *Handbook of Child Psychology* (5th ed., pp. 939–991). New York: Wiley.

Emirbayer, M., and Mische, A. (1998). What is agency? *American Journal of Sociology, 103*(4), 962–1023.

Erickson, F. (1986). Qualitative methods in research on teaching. In M. C. Wittrock (Ed.), *Handbook of research on teaching* (3rd ed., pp. 119–161). New York: Macmillan.

Erikson, E. H. (1993). *Childhood and Society*. New York: W. W. Norton and Company.

Erskine, W., and Spalter-Roth, R. (2005). Beyond the fear factor. *Change, 37*(6), 18–25.

Everson, S. (2006). The role of partnerships in the professional doctorate in education: A program application in educational leadership. *Educational Considerations, 33*(2), 1–15.

Fairweather, J. S. (1993). *Teaching, research and faculty rewards*. University Park, PA: National Center on Postsecondary Teaching, Learning, and Assessment.

Fairweather, J. S. (1996). *Faculty work and public trust: Restoring the value of teaching and public service in American academic life*. Boston: Allyn and Bacon.

Fairweather, J. S. (2003). The mythologies of faculty productivity. *Journal of Higher Education, 73*(1), 26–48.

Fairweather, J. S. (2005). Beyond the rhetoric: Trends in the relative value of teaching and research in faculty salaries. *Journal of Higher Education, 76*(4), 401–422.

Fear, F., and Sandmann, L. (1995). Unpacking the service category: Reconceptualizing university outreach for the 21st century. *Continuing Higher Education Review, 59*(3), 110–122.

Finkel, S. K., and Olswang, S. G. (1996). Child rearing as a career impediment to women assistant professors. *Review of Higher Education, 19*(2), 123–39.

Finkelstein, M. (1984). *The American academic profession: A synthesis of social scientific inquiry since WWII.* Columbus: Ohio State University Press.

Finkelstein, M. (2007). From tutor to specialized scholar. In L. F. Goodchild and H. S. Wechsler (Eds.), *History of American higher education* (3rd ed.). ASHE reader series (pp. 80–90). Boston: Pearson Custom Publishing.

Finkelstein, M. J., and Schuster, J. H. (2001). Assessing the silent revolution: How changing demographics are reshaping the academic profession. *AAHE Bulletin, 54,* 3–7.

Finkelstein, M. J., Seal, R. K., and Schuster, J. H. (1998). *The new academic generation: A profession in transformation.* Baltimore: Johns Hopkins University Press.

Finnegan, D. E. (1996). Segmentation in the academic labor market: Hiring cohorts in comprehensive universities. In D. E. Finnegan, D. Webster, and Z. F. Gamson, *Faculty and faculty issues in colleges and universities* (2nd ed.). ASHE reader series (pp. 79–101). Boston: Simon & Schuster.

Finnegan, D. E., and Gamson, Z. F. (1996). Disciplinary adaptations to research culture in comprehensive institutions. *Review of Higher Education, 19*(2), 141–177.

Fisher, C., Hall, L., and Musanti, S. (2006). Professional development in teacher education: What can we learn from PT3? *TechTrends, 50*(3), 25–31.

Fitzpatrick, J., and Sloma, L. (2007, November 8). *Examining experiences of isolation among women faculty in academic medicine: The case of ELAM.* Paper presented at the annual conference of the Association for the Study of Higher Education, Louisville, KY.

Ford, M. E. (1992). *Motivating humans: Goals, emotions, and personal agency beliefs.* Newbury Park, CA: Sage Publications.

Gappa, J. M. (1996). *Off the tenure track: Six models for full-time, nontenurable appointments.* New pathways: Faculty career and employment for the 21st century working paper series, inquiry, no. 10. Washington, DC: American Association for Higher Education.

Gappa, J. M. (2000). *The new faculty majority: Somewhat satisfied but not eligible for tenure.* New directions for institutional research, no. 27. San Francisco: Jossey-Bass.

Gappa, J. M., Austin, A. E., and Trice, A. G. (2005). Rethinking academic work and workplaces. *Change, 37*(6), 32–39.

Gappa, J. M., Austin, A. E., and Trice, A. G. (2007). *Rethinking faculty work: Higher education's strategic imperative.* San Francisco: Jossey-Bass.

Gappa, J. M., and Leslie, D. W. (1993). *The Invisible faculty: Improving the status of part-timers in higher education.* San Francisco: Jossey-Bass.

Geiger, R. L. (2004). *Knowledge and money: Research universities and the paradox of the marketplace.* Palo Alto, CA: Stanford University Press.

Gibson, S., and Peacock, K. (2006). What makes an effective virtual learning experience for promoting faculty use of technology? *Journal of Distance Education, 21*(1), 62–74.

Giele, J. Z., and Elder, G. H. (1998). *Methods of life course research: Qualitative and quantitative approaches.* Thousand Oaks, CA: Sage Publications.

Gilligan, C. (1982). *In a different voice: Psychological theory and women's development.* Cambridge, MA: Harvard University Press.

Giroux, H. A. (1993). *Between borders: Pedagogy and the politics of culture.* New York: Routledge.

Glaser, B., and Strauss, A. L. (1967). *The discovery of grounded theory: Strategies for qualitative research.* Chicago: Aldine.

Glassick, C. E., Huber, M. T., and Maeroff, G. I. (1997). *Scholarship assessed: Evaluation of the professoriate.* San Francisco: Jossey-Bass.

Glazer-Raymo, J. (1999). *Shattering the myths: Women in academe.* Baltimore: Johns Hopkins University Press.

Glazer-Raymo, J. (Ed.). (2008). *Unfinished agendas: New and continuing gender challenges in higher education.* Baltimore: Johns Hopkins University Press.

Golde, C. (2008). Applying lessons from professional education to the preparation of the professoriate. In C. L. Colbeck, K. O'Meara, and A. Austin (Eds.), *Educating integrated professionals: Theory and practice on preparation for the professoriate.* New directions for teaching and learning, no. 113 (pp. 17–26). San Francisco: Jossey-Bass.

Golde, C. M., and Walker, G. E. (Eds.). (2006). *Envisioning the future of doctoral education: Preparing stewards of the discipline.* San Francisco: Jossey-Bass.

Goodchild, L. F., and Wechsler, H. S. (1997). *History of American higher education,* (2nd ed.). ASHE reader series. Boston: Pearson Custom Publishing.

Gouldner, A.W. (1960). The norm of reciprocity: A preliminary statement. *American Sociological Review, 25,* 161–177.

Greenwald, A., and Gilmore, G. (1997). Grading leniency is a removable contaminant of student ratings. *American Psychologist, 52*(11), 1209–1212.

Groves, M., and Zemel, P. (2000). Instructional technology adoption in higher education: An action research case study. *International Journal of Instructional Media, 27*(1), 57–65.

Guinier, L., Fine, M., and Balin, J. (1997). *Women, law school, and institutional change.* Boston: Beacon Press.

Gumport, P. J. (1990). Feminist scholarship as a vocation. *Higher Education, 20,* 231–243.

Gumport, P. J. (2000). Academic restructuring: Organizational change and institutional imperatives. *Higher Education, 39,* 67–91.

Gumport, P. J. (2002). *Academic pathfinders: Knowledge creation and feminist scholarship.* Westport, CT: Greenwood Press.

Gumport, P. J., and Pusser, B. (1999). University restructuring: The role of economic and political contexts. In J. C. Smart (Ed.), *Higher education: Handbook of theory and research* (pp. 146–200). Edison, NJ: Agathon Press.

Hagedorn, L. S. (1996). Wage equity and female faculty job satisfaction: The role of wage differentials in a job satisfaction causal model. *Research in Higher Education, 37*(5), 569–598.

Hagedorn, L. S. (2000). *What contributes to job satisfaction among faculty and staff.* New directions for institutional research, no. 105. San Francisco: Jossey-Bass.

Hamilton, N. (2006). Faculty professionalism: Failures of socialization and the road to loss of professional autonomy. *Liberal Education, 92*(4), 14–21.

Handy, C. (1994). *The age of unreason.* Boston: Harvard Business School Press.

Hansen, D. T. (1995). *The call to teach.* New York: Teachers College Press.

Haraway, D. (1988). Situated knowledges: The science question in feminism as a site of discourse on the privilege of partial perspective. *Feminist Studies, 14*(3), 575–599.

Harding, S. (1986). *The science question in feminism.* Ithaca, NY: Cornell University Press.

Harding, S. G. (1991). *Whose science? Whose knowledge? Thinking from women's lives.* Ithaca, NY: Cornell University Press.

Hargens, L., and Long, S. (2002). Demographic inertia and women's representation among faculty in higher education. *Journal of Higher Education, 73*(4), 498–517.

Harlow, R. (2003). Race doesn't matter, but. The effect of race on professors' experiences and emotion management in the undergraduate classroom. *Social Psychology Quarterly, 66*(4), 348–363.

Harper, E. P., Baldwin, R. G., Gansneder, B. G., and Chronister, J. L. (2001). Full-time women faculty off the tenure track: Profile and practice. *Review of Higher Education, 24*(3), 237–257.

Harrington, C., and Schibik, T. (2001, June). *Caveat emptor: Is there a relationship between part-time faculty utilization and student learning outcomes and retention?* Paper presented at the Association of Institutional Research Annual Forum, Long Beach, CA.

Hearn, J. C. (1999). Pay and performance in the university: An examination of faculty salaries. *The Review of Higher Education, 22*(4), 391–410.

Heilman, M. (2001). Description and prescription: How gender stereotypes prevent women's ascent up the organizational ladder. *Journal of Social Issues, 57,* 657–674.

Helmke, L., Kurtz-Costes, B., and Ülkü-Steiner, B. (2006). Gender and doctoral studies: The perceptions of Ph.D. students in an American university. *Gender & Education, 18*(2), 137–155.

Hermanowicz, J. C. (1998). *The stars are not enough: Scientists, their passions and professions.* Chicago: University of Chicago Press.

Hermanowicz, J. C. (2009). *Lives in science: How institutions affect academic careers.* Chicago: University of Chicago Press.

Herzberg, F. (1966). *Work and the nature of man.* Cleveland, OH: World.

Hill Collins, P. (1990). *Black feminist thought: Knowledge, consciousness, and the politics of empowerment.* Boston: Unwin Hyman.

Hochschild, A. R. (1997). *The time bind: When work becomes home and home becomes work.* New York: Metropolitan Books.

Hoffer, T. B., Welch, V., Jr., Williams, K., Hess, M., Webber, K., Lisek, B., Lowew, D., et al. (2005). *Doctorate recipients from United States universities. Summary report 2004.* Chicago: National Opinion Research Center.

Hollander, E., and Hartley, M. (2000). Civic renewal in higher education: The state of the movement and the need for a natural network. In T. Ehrlich (Ed.), *Higher education and civic responsibility* (pp. 345–366). Phoenix, AZ: Oryx Press.

Honan, J., and Teferra, D. (2001). The US academic profession: Key policy changes. *Higher Education, 41*(1), 183–204.

Howell, A., and Tuitt, F. (Eds.). (2003). *Race and higher education: Rethinking pedagogy in diverse college classrooms.* Cambridge, MA: Harvard Educational Review.

Huber, M. T. (2002). Faculty evaluation and the development of academic careers. In C. L. Colbeck (Ed.), *Evaluating faculty performance.* New directions for institutional research, no. 114 (pp. 17–26). San Francisco: Jossey-Bass.

Huber, M. T. (2004). *Balancing acts: The scholarship of teaching and learning in academic careers.* Washington, DC: American Association for Higher Education and the Carnegie Foundation for the Advancement of Teaching.

Huston, T. A., Norman, M., and Ambrose, S. A. (2007). Expanding the discussion of faculty vitality to include productive but disengaged senior faculty. *Journal of Higher Education, 78*(5), 493–522.

Hutchings, P., and Shulman, L. S. (1999). The scholarship of teaching: New elaborations. New developments. *Change, 31*(5), 11–15.

Infanger, S. (2007). *What is narrative?* Retrieved July 7, 2008, from www.class.vidaho.edu/ narrative/theory/what_narrative.htm.

Jacoby, D. (2006). Effects of part-time faculty employment on community college graduation rates. *Journal of Higher Education, 77*(6), 1081–1103.

Jaeger, A., and Thornton, C. (2006). Neither honor nor compensation: Faculty and public service. *Educational Policy, 20*(2), 345–366.

Jaeger, A., Thornton, C., and Eagan, K. (2007, November 9). *Effects of faculty type on first year student retention and performance.* Paper presented at the Annual Conference for the Association for the Study of Higher Education, Louisville, KY.

Jaffee, D. (2003). Virtual transformation: Web-based technology and pedagogical change. *Teaching Sociology, 31*(2), 227–237.

Jencks, C., and Riesman, D. (1968). *The academic revolution.* Garden City, NY: Doubleday.

Johnson, E. (2007). Misconceptions about the early land-grant colleges. In L. F. Goodchild and H. S. Wechsler (Eds.), *History of American higher education* (3rd ed.). ASHE Reader Series (pp. 280–290). Boston: Pearson Custom Publishing.

Johnsrud, L. K., and Rosser, V. J. (2002). Faculty members' morale and their intentions to leave a multi-level explanation. *Journal of Higher Education, 71*(1), 34–59.

Johnsrud, L. K., and Sadao, K. C. (1998). The common experience of "otherness": Ethnic and racial minority faculty. *Review of Higher Education, 21*(4), 315–342.

Kadar, R. S. (2005). *Peer-mentoring relationships: Toward a non-hierarchical mentoring approach for faculty women.* Unpublished doctoral dissertation, Teachers College, Columbia University, New York.

Kanter, R. M. (1977). *Men and women of the corporation.* New York: Basic Books.

Kast, F. E., and Rosenzweig, J. E. (1985). *Organization and management: A systems and contingency approach* (4th ed.). New York: McGraw-Hill.

Katz, D., and Kahn, R. L. (1978). *The social psychology of organizations* (2nd ed.). New York: Wiley.

Kezar, A. (2001). *Understanding and facilitating organizational change in the 21st century.* ASHE-ERIC higher education report, no. 28(4). San Francisco: Jossey-Bass.

Kezar, A. (2005). Moving from I to we: Reorganizing for collaboration in higher education. *Change, 37*(6), 50–57.

Kezar, A., and Eckel, P. (2002). The effect of institutional culture on change strategies in higher education: Universal principles of culturally responsive concepts. *Journal of Higher Education, 73*(4), 435–460.

Kezar, A. J., Lester, J., and Anderson, G. (2006, Fall). Challenging stereotypes that interfere with effective governance. *Thought and Action,* 121–134.

Kondo, D. K. (1990). *Crafting delves: Power, gender, and discourses of identity in a Japanese workplace.* Chicago: University of Chicago Press.

Kuh, G. D., and Whitt, E. J. (1988) *The invisible tapestry: Culture in American colleges and universities.* ASHE-ERIC higher education report, no. 1. Washington, DC: Association for the Study of Higher Education.

Kuntz, A. (2005). Academic citizenship: The risks and responsibility of reframing faculty work. *Journal of College and Character, 7*(5), 2–9.

Lackritz, J. (2004). Exploring burnout among university faculty: Incidence, performance, and demographic issues. *Teaching and Teacher Education: An International Journal of Research and Studies, 20*(7), 713–729.

Ladson-Billings, G. (1997). For colored girls who have considered suicide when the academy's not enough: Reflections of an African American woman scholar. In A. Neumann and P. L. Peterson (Eds.), *Learning from our lives: Women, research, and autobiography in education* (pp. 52–70). New York: Teachers College Press.

Latack, J. C. (1984). Career transitions within organizations: An exploratory study of work, nonwork, and coping strategies. *Organizational Behavior and Human Decision Processes, 34*(3), 296–322.

Lattuca, L. R. (2001). *Creating interdisciplinarity: Interdisciplinarity research and teaching among college and university faculty.* Nashville, TN: Vanderbilt University Press.

Laursen, S., Marschke, R., McCarl Nielsen, J., and Rankin, P. (2007). Demographic inertia revisited: An immodest proposition to achieve equitable gender representation among faculty in higher education. *Journal of Higher Education, 78*(1), 1–26.

Lee, E., and Kutina, K. L. (1974). Sampling and measurement error in faculty activity and effort reporting. *Journal of Medical Education, 49,* 989–991.

Leh, A. (2005). Lessons learned from service learning and reverse mentoring in faculty development: A case study in technology training. *Journal of Technology and Teacher Education, 13*(1), 25–41.

Lessen, E., and Sorensen, C. (2006). Integrating technology in schools, colleges, and departments of education. *Change, 38*(2), 44–49.

Levinson, D. J. (1978). *The seasons of a man's life.* New York: Alfred A. Knopf.

Levinson, D. J., in collaboration with Judy D. Levinson. (1996). *The seasons of a woman's life.* New York: Alfred A. Knopf.

Licata, C. M. (1999). Precepts for post-tenure review. *Trusteeship, 7,* 8–13.

Licata, C. M., and Morreale, J. C. (1997). Post-tenure review: Policies, practices, precautions, new pathways. In *Faculty careers and employment for the 21st century.* Washington, DC: American Association for Higher Education.

Licata, C. M., and Morreale, J. C. (2002). *Post-tenure faculty review and renewal: Experienced voices.* New pathways series, American Association for Higher Education. Sterling, VA: Stylus.

Liden, R. C., Wayne, S. J., Kraimer, M. L., and Sparrowe, R. T. (2003). The dual commitments of contingent workers: An examination of contingents' commitment to the agency and the organization. *Journal of Organizational Behavior, 24,* 609–625.

Lindholm, J. (2003). Perceived organizational fit: Nurturing the minds, hearts, and personal ambitions of university faculty. *Review of Higher Education, 27*(1), 125–149.

Lindholm, J. (2004). Pathways to the professoriate: The role of self, others, and environment in shaping academic career aspirations. *Journal of Higher Education, 75*(6), 603–635.

Lindholm, J. A., Szelenyi, K., Hurtado, S., and Korn, W. S. (2005). *The American college teacher: National norms for the 2004–2005 HERI faculty survey.* Los Angeles: Higher Education Research Institute, UCLA.

Lynton, E. A. (1995). *Making the case for professional service.* Washington, DC: American Association for Higher Education.

Lynton, E. A., and Elman, S. E. (1987). *New priorities for the university: Meeting society's needs for applied knowledge and competent individuals.* San Francisco: Jossey-Bass.

Ma, Y., and Runyon, L. (2004). Academic synergy in the age of technology: A new instructional paradigm. *Journal of Education for Business, 79*(6), 367–71.

Maeroff, G. I. (1993). *Team building for school change: Equipping teachers for new roles.* New York: Teachers College Press.

Magnusson, D. (1995). Individual development: A holistic, integrated model. In P. Moen, G. H. Elder, and K. Lusher (Eds.), *Examining lives in contexts: Perspectives on the ecology of human development.* Washington, DC: American Psychological Association.

Mallon, W. (2002). *Abolishing and instituting tenure: Four case studies of change in faculty employment policies.* Unpublished doctoral dissertation, Harvard University, Cambridge, MA.

Marshall, V. (2000, August). *Agency, structure and the life course in the era of reflexive modernization.* Paper presented at the American Sociological Association Annual Meeting, Washington, DC.

Martinez, M., and Nilson, M. (2006). Assessing the connection between higher education policy and performance. *Educational Policy, 20*(2), 299–322.

Mason, M., and Goulden, M. (2002). Do babies matter: The effect of family formation on the life long careers of academic men and women. *Academe, 88*(6), 21–28.

McAfee, N. (2000). *Habermans, Kristeva, and citizenship.* Ithaca, NY: Cornell University Press.

McArthur, R. C. (1999). A comparison of grading patterns between full- and part-time humanities faculty: A preliminary study. *Community College Review, 27*(3), 65–76.

McCallum, C. A. (1994). The bottom line: Broadening the faculty reward system. *Teachers College Record, 95*(3), 332–36.

McMillan, L. A., and Berberet, W. G. (2002). *New academic compact: Revisioning the relationship between faculty and their institutions.* Bolton, MA: Anker.

McNaron, T. A. H. (1997). *Poisoned ivy: Lesbian and gay academics confronting homophobia.* Philadelphia: Temple University Press.

Mendoza, P. (2007). Academic capitalism and doctoral student socialization: A case study. *The Journal of Higher Education, 78*(1), 77–96.

Menges, R. J., and Austin, A. E. (2001). Teaching in higher education. In V. Richardson (Ed.), *Handbook of research on teaching* (4th ed., pp. 1122–1156). Washington, DC: American Education Research Association.

Menges, R. J., and Exum, W. H. (1983). Barriers to the progress of women and minority faculty. *Journal of Higher Education, 54,* 123–144.

Milem, J. F., Sherlin, J., and Irwin, L. (2001). The importance of collegial networks to college and university faculty. In E. G. Creamer (Ed.), *Working equal: Academic couples as collaborators* (pp. 146–166). New York: Routledge Falmer.

Miller, D. C., and Skeen, A. (1997). POSSLQs and PSSSLQs: Unmarried academic couples. In M. A. Ferber and J. W. Loeb (Eds.), *Academic couples: Problems and promises* (pp. 106–127). Urbana: University of Illinois Press.

Mills, C. W. (1959). *The Sociological imagination.* New York: Oxford University Press.

Mills, M., Bettis, P., Miller, J., and Nolan, R. (2005). Experiences of academic unit reorganization. Organizational identity and identification in organizational change. *Review of Higher Education, 28*(4), 597–619.

Mishra, P., and Koehler, M. J. (2006). Technological pedagogical content knowledge: A framework for teacher knowledge. *Teachers College Record, 108*(6), 1017–1054.

Morphew, C. C., and Huisman, J. (2002). Using institutional theory to reframe research on academic drift. *Higher Education in Europe, 27*(4), 491–506.

Morrison, E., Rudd, E., Nerad, M., and Picciano, J. (2007, November 8). *The more things change? Gender inequality in careers of recent social science Ph.D's.* Paper presented at the annual conference of the Association for the Study of Higher Education, Louisville, KY.

National Center for Education Statistics. (2001). *National survey of postsecondary faculty.* Retrieved June 15, 2007 from http://nces.ed.gov/surveys/nsopf.

NEA Higher Education Advocate. (2007). *Special issue.* Washington, DC: National Education Association.

Nettles, M., Perna, L., Bradburn, E., and Zimbler, L. (2000). *Salary, promotion and tenure status of minority and women faculty in U.S. colleges and universities. Statistical analysis report. Institute of education sciences.* Washington, DC: U.S. Department of Education.

Neugarten, B. L. (Ed.). (1968). *Middle age and aging.* Chicago: University of Chicago Press.

Neumann, A. (1995). On the making of hard times and good times: The social construction of resource stress. *Review of Higher Education, 66*(1), 3–31.

Neumann, A. (1999a). *Between the work I love and the work I do: Creating professors and scholars in the early post-tenure career.* Occasional paper series, no. 57. Ann Arbor: University of Michigan Center for the Education of Women and Institute for Research on Women and Gender.

Neumann, A. (1999b). Inventing a labor of love: Scholarship as a woman's work. In M. Romero and A. J. Stewart (Eds.), *Women's untold stories: Breaking silence, talking back, voicing complexity* (pp. 243–255). New York: Routledge.

Neumann, A. (2005). Observations: Taking seriously the topic of learning in studies of faculty work and careers. In E. G. Creamer and L. R. Lattuca (Eds.), *Advancing faculty learning through interdisciplinary collaboration.* New directions for teaching and learning, no. 102 (pp. 63–83). San Francisco: Jossey-Bass.

Neumann, A. (2006). Professing passion: Emotion in the scholarship of professors at research universities. *American Educational Research Journal, 43*(3), 381–424.

Neumann, A. (in press). *Professing to learn: Creating tenured lives and careers in the American research university.* Baltimore: Johns Hopkins University Press.

Neumann, A., and Peterson, P. (1997). *Learning from our lives: Women, research, and autobiography in education.* New York: Teachers College Press.

Neumann, A., Schell, J. A., and Charron, K. J. (2005, April). *The interrelation of self and work: Exploring the personal sources of university professors' scholarly endeavors.* Paper presented at the Annual Meeting of the American Education Research Association, Montreal, Canada.

Neumann, A., and Terosky, A. L. (2007). To give and to receive: Recently tenured professors' experiences of service in major research universities. *Journal of Higher Education, 78*(3), 282–310.

Neumann, A., Terosky, A. L., and Schell, J. (2006). Agents of learning: Strategies for assuming agency, for learning, in tenured faculty careers. In S. Bracken, J. Allen, and D. Dean (Eds.), *The balancing act: Gendered perspectives in faculty roles and work lives* (pp. 91–120). Sterling, VA: Stylus.

Nevill, S. C., and Bradburn, E. M. (2006). *Institutional policies and practices regarding postsecondary faculty: Fall 2003 (NCES 2007–157).* Washington, DC: National Center for Education Statistics. Retrieved June 7, 2007, from http://nces.ed.gov/pubsearch.

Niess, M. L. (2005). Preparing teachers to teach science and mathematics with technology: Developing a technology pedagogical content knowledge. *Teaching and Teacher Education, 21*(5), 509–523.

Nworie, J. (2006). Academic technology in higher education: Organizing for better results. *Journal of Educational Technology Systems, 35*(1), 105–128.

Okojie, M., and Olinzock, A. (2006). Developing a positive mind-set toward the use of technology for classroom instruction. *International Journal of Instructional Media, 33*(1), 33–41.

O'Meara, K. A. (1996). *Faculty workload study.* Unpublished manuscript. University of Maryland, College Park.

O'Meara, K. A. (2002a). *Scholarship unbound: Assessing service as a scholarship for promotion and tenure.* New York: Routledge Falmer.

O'Meara, K. A. (2002b). Uncovering the values in faculty evaluation of service as scholarship. *Review of Higher Education, 26,* 57–80.

O'Meara, K. A. (2003). Believing is seeing: The influence of beliefs and expectations on post-tenure review in one state system. *Review of Higher Education, 27*(1), 17–44.

O'Meara, K. A. (2004a). Beliefs about post-tenure review: The influence of autonomy, collegiality, career stage, and institutional context. *The Journal of Higher Education, 75*(2), 178–202.

O'Meara, K. A. (2004b). Reframing incentives and rewards for community service-learning and academic outreach. *Journal of Higher Education Outreach and Engagement, 8*(2), 201–220.

O'Meara, K. A. (2005a). Effects of encouraging multiple forms of scholarship nationwide and across institutional types. In K. A. O'Meara and R. E. Rice (Eds.), *Faculty priorities reconsidered: Encouraging multiple forms of scholarship* (pp. 77–95). San Francisco: Jossey-Bass.

O'Meara, K. (2005b). The Courage to be experimental: How one faculty learning community influenced faculty teaching careers, understanding of how students learn and assessment. *Journal of Faculty Development, 20*(3), 153–160.

O'Meara, K. (2007a). *Striving for what? Exploring the pursuit of prestige.* J. C. Smart (Ed.). Higher Education: Handbook of Theory and Research, Vol. XXII (pp. 121–179).

O'Meara, K. (2007b). Stepping up: How one faculty learning community influenced faculty members' understanding and use of active learning methods and course design. *Journal on Excellence in College Teaching, 18*(2), 97–118.

O'Meara, K. A. (2008) Motivation for faculty community engagement: Learning from exemplars. *Journal of Higher Education Outreach and Engagement, 12*(1), 7–29.

O'Meara, K. A., and Jaeger, A. (2007). Preparing future faculty for community engagement: History, barriers, facilitators, models and recommendations. *Journal of Higher Education Outreach and Engagement, 11*(4), 3–26.

O'Meara, K. A., Kaufman, R., and Kuntz, A. (2003). Faculty work in challenging times: Trends, consequences and implications. *Liberal Education, 89*(4), 16–23.

O'Meara, K. A., and Rice, R. E. (Eds.). (2005). *Faculty priorities reconsidered: Encouraging multiple forms of scholarship.* San Francisco: Jossey-Bass.

Pallas, A. (2001). Preparing education doctoral students for epistemological diversity. *Educational Researcher, 30*(5), 6–11.

Pallas, A. (2007). A subjective approach to schooling and the transition to adulthood. In R. Macmillan (Ed.), *Constructing adulthood: Agency and subjectivity in adolescence and adulthood* (vol. 11, pp. 173–198). Amsterdam: Elsevier, JAI.

Park, S. M. (1996). Research, teaching and service: Why shouldn't women's work count? *Journal of Higher Education, 67*(1), 46–84.

Pascarella, E. T., and Terenzini, P. T. (2005). *How college affects students: A third decade of research.* San Francisco: Jossey-Bass.

Perna, L. W. (2001a). Sex and race differences in faculty tenure and promotion. *Research in Higher Education, 42*(5), 541–567.

Perna, L. W. (2001b). Sex differences in faculty salaries: A cohort analysis. *Review of Higher Education, 24*(3), 283–307.

Perna, L. W. (2005). Sex differences in faculty tenure and promotion: The contribution of family ties. *Research in Higher Education, 46*(3), 277–307.

Perry, W. G. (1968). *Forms of intellectual and ethical development in the college years: A scheme.* Orlando, FL: Holt, Rhinehart, and Winston.

Peters, S. (2006). *Changing the story about higher education's public purposes and work: Land-grants, liberty and the little country theater.* Ann Arbor, MI: Imagining America.

Peters, S., and Alter, T. (2006, November 4). *If not for the rewards. . .Why? Theory-based research about what motivates faculty to engage in public scholarship.* Symposium presentation at the Annual Conference of the Association for the Study of Higher Education, Anaheim, CA.

Peters, S. J., Jordan, N. R., Adamek, M., and Alter, T. (Eds.). (2005). *Engaging campus and community: The practice of public scholarship in the state and land-grant university system.* Dayton, OH: Kettering Foundation Press.

Peterson, M. W., Dill, D. D., and Mets, L. (Eds.). (1997). *Planning and management for a changing environment: A Handbook on redesigning postsecondary institutions.* San Francisco: Jossey-Bass.

Pfeffer, J., and Salancik, G. R. (1978). *The external control of organizations: A resource dependence perspective.* New York: Harper & Row.

Polachek, S., Robst, J., and VanGilderb, J. (2003). Perceptions of female faculty treatment in higher education: Which institutions treat women more fairly? *Economics of Education Review, 22*(1), 59–67.

Porter, S. (2007, November 8). *Does increased representation help or hurt female faculty. A multi-level analysis of research productivity and departmental context.* Paper presented at the Annual Conference of the Association for the Study of Higher Education, Louisville, KY.

Postman, N. (1995). *The End of education: Redefining the value of school.* New York: Knopf.

Rayle, A. D., Bordes, V., Zapata, A., Arrendondo, P., Rutter, M., and Howard, C. (2006). Mentoring experiences of women in graduate education: Factors that matter. *Current Issues in Education, 9*(6). Retrieved July 3, 2008, from http://cie.asu.edu/volume9/number6/index.html.

Rhoades, G. (1998). *Managed professionals: Unionized faculty and restructuring academic labor.* Albany: State University of New York Press.

Rhoades, G. (2007). The study of the academic profession. In P. J. Gumport (Ed.), *Sociology of higher education: Contributions and their contexts* (pp. 113–146). Baltimore: Johns Hopkins University Press.

Rhoades, L., Eisenberger, R., and Armeli, S. (2001). Affective commitment to an organization: The contribution of perceived organizational support. *Journal of Applied Psychology, 86,* 825–836.

Rhoades, G., Kiyama, J. M., McCormick, R., and Quiroz, M. (2008). Local cosmopolitans and cosmopolitan locals: New models of professionals in the academy. *Review of Higher Education, 31*(2), 209–235.

Rice, R. E. (1996). *Making a place for the new American scholar.* New pathways, inquiry no. 1. Washington, DC: American Association for Higher Education.

Rice, R. E. (2006). From Athens to Berlin to LA: Faculty work and the new academy. *Liberal Education, 92*(4), 6–13.

Rice, R. E., and Sorcinelli, M. D. (2002). Can the tenure process be improved? In R. Chait (Ed.), *The questions of tenure* (pp. 101–124). Cambridge, MA: Harvard University Press.

Rice, R. E., Sorcinelli, M. D., and Austin, A. E. (2000). *Heeding new voices: Academic careers for a new generation.* New pathways, inquiry no. 7. Washington, DC: American Association for Higher Education.

Richardson, L. (1997). *Fields of play: Constructing an academic life.* New York: Routledge.

Riger, S., Stokes, J., Raja, S., and Sullivan, M. (1997). Measuring perceptions of the work environment for female faculty. *Review of Higher Education, 21*(1), 63–78.

Ring, P. S., and Rands, G. P. (1989). Sense-making, understanding, and committing: Emergent interpersonal transaction processes in the evolution of 3M's micro-gravity research program. In A. H. Van de Ven, H. L. Angle, and M. S. Poole (Eds.), *Research on the management of innovation: The Minnesota studies* (pp. 337–366). New York: Ballinger.

Robst, J., VanGilder, J., and Polachek, S. (2003). Perceptions of female faculty treatment in higher education: Which institutions treat women more fairly? *Economics of Education Review, 22*(1), 59–67.

Romero, M., and Stewart, A. J. (Eds.). (1999). *Women's untold stories: Breaking silence, talking back, voicing complexity.* New York: Routledge.

Ropers-Huilman, B. (2000). Aren't you satisfied yet? Women faculty members' interpretations of their academic work. In L. H. Hagedorn (Ed.), *What contributes to job satisfaction among faculty and staff.* New directions for institutional research, no. 105 (pp. 21–32). San Francisco: Jossey-Bass.

Rosser, V. J. (2004). Faculty members' intentions to leave: A national study on their worklife and satisfaction. *Research in Higher Education, 45*(3), 285–309.

Rosser, V. J. (2005a). Measuring the change in faculty perceptions over time: An examination of their worklife and satisfaction. *Research in Higher Education, 46*(1), 81–107.

Rosser, V. J. (2005b, April). *Women and ethnic minority faculty members: Examining changes in their workload responsibilities over time.* Paper presented at the Annual Meeting of the American Educational Research Association, Montreal, Canada.

Rossiter, M. W. (1982). *Women scientists in America: Struggles and strategies to 1940.* Baltimore: Johns Hopkins University Press.

Sandmann, L., Saltmarsh, J., and O'Meara, K. (2008). Creating academic homes: An integrated model for advancing the scholarship of engagement. *Journal of Higher Education Outreach and Engagement, 12*(1), 47–63.

Sandmann, L. R., and Weerts, D. J. (2007, April). Reshaping institutional boundaries to accommodate an engagement agenda. Presentation at Annual Meeting of the American Education Research Association, Chicago, IL.

Schein, E. (1985). *Organizational culture and leadership: A dynamic view.* San Francisco: Jossey-Bass.

Schön, D. (1983). *The Reflective practitioner: How professionals think in action.* London: Temple Smith.

Schrier, R. W. (1997). Ensuring the survival of the clinician-scientist. *Academic Medicine, 72,* 589–594.

Shulman, L. S. (2004). *Teaching as community property: Essays on higher education.* San Francisco: Jossey-Bass.

Schuster, J. H., and Finkelstein, M. J. (2006). *The American faculty: The restructuring of academic work and careers.* Baltimore: Johns Hopkins University Press.

Scott, R. W. (1987). *Organizations: Rational, natural, and open.* Englewood Cliffs, NJ: Prentice-Hall.

Seligman, M.E.P., and Csikszentmihalyi, M. (2000). Positive psychology: An introduction. *American Psychologist, 55*(1), 5–14.

Senge, P. S. (1990). *The fifth discipline.* New York: Currency Doubleday.

Shaw, I. S., Leder, S., and Harris, B. J. (2007). Special issue: Women, tenure and promotion. *NWSA Journal, 19*(3), vii–viii.

Shulman, L. (2004). Problem-based learning: The pedagogies of uncertainty. In P. Hutchings (Ed.), *Teaching as community property: Essays on higher education* (pp. 49–62). San Francisco: Jossey-Bass.

Slaughter, S. (1997). *Academic capitalism: Politics, policies, and the entrepreneurial university.* Baltimore: Johns Hopkins University Press.

Slaughter, S., and Leslie, L. (1997). *Academic capitalism: Politics, policies and the entrepreneurial university.* Baltimore: Johns Hopkins University Press.

Slaughter, S., and Rhoades, G. (2004). *Academic capitalism and the new economy: Markets, states, and higher education.* Baltimore: Johns Hopkins University Press.

Smith, D. E. (1987). *The everyday world as problematic: A feminist sociology.* Boston: Northeastern University Press.

Smith, D., Turner, C., and Osei-Kofi, N. (2004). Interrupting the usual: Successful strategies for hiring diverse faculty. *Journal of Higher Education, 75*(2), 133–160.

Sorcinelli, M.D., and Austin, A. E. (Eds.). (1992). *Developing new and junior faculty.* New Directions for Teaching and Learning, no. 50. San Francisco: Jossey-Bass.

Sorcinelli, M. D., Austin, A. E., Eddy, P. L., and Beach, A. L. (2005). *Creating the future of faculty development: Learning from the past, understanding the present.* San Francisco: Jossey-Bass.

Sullivan, W. M. (2005). *Work and integrity. The crisis and promise of professionalism in American society* (2nd ed.) San Francisco: Jossey-Bass.

Survey of Earned Doctorates. (2005). Retrieved July 7, 2008, from www.aacu.org/ocww/volume35.

Swartzman, H. B. (1987). The significance of meeting in an American mental health center. *American Ethnologist, 14,* 271–294.

Sweitzer, V. L. (2008). Networking to develop a professional identity: A look at the first semester experience of doctoral students in business. In C. L. Colbeck, K. O'Meara, and A. Austin (Eds.), *Educating integrated professionals: Theory and practice on preparation for the professoriate.* New directions for teaching and learning, no. 113 (pp. 43–56). San Francisco: Jossey-Bass.

Sykes, C. (1988). *Profscam.* New York: St. Martin's Press.

Talburt, S. (2000). *Subject to identity: Knowledge, sexuality, and academic practices in higher education.* Albany: State University of New York Press.

Taylor, H. L. (1997). No more ivory towers: Connecting the research university to the community. *Journal of Planning Literature, 11*(3), 327–332.

Terosky, A. L. (2005). *Taking teaching seriously: A study of university professors and their undergraduate teaching.* New York: Teachers College, Columbia University.

Terosky, A., Phifer, T., and Neumann, A. (2008). Shattering plexiglass: Continuing challenges for women professors in research universities. In J. Glazer-Raymo (Ed.), *Unfinished agendas: New and continuing gender challenges in higher education* (pp. 52–79). Baltimore: Johns Hopkins University Press.

Terpestra, V., and Honoree, A. (2004). Job satisfaction and pay satisfaction levels of university faculty by discipline type and by geographic region. *Education, 124*(3), 528–539.

Tierney, W. G. (Ed.). (1997). *Academic outlaws: Queer theory and cultural studies in the academy.* Thousand Oaks, CA: Sage Publications.

Tierney, W. G. (2004). Academic freedom and tenure: Between fiction and reality. *Journal of Higher Education, 75*(2), 161–77.

Tierney, W. G. (2005). When divorce is not an option. *Academe, 91*(3), 43–46.

Tierney, W. G., and Bensimon, E. M. (1996). *Promotion and tenure: Community and socialization in academe.* Albany: State University of New York.

Toutkoushian, R. K., Bellas, M. L., and Moore, J. V. (2007). The interaction effects of gender, race and marital status on faculty salaries. *The Journal of Higher Education, 78* (5), 572–601.

Toutkoushian, R. K., and Conley, V. M. (2005). Progress for women in academe, yet inequities persist: Evidence from NSOPF:99. *Research in Higher Education, 46*(1), 1–28.

Trower, C. A. (2008, January 28). *Promoting interdisciplinarity: Aligning faculty rewards with curricular and institutional realities.* Presentation at the American Association of Colleges and Universities Annual Conference.

Trower, C. A. (2002). Can colleges competitively recruit faculty without the prospect of tenure. In, R. Chait (Ed.), *Questions of tenure.* Cambridge, MA: Harvard University Press.

Trower, C. A., and Bleak, J. L. (2004a). *Study of new scholars: Gender: Statistical report [Universities].* Cambridge, MA: Harvard Graduate School of Education. Retrieved February 15, 2007, from http://www.gse.harvard.edu/news/features/trower04122004.pdf.

Trower, C. A., and Bleak, J. L. (2004b). *Study of new scholars: Race: Statistical report [Universities]*. Cambridge, MA: Harvard Graduate School of Education. Retrieved February 15, 2007, from http://www.gse.harvard.edu/~newscholars/newscholars/downloads/racereport.pdf.

Trower, C. A., and Chait, R. (2002). Faculty diversity: Too little for too long. *Harvard Magazine, 104*(4), 33-38.

Turner, C. S. (2002). Women of color in academe: Living with multiple marginality. *Journal of Higher Education, 73*(1), 74–93.

Turner, C. S. (2003). Incorporation and marginalization in the academy: From border toward center for faculty of color. *Journal of Black Studies, 34*(1), 112–125.

Turner, C. S., and Myers, S. L., Jr. (1999). *Faculty of color in academe: Bittersweet success.* Boston: Allyn and Bacon.

Turner, C. S., Myers, S. L., Jr., and Creswell, J. W. (1999). Exploring underrepresentation: The case of faculty of color in the Midwest. *Review of Higher Education, 70*(1), 27–59.

Umbach, P. D. (2006). The contribution of faculty of color to undergraduate education. *Research in Higher Education, 47*(3), 317–345.

Umbach, P. D. (2007a). Gender equity in the academic labor market: An analysis of academic disciplines. *Research in Higher Education, 48*(2), 169–192.

Umbach, P. D. (2007b). How effective are they? Exploring the impact of contingent faculty on undergraduate education. *Review of Higher Education, 30*(2), 91–123.

Umbach, P. D., and Wawryznski, M. R. (2005). Faculty do matter: The role of college faculty in student learning and engagement. *Research in Higher Education, 46*(2), 153–184.

U. S. Department of Education. (2006). *A test of leadership: Charting the future of U.S. higher education.* Washington, DC: Author.

Valian, V. (2000). Schemas that explain behavior. In J. Glazer-Raymo, B. K. Townsend, and B. Ropers-Huilman (Eds.), *Women in higher education: A feminist perspective* (2nd ed.). ASHE Reader Series (pp. 22–33). Boston: Pearson Custom Publishing.

Van Ummersen, C. (2005). No talent left behind. *Change, 37*(6), 26–31.

Vroom, V. H. (1964). *Work and motivation.* New York: Wiley.

Walker, C. J. (2002). Faculty well-being review: An alternative to post-tenure review? In C. M. Licata and J. C. Morreale (Eds.), *Post-tenure faculty review and renewal: Experienced voices.* Washington, DC: American Association for Higher Education Forum on Faculty Roles and Rewards.

Ward, K. (2003). *Faculty service roles and the scholarship of engagement.* ASHE-ERIC higher education report, no. 29(5). San Francisco: Jossey-Bass.

Ward, K., and Wolf-Wendel, L. (2003, November 14). *Academic life and motherhood: Variations by institutional type.* Paper presented at the Annual Conference of the Association for the Study of Higher Education, Portland, Oregon.

Ward, K., and Wolf-Wendel, L. (2007). Academic life and motherhood: Variations by institutional type. *Higher Education, 52*(3), 487–521.

Waskel, S. A., and Owens, R. (1991). Frequency distribution of trigger events identified by people ages 30 through 60. *College Student Journal, 25*(2), 235–239.

Waterman, R. H. (1990). *Adhocracy: The power to change.* Memphis, TN: WhittleDirect Books.

Weick, K. E. (1979). *The social psychology of organizing.* New York: Random House.

Weick, K. E. (1995). *Sensemaking in organizations.* Thousand Oaks, CA: Sage.

Weidman, J. C., Twale, D. J., and Stein, E. L. (2001). *Socialization of graduate and professional students in higher education—A perilous passage?* ASHE-ERIC higher education report, no. 28(3). Washington, DC: The George Washington University, School of Education and Human Development.

Weimer, M. (1997). *Integration of teaching and research: Myth, reality, and possibility.* New directions for teaching and learning, no. 72. San Francisco: Jossey-Bass.

Welsh, J., and Metcalf, J. (2003). Faculty and administrative support for institutional effectiveness activities: A bridge across the chasm? *Journal of Higher Education, 74*(4), 445–468.

Wertsch, J. V. (1985). *Vygotsky and the social formation of mind.* Cambridge, MA: Harvard University Press.

Wertsch, J. V., Del Rio, P., and Alvarez, A. (Eds.). (1995). *Sociocultural studies of mind.* Cambridge, MA: Cambridge University Press.

West, M. S., and Curtis, J. W. (2006). *AAUP gender equity indicators 2006.* Washington, DC: American Association of Colleges and University Professors.

Whitt, E. (1991). Hit the ground running: Experiences of new faculty in a school of education. *The Review of Higher Education, 14*(2), 177–197.

Whyte, W. H., Jr. (1956). *The organization man.* New York: Simon & Schuster.

Williams, J. C. (1999). *Unbending gender: Why family and work conflict and what to do about it.* New York: Oxford Press.

Williams, J. C., Alon, T., and Bornstein, S. (2006). Beyond the 'Chilly Climate': Eliminating bias against women. *Thought & Action, 22,* 79–96.

Williams, P. (1991). *The alchemy of race and rights: Diary of a law professor.* Cambridge, MA: Harvard University Press.

Wimsatt, L. A., and Trice, A. G. (2006). *A profile of grant administration burden among faculty within the Federal Demonstration Partnership: A report of the faculty advisory committee of the Federal Demonstration Partnership.* Washington, DC: The National Academy of Sciences.

Wing, A. (Ed.). (2000). *Global critical race feminism: An international reader.* New York: NYU Press.

Wood, M., and Johnsrud, L. K. (2005). Post-tenure review. What matters to faculty. *The Review of Higher Education, 28*(3), 393–420.

Wolfinger, N., Mason, M., and Goulden, M. (2004, August). *Problems in the pipeline: Gender, marriage and fertility in the ivory tower.* Paper presented at the Annual Meeting of the American Sociological Association, San Francisco.

Wolfinger, N., Mason, M. A., and Goulden, M. (2006, August). *Dispelling the pipeline myth: Gender, family formation and alternative trajectories in the academic life course.* Paper presented at the Annual Meeting of the American Sociological Association, Montreal, Quebec, Canada.

Wright, M. (2006). Always at odds?: Congruence in faculty beliefs about teaching at a research university. *Journal of Higher Education, 76*(3), 331–53.

Wulff, D. H., Austin, A. E., Nyquist, J. D., and Sprague, J. (2004). The development of graduate students as teaching scholars: A four-year longitudinal study. In D. H. Wulff, A. E. Austin, and Associates (Eds.), *Paths to the professoriate: Strategies for enriching the preparation of future faculty.* San Francisco: Jossey-Bass.

Yin, R. K. (2003). *Case study research.* Thousand Oaks, CA: Sage Publications.

Name Index

A

Adamek, M., 31
Aguirre, A., 14, 40, 41, 42, 47, 53, 127, 159, 169
Alderfer, C. P., 139
Alexander, P. A., 168
Allan, E., 155
Allen, J. K., 21, 113
Alon, T., 100, 101, 110, 111
Altbach, P., 4, 14, 17
Alter, T., 31, 177
Ambrose, S. A., 25, 89, 161
Amey, M. J., 143
Anderson, G., 68, 145
Angelo, T. A., 12
Anthony, N., 56–57
Antonio, A. L., 130, 146
Antony, J., 59, 62, 64, 67
Argyris, C., 30
Armenti, C., 17, 85, 112
Astin, H. S., 86, 128
Austin, A. E., 2, 4, 14, 15, 17, 20, 28, 30, 57, 74, 80, 81, 82, 84, 85, 86, 87, 89, 92, 94, 127, 130, 139, 159, 161, 162, 167, 171, 180

B

Baez, B., 28, 155, 158, 163
Bailyn, L., 130
Baldwin, R. L., 24, 64, 68, 102
Baldwin, R. G., 14, 24, 57, 61, 98, 138, 169

Balin, J., 145
Baltes, M. M., 131
Baltes, P. B., 131
Barr, R. B., 12
Bass, R., 12
Bayer, A. E., 14
Beach, A. L., 167
Bean, J. P., 141
Becher, T., 127
Behar, R., 145
Bellas, M. L., 99
Benjamin, E., 57, 64, 65, 66
Bensimon, E. M., 14, 30, 86, 112, 127, 133, 141, 145, 155
Berberet, W. G., 14, 107
Bergquist, W. H., 14, 97, 127
Berry, T. R., 146
Bettis, P., 141, 142
Bieber, J. P., 86
Biglan, A., 127
Birnbaum, R., 10, 69, 83, 106, 128, 134, 141, 142, 152
Blackburn, R. T., 30, 95, 97, 98, 132, 138, 142, 162
Bland, C. J., 14, 57, 61, 62, 63, 64, 66, 79, 95, 96, 97, 115, 162
Bloomgarden, A., 77, 178
Boice, R., 24
Bornstein, S., 100, 101, 110, 111
Bowen, H. R., 13, 17, 22, 76
Boyer, E., 1, 10, 11, 13, 17, 108, 109
Boyte, H. C., 118, 169

Bracken, S. J., 21, 113
Bradburn, E., 99
Braskamp, L. A., 14, 20, 176, 177
Braxton, J. M., 11, 14, 107, 109
Breneman, D. W., 14
Bronfenbreener, U., 24, 129, 140
Brown, D. F., 143
Burgess, L. A., 65
Burns, G. M., 178

C

Callister, R., 102
Carlin, J. F., 6
Center, B., 66, 96
Centra, J., 76
Chaffee, E. E., 137
Chait, R., 6, 13, 14
Checkoway, B., 5, 76
Chism, N.V.N., 14
Chronister, J., 14, 57, 64, 68, 102
Chronister, J. L., 61
Clark, B. R., 87, 97, 101, 127, 128, 129, 162
Clark, S., 130, 162
Clausen, J. A., 131
Clotfelter, C. T., 136
Colbeck, C. L., 4, 77, 78, 79, 80, 110, 113, 164, 167, 170, 171
Colby, A., 118
Collins, P. H., 144
Conley, V. M., 59, 60
Connolly, M. R., 171
Cook, S. G., 169
Corcoran, M., 130, 162
Creamer, E. G., 21, 26, 30, 78, 113, 143, 147, 159
Creswell, J. W., 130, 146
Cross, P. K., 12
Csikszentmihalyi, M., 22
Curtis, J. W., 61, 99

D

Daloz, L. A., 32, 118, 176
Daly, C., 139, 159, 161
Damon, W., 118
Davis, D. E., 30, 86

Dean, D. R., 21, 113
Dee, J., 139, 159, 161
Delgado, R., 146
Deming, W. E., 97
Diamond, R., 11, 14
Dickens, C. S., 30, 159, 172
Dill, D. D., 134
DiMaggio, P., 132
Drago, R., 77, 110, 113, 170
Dweck, C., 24, 25, 27, 89

E

Eagan, K., 8, 57, 63, 66, 97
Eckel, P., 142
Eddy, P. L., 167
Elder, G. H., 28, 29, 131
Elman, S. E., 75
Emirbayer, M., 29
Erickson, E. H., 128
Erikson, E. H., 24, 27, 138
Erskine, W., 110, 111

F

Fairweather, J. A., 13, 95, 162
Fear, F., 75, 76
Fine, M., 145
Finkel, S. K., 85
Finkelstein, M. J., 1, 4, 13, 14, 15, 20, 58, 59, 61, 67, 68, 74, 75, 78, 79, 82, 84, 85, 96, 98, 99, 125, 126, 139, 180
Finnegan, D. E., 125, 126
Finstad, D., 66, 96
Fitzpatrick, J., 135

G

Gamson, Z. F., 4, 30, 94, 126, 162
Gansneder, B. G., 61, 64, 102
Gappa, J. M., 2, 4, 14, 15, 17, 20, 28, 57, 58, 59, 60, 62, 64, 65, 67, 68, 70, 74, 79, 80, 81, 82, 84, 85, 87, 130, 139, 161, 180
Geiger, R. L., 15, 126
Giele, J. Z., 131
Gilmore, G., 68
Giroux, H. A., 155

Rosser, V. J., 30, 84, 103, 139, 161, 169
Rudd, E., 113
Runyon, L., 83

S

Sagaria, M. D., 30, 159, 172
Salancik, G. R., 134
Saltmarsh, J., 119
Samson, J., 73–74
Samuels, C., 65
Sandmann, L., 75, 76, 119, 172
Schein, E., 127
Schell, J., 28, 29, 74, 86, 90, 118, 131, 134, 163, 169, 170
Schibik, T., 65
Schön, D., 12
Schrier, R. W., 17
Schuster, J. H., 1, 4, 13, 14, 15, 17, 20, 58, 59, 61, 67, 68, 74, 75, 76, 78, 79, 82, 84, 85, 96, 98, 99, 139, 180
Scott, R. W., 133
Seal, R. K., 14
Seligman, M.E.P., 22
Senge, P. S., 97
Shaw, I. S., 145
Sherlin, J., 72
Shulman, L. S., 1, 10, 12, 13, 75
Slaughter, S., 15, 80, 81, 137
Sloma, L., 135
Smith, D. E., 140, 144
Smith, T., 55, 57
Sorcinelli, M. D., 11, 14, 20, 85, 86, 92, 159, 167
Spalter-Roth, R., 110, 111
Sprague, J., 14
Stein, E. L., 14, 20, 127
Stewart, A., 145
Stokes, J., 86
Strauss, A. L., 128
Sullivan, K., 102
Sullivan, M., 86
Sullivan, W. M., 4, 5, 6, 29, 32, 164, 175, 177
Swartzman, H. B., 141

Sweitzer, V. L., 20
Sykes, C., 5, 10, 80, 164, 171
Szelenyi, K., 85, 86

T

Tagg, J., 12
Talburt, S., 14, 145
Taylor, H. L., 76
Teferra, D., 80
Terosky, A., 1, 21, 27, 28, 29, 31, 74, 75, 76, 77, 86, 90, 118, 131, 134, 148, 161, 163, 169, 170, 171, 174
Thornton, C., 8, 57, 63, 66, 97, 164
Tierney, W. G., 14, 30, 86, 127
Toutkoushian, R. K., 99
Trautvetter, L. C., 20, 176, 177
Trice, A. G., 2, 4, 15, 17, 20, 28, 57, 74, 80, 81, 82, 84, 85, 86, 87, 130, 139, 161, 180
Trower, C. A., 78
Tuitt, F., 146
Turner, C. S., 14, 130, 146
Twale, D. J., 14, 20, 127

U

Umbach, P. D., 8, 57, 63, 64, 65, 97, 99

V

Valadez, J., 59, 62, 64, 67
VanderLinden, K. E., 138, 169
VanGilder, J., 101
Vroom, V. H., 142

W

Walker, C. J., 97
Walker, G. E., 4
Ward, K., 12, 20, 76, 77, 85, 87, 130, 164, 174, 176, 177
Waskel, S. A., 139
Waterman, R. H., 142
Weertz, D. J., 172
Weick, K. E., 141, 142

Weidman, J. C., 14, 20, 127
Wertsch, J. V., 140, 142
West, M. S., 99
Whyte, W. H., Jr., 130
Williams, J. C., 100, 101, 110, 111, 130
Williams, P., 146
Wimsatt, L. A., 86
Wing, A., 146
Wolf-Wendel, L., 85, 87, 130, 174
Wolfinger, N., 86, 130
Wood, M., 106

Worley, L. K., 86
Wulff, D. H., 14

Y
Yin, R. K., 128
Youn, T. K., 14

Z
Zemel, P., 82
Zimbler, L., 99

Subject Index

Full-time non-tenure-track faculty appointments: analyzing performance of, 63–69; description of, 60–61; examining the rise in, 61–62; implications of, 69–72

G

Gay faculty, 115
Gender differences: full-time non-tenure-track faculty percentage, 61; part-time faculty percentage, 59–60; salary gap as, 98–103; study on "ceilings" and opportunities related to, 145
Generation X and Y faculty, 169

H

Harvard Project on Faculty Appointments, 104
Higher education: fiscal challenges, competition, and entrepreneurism in, 80–81; great critique (1980s–1990s) of, 5–9; impact of technology on, 82–84; measures of accountability in, 79–80; new period of reform in, 9–13
Higher Education Research Institute (HERI), 15, 60, 172
Higher Education Research Institute (HERI) survey, 100
Historic-shift perspective, 125–127
Human capital theory, 99
Human developmental theories, 138

I

"Ideal worker," 130, 132
Indiana's University's Faculty Survey on Student Engagement (2003–2004), 64, 65
Institute for Scientific Information, 107
Institutions: fiscal challenges, competition, and entrepreneurism in, 80–81; parental leave policies by, 110–113. *See also* Chief academic officers (CAOs); Faculty
Integrative theory of development, 24
The Invisible Faculty (Gappa and Leslie), 14

J

Job satisfaction. *See Faculty* satisfaction
Journal of the Professoriate, 20

K

Knowledge: faculty's self-knowledge and social, 138; standpoint theory on "official," 143

L

Learning: as center of faculty work, 166–169; counternarrative on faculty being shaped by, 173–175; as faculty growth aspect, 26–28; "fragile competence" and continuous, 168; notions of "scholarly," 75, 148; relationship between nature of content and, 166
Lesbian faculty, 115
Life course, 131–132
Life-stage theories, 138
Lone ranger narrative, 159–160

M

Magnusson's integrative theory of development, 24
Market perspective, 136–137
Maryland General Assembly, 8
Maryland Higher Education Commission, 8
"Master learners," 26
MIT, 100, 169

N

Narrative of constraint: definition of, 16; features of prevailing, 157–165; overview of, 15–19, 155–157; what it emphasizes and obscures, 18e. *See also* Counternarrative; Faculty growth
Narrative images: academic as lone ranger, 158–160; faculty development to redirect faculty, 161–163; faculty as disinterested/disengaged intellectuals, 163–164; faculty as victims as opposed to agents, 158; faculty work as accrual of resources, prestige, and standing, 164–165

About the Authors

KerryAnn O'Meara is Associate Professor of Higher Education at the University of Maryland. Her research explores the structures, cultures, and systems in colleges and universities that support and sometimes impede faculty careers, the ability of faculty to develop as well-rounded scholars, and thereby contribute to the development of others. She is particularly interested in how faculty grow and develop in the areas of community engagement and teaching. She has written extensively in the area of faculty roles and rewards, considering efforts to redefine scholarship for promotion and tenure, to assess faculty community engagement, and to implement post-tenure review. She has recently completed studies of faculty work life in striving institutions, and graduate education and community engagement. Currently she is collaborating on a study on faculty and work life balance, and on several studies on the lives of community engaged faculty. She serves as the Associate Editor of the *Journal of Higher Education Outreach and Engagement.* O'Meara's work has appeared in the *Review of Higher Education, Journal of Higher Education, Research in Higher Education, the NASPA Journal, Planning in Higher Education, Journal of Higher Education Outreach and Engagement, Community College Review, Journal of Teaching Excellence, Journal of Faculty Development*, and *Liberal Education.* In 2005, a book she co-edited with Gene Rice, *Faculty Priorities Reconsidered: Encouraging Multiple Forms of Scholarship,* was published with Jossey-Bass.

Aimee LaPointe Terosky is an adjunct assistant professor of Higher and Postsecondary Education at Teachers College, Columbia University. She teaches courses on teaching and learning in postsecondary settings and faculty development. She is also the assistant principal of The Anderson School (P.S. 334), a public school in New York City, which received the 2007 New York City Blackboard Award for Outstanding Public Middle School. She received her B.S. in Secondary Education (Social Studies) from The Pennsylvania State University, her M.A. in School Leadership from Villanova University, her New York State School Building Leadership Certificate from Teachers College, Columbia University, and her Ed.D. in Higher and Postsecondary Education from Teachers College, Columbia University. Aimee's research concentrates on teaching and learning in K–12 and higher education, faculty careers, and women/girls in education. Her dissertation, *Taking Teaching Seriously: A Study of Professors and Their Undergraduate Teaching,* was awarded the 2005 Bobby Wright Dissertation of the Year from the Association for the Study of Higher Education. Along with Anna Neumann, Terosky's work has appeared in the *Journal of Higher Education,* in the book *Unfinished Agendas: New and Continuing Gender Challenges in Higher Education* edited by Judith Glazer-Raymo, and in the book *The Balancing Act: Gendered Perspectives in Faculty Roles and Worklives.*

Anna Neumann is Professor of Higher and Postsecondary Education at Teachers College, Columbia University and former program coordinator. She previously served on the faculty at Michigan State University with appointments in Educational Psychology (Learning and Development) and Higher Education. Neumann's research addresses professors and their intellectual careers, teaching and learning in higher education, women's scholarly development, doctoral students' and early career scholars' learning of research and development as researchers, and academic leadership and cultures. She recently completed a study, funded by the Spencer Foundation's Major Grants Program, of early midcareer professors' scholarly learning and development. A book reporting study findings is in press (to be released in early 2009 by Johns Hopkins University Press) under the title: *Professing to Learn: Creating Tenured Lives and Careers in the American Research University.* She is currently engaged in classroom-based research on undergraduate teaching and learning in the liberal arts curriculum in high minority-serving institutions in the New York City metropolitan area. Neumann's earlier books include *Learning from*

Our Lives: Women, Research, and Autobiography in Education (with Penelope L. Peterson, Teachers College Press, 1997), *Redesigning Collegiate Leadership: Teams and Teamwork in Higher Education* (with Estela M. Bensimon, Johns Hopkins University Press, 1993), and other volumes on academic leadership and qualitative research methods. Her research has appeared in the *Journal of Higher Education, Review of Higher Education, American Educational Research Journal, Curriculum Inquiry,* among others. Neumann's research has been funded by the Spencer Foundation, the Office of Educational Research and Improvement (OERI) of the U.S. Office of Education, the Lilly Foundation, and TIAA-CREF.

About the ASHE Higher Education Report Series

Since 1983, the ASHE (formerly ASHE-ERIC) Higher Education Report Series has been providing researchers, scholars, and practitioners with timely and substantive information on the critical issues facing higher education. Each monograph presents a definitive analysis of a higher education problem or issue, based on a thorough synthesis of significant literature and institutional experiences. Topics range from planning to diversity and multiculturalism, to performance indicators, to curricular innovations. The mission of the Series is to link the best of higher education research and practice to inform decision making and policy. The reports connect conventional wisdom with research and are designed to help busy individuals keep up with the higher education literature. Authors are scholars and practitioners in the academic community. Each report includes an executive summary, review of the pertinent literature, descriptions of effective educational practices, and a summary of key issues to keep in mind to improve educational policies and practice.

The Series is one of the most peer reviewed in higher education. A National Advisory Board made up of ASHE members reviews proposals. A National Review Board of ASHE scholars and practitioners reviews completed manuscripts. Six monographs are published each year and they are approximately 120 pages in length. The reports are widely disseminated through Jossey-Bass and John Wiley & Sons, and they are available online to subscribing institutions through Wiley InterScience (http://www.interscience.wiley.com).

Call for Proposals

The ASHE Higher Education Report Series is actively looking for proposals. We encourage you to contact one of the editors, Dr. Kelly Ward (kaward@wsu.edu) or Dr. Lisa Wolf-Wendel (lwolf@ku.edu), with your ideas.

Recent Titles

ASHE HIGHER EDUCATION REPORT
Order Form
SUBSCRIPTIONS AND SINGLE ISSUES

DISCOUNTED BACK ISSUES:

Use this form to receive **20% off** all back issues of ASHE Higher Education Report. All single issues priced at **$22.40** (normally $29.00)

TITLE	ISSUE NO.	ISBN
_____	_____	_____
_____	_____	_____
_____	_____	_____

Call 888-378-2537 or see mailing instructions below. When calling, mention the promotional code, JB7ND, to receive your discount.

SUBSCRIPTIONS: *(1 year, 6 issues)*

☐ New Order   ☐ Renewal

U.S.	☐ Individual: $174	☐ Institutional: $228
Canada/Mexico	☐ Individual: $174	☐ Institutional: $288
All Others	☐ Individual: $210	☐ Institutional: $339

Call 888-378-2537 or see mailing and pricing instructions below. Online subscriptions are available at www.interscience.wiley.com.

Copy or detach page and send to:
John Wiley & Sons, Journals Dept., 5th Floor
989 Market Street, San Francisco, CA 94103-1741
Order Form can also be faxed to: 888-481-2665

Issue/Subscription Amount: $ _____
Shipping Amount: $ _____
(for single issues only—subscription prices include shipping)
Total Amount: $ _____

SHIPPING CHARGES:

SURFACE	Domestic	Canadian
First Item	$5.00	$6.00
Each Add'l Item	$3.00	$1.50

(No sales tax for U.S. subscriptions. Canadian residents, add GST for subscription orders. Individual rate subscriptions must be paid by personal check or credit card. Individual rate subscriptions may not be resold as library copies.)

☐ Payment enclosed (U.S. check or money order only. All payments must be in U.S. dollars.)

☐ VISA   ☐ MC   ☐ Amex # _____ Exp. Date _____

Card Holder Name _____ Card Issue # _____

Signature _____ Day Phone _____

☐ Bill Me (U.S. institutional orders only. Purchase order required.)

Purchase order # _____
Federal Tax ID13559302   GST 89102 8052

Name _____

Address _____

Phone _____ E-mail _____

JB7ND

ASHE-ERIC HIGHER EDUCATION REPORT IS NOW AVAILABLE ONLINE AT WILEY INTERSCIENCE

What is Wiley InterScience?

Wiley InterScience is the dynamic online content service from John Wiley & Sons delivering the full text of over 300 leading scientific, technical, medical, and professional journals, plus major reference works, the acclaimed Current Protocols laboratory manuals, and even the full text of select Wiley print books online.

What are some special features of Wiley InterScience?

Wiley Interscience Alerts is a service that delivers table of contents via e-mail for any journal available on Wiley InterScience as soon as a new issue is published online.
Early View is Wiley's exclusive service presenting individual articles online as soon as they are ready, even before the release of the compiled print issue. These articles are complete, peer-reviewed, and citable.
CrossRef is the innovative multi-publisher reference linking system enabling readers to move seamlessly from a reference in a journal article to the cited publication, typically located on a different server and published by a different publisher.

How can I access Wiley InterScience?

Visit http://www.interscience.wiley.com.

Guest Users can browse Wiley InterScience for unrestricted access to journal Tables of Contents and Article Abstracts, or use the powerful search engine.
Registered Users are provided with a *Personal Home Page* to store and manage customized alerts, searches, and links to favorite journals and articles. Additionally, Registered Users can view free Online Sample Issues and preview selected material from major reference works.
Licensed Customers are entitled to access full-text journal articles in PDF, with select journals also offering full-text HTML.

How do I become an Authorized User?

Authorized Users are individuals authorized by a paying Customer to have access to the journals in Wiley InterScience. For example, a University that subscribes to Wiley journals is considered to be the Customer.

Faculty, staff and students authorized by the University to have access to those journals in Wiley InterScience are Authorized Users. Users should contact their Library for information on which Wiley journals they have access to in Wiley InterScience.